This study identifies key mechanisms through which a young child operates with external knowledge in her immediate social context. Central to this is the child's capacity to draw on discourse-based understandings which have become evident in prior interaction. These understandings are shown to inform and shape various aspects of the child's behaviour, notably request selection, the emergence of new request forms and various kinds of child distress, and they form the 'context' to which the child's actions come to be increasingly sensitive. In contrast to studies which analyse development under different headings, such as language, emotions and cognition, Tony Wootton links these aspects in his examination of the state of understanding which exists at any given moment in interaction. The result is a distinctive social constructivist approach to children's development.

Studies in interactional sociolinguistics 14

EDITORS

*Paul Drew, Marjorie Harness Goodwin, John J. Gumperz,
Deborah Schiffrin*

Interaction and the development of mind

Studies in Interactional Sociolinguistics

Interaction and the development of mind

A. J. WOOTTON
University of York

CAMBRIDGE
UNIVERSITY PRESS

Published by the Press Syndicate of the University of Cambridge
The Pitt Building, Trumpington Street, Cambridge CB2 1RP
40 West 20th Street, New York, NY 10011–4211, USA
10 Stamford Road, Oakleigh, Melbourne 3166, Australia

© Cambridge University Press 1997

First published 1997

Printed in the United Kingdom at the University Press, Cambridge

A catalogue record for this book is available from the British Library

Library of Congress cataloguing in publication data applied for

Wootton, A. J.
    Interaction and the development of mind / A. J. Wootton.
        p.   cm. – (Studies in interactional sociolinguistics; 14)
    Includes bibliographical references and index.
    ISBN 0 521 57341 6 (hardback)
    1. Social perception in children.   2. Social interaction in
children.   3. Cognition in children.   4. Interpersonal relations in
children.   5. Interpersonal communication in children.   I. Title.
II. Series.
BF723.S6W66   1997
155.4'13–dc20   96-26540   CIP

ISBN 0 521 573416 hardback

Contents

Preface

Several years ago, after publishing one or two small-scale studies relating to children's requests, I sat down to think through the relationship between these studies and the spectrum of research carried out on children. The approach I had been taking was a minority interest, one which placed its methodological emphasis on the rigorous analysis of small numbers of sequences. Here, 'rigour' meant identifying the details within these exchanges which documented the understandings of the participants involved. It seemed fairly clear that by proceeding in this way one could tap into forms of interactional organization which seemed quite powerful, but the question arose as to how these findings meshed in with the large amount of other knowledge about young children's behaviour which had been generated by alternative and more conventional modes of research. This was the issue I sat down to address.

I found this task very difficult. Much of this other research was heavily quantitative, and thus generated through the application of various kinds of pre-specified taxonomy to the flow of what took place in children's interaction. These taxonomies usually came with some evidence of high reliability, in the technical sense, but there was little compelling basis for selecting one taxonomy rather than another. And, more importantly, in spite of pioneering work by people such as Carter (1975, 1978), there was little systematic attention paid to finding ways of figuring out the significance which these different forms of speech act had for the children themselves. Rather reluctantly, therefore, when confronted by categories like 'imperatives' I found myself reaching back into the main corpus of recorded data which I had available in order to learn more about the ways in which the child studied employed these devices.

In the weeks that followed various systematic patternings began to emerge, especially as regards 'imperatives'; and other lines of analysis also suggested themselves, ones which come to form core themes of this book. In the course of this, however, it also became clear that the contours of these findings had important implications for various issues in developmental research. One of these was the matter of how the child first accessed contextual knowledge, how contextual awareness was built into the ways in which her conduct was organized. Another related to the question of how the child comes to have knowledge of the 'internal' states of other people, how knowledge of other minds first enters into her everyday behaviour. A third concerned the relative parts played by agreement and disagreement in development: if my observations were correct then rather than the conflict emphasized within the Piagetian tradition it was agreement that played the more pivotal role. And, at the same time, important links began to emerge between aspects of the child's behaviour which were normally given discrete treatment in the research literature, aspects such as the emotional and the cognitive.

This is not the place to anticipate all these more general themes, but what has emerged from my 'case study' is a general developmental statement that is in its own way distinctive. It is a statement about how one child enters the world of culture, and the central processes involved here turn out to be those through which her conduct comes to be connected to publicly established understandings which have emerged in interaction. I argue that it is these understandings which play a pivotal role both as regards her grasp of the culture which surrounds her and as regards the ways in which she employs the language which is at her disposal. It is they, rather than internal psychological representations or external cultural scripts, which come to matter for the child in the on-line management of her conduct; and I suggest that it is they which lie at the heart of a variety of more specific developmental accomplishments which children normally attain in the months after their second birthday.

This book is rather different, therefore, from that which I first sat down to write. Furthermore, input from other people has further served to alter its shape. In particular, I thank Maureen Cox, Derek Edwards and Michael Forrester for their pertinent and helpful comments on earlier drafts.

1

Overview of arguments and procedures

Several strands of social theory have long insisted on the existence of social facts. These are normally thought of as features of social organization which shape the actions of individuals whilst, at the same time, being in some sense independent of those individuals. Within my home discipline, sociology, the most famous articulation of such a position is in the writings of Durkheim (1901/1938). For him the representations of the 'collective conscience', the stuff of law, customs and such like, are separable from individual representations, those which are person specific, even though both co-exist within particular human practices. The business of sociology was to be the analysis of collective representations, and, by implication, the study of childhood becomes an occasion for examining how these representations are acquired by the child; he writes, for example, that education is 'a continuous effort to impose on the child ways of seeing, feeling and acting at which he would not have arrived spontaneously' (1938:6, cited in Lukes 1973:12).

If we accept that human thought and action are informed by the existence of some such shared social component the question then arises as to how the young child gains access to it. Within sociology this has often been glossed as a process in which the child's actions are shaped by the norms of the society, as though the child is exposed to various regulative rules which serve to guide her production of appropriate conduct, and which act as yardsticks against which her actions are evaluated by her parents. This kind of imagery, partially articulated in the above quotation from Durkheim, has an obvious plausibility when considering certain aspects of the child's experience. For example, when she goes to school there are certain rules about participation and involvement in activities to which she is required to adapt. But in such cases, where people are placed in the position of adapting to pre-existing rules, it has in fact proven a

1

tricky matter to identify the precise manner in which this adaptation takes place. Following such rules appears to involve the learner in mastering and deploying various further forms of knowledge in order to follow the rule; and it involves mastering the various modes of interactional involvement through which some form of recognition of the existence of such rules can be made. Deciding on how to handle such complications remains a problematic matter for sociology.[1] Fortunately, I think we can by-pass these matters as there are a number of reasons why this kind of 'normative imposition' imagery is clearly inappropriate for the age group of primary concern in this book, children between about one and three years old, that is children in the initial and primordial stages of becoming social beings.

The reasons in question here are both negative and positive. On the negative side is the relative absence of overt instruction *which is framed in terms of explicit rules*. If we take untoward misbehaviour of the child as an example we find that the child is often reprimanded, or told not to do things, but these injunctions and the like are rarely stated in the form of an explicit rule – instead, parents say things like 'Don't do that, you'll hurt him' or 'Give it back' or 'If you do that again I'm going to get angry' or just 'No'. Such statements, of course, simply identify some current, or projected, act as untoward: they do not explicitly set out a guideline/rule which acts as a precept for a more general set of circumstances in which the child may find herself in the future. A more concrete example of this, and one which I discuss further in both chapter 2 and chapter 6, concerns the young child's use of the word 'please' in requests. On those rare occasions in which the parent chooses to address the child's omission of this word from a request, the parents I have studied can act as though a rule has been broken, but they never explicitly state the circumstances in which, in future, the child should use 'please'. They address the omission by saying things like 'What do you say?', and when the child comes up with 'please' they take that in itself to be a successful outcome. In short, the point I am making is this: parents do not, on the whole, actually treat the induction of their young child into the social world as though it were like an induc-

---

[1] The question of how rules are followed is addressed most thoroughly in a conceptual fashion in the analytic tradition within philosophy which has emerged from the later work of Wittgenstein (1953). Somewhat parallel considerations emerged in sociology through the conceptual critique of the work of Parsons by his student Garfinkel, and through Garfinkel's empirical explorations of these matters (brought together in Garfinkel 1967; see Heritage 1984 for a good historical overview of such matters). Much recent social theory (e.g. Giddens 1976; Turner 1994) can be read, in part, as an attempt to come to grips with the considerations raised within these earlier bodies of work.

tion into a formal organization, where their job is to tell the child what the rules are.[2]

There are also positive reasons for treating the imagery of the normative imposition model as misleading for the study of very young children. One of the main things we have learned from various studies of children of this age is that they have a phenomenal capacity to detect orderliness in the information with which they are presented. The absence of overt rule-like instruction with regard to such things as the properties of objects, the referential relationships of words to things, the rules of grammar and moral concerns does not normally appear to hinder the emergence of an impressive order of competence in all such spheres. With regard to language itself, Lock (1980) captures the key features here in his excellent book title, **The Guided Reinvention of Language**. In acquiring a language there is every suggestion that the child is, in effect, reinventing it, rather than, for example, simply copying it; and similar processes seem to be at work with regard to other aspects of knowledge acquisition, even though they might now often be expressed in the less anthropomorphic language of connectionism rather than through more metaphorical terms such as 'invention' (Plunkett and Sinha 1992). While it is true that the parent can exercise various forms of guidance in this process, a matter to which I shall return, there is a predominant sense that the child is making developmental headway by actively assembling various orders of sense in the world to which she is being exposed. And, in these respects, culture is as much a candidate for 'reinvention' as is language.

If we leave aside the 'normative imposition' model of cultural acquisition, and if our inclinations lead us towards a more constructivist, child-centred position, we are still left with the question of *how* the child accesses her local culture at this early stage of her life, how she becomes acculturated. After all, one of the hallmarks of social and cultural facts, as Durkheim reminded us, is their shared, intersubjective nature. How is it possible for the child to build for herself an understanding of the world which is commensurate with that of her parents? Imagine for a moment that you are a child aged 18 months. By then you may just be putting together two-word sentences; you have a capacity to draw attention to, and make requests regarding, objects and actions in your immediate environment; you will have a fairly secure grasp of the functions of various every-

---

[2] The observations in this paragraph are more fully elaborated in Wootton 1986; for a useful, and consistent, Wittgensteinian account of issues touched on here see Pitkin (1972: chapter 3).

day objects; you have a capacity to engage in simple games such as peeka-boo;[3] you can understand much of what is said to you if it is phrased in simple ways and if it relates to matters in your immediate environment. In what sense, though, do you share a culture with your parent, and what are the mechanisms through which this takes place, and in what respects does change take place in subsequent months, at this time of rapid human development?

In the following chapters I develop a distinctive kind of account of the processes which are involved in this initial accculturation. Whereas the accounts of others who have most directly addressed this issue empha-size the child's early capacity to grasp and store the general social pat-terns which she can detect in her social environment, my account lays emphasis on what takes place in the local sequence of action in which the child is engaged. I shall argue that it is through taking account of what has taken place within the local sequence that her actions come to be shaped by the local culture which surrounds her; that she comes to be social by acting strategically so as to take account of what has happened in any given encounter. It is in the detailed management of encounters that the seeds of social being are laid. Before giving serious explication of my own position, however, I shall first enlarge on what I see as the main counterposition. Those whom I shall treat as working within this latter framework have seen the child as becoming social through build-ing up a store of social and cultural knowledge which is of potential relevance in a variety of specific situations. This knowledge is, there-fore, trans-situational in its potential application, and, consequently, I shall loosely refer to this counterposition as 'the trans-situational position'.

The trans-situational position

Under this heading I am, in fact, grouping a range of rather different per-spectives and research traditions which relate to children aged between about 18 and 36 months. To my mind, however, they have certain features in common which it is useful to highlight. One person whose views encap-sulate core features of this position is the American philosopher G. H. Mead, a figure who has exercised a major influence on certain branches of

---

[3] An interesting and detailed account of the kinds of participation which young children can have in one type of game at around 12 months of age can be found in Bruner and Sherwood (1976).

sociology, and some on child language study. Writing about our thoughts when about to carry out a certain action he suggests that they call up:

memory images of the responses of those about us, the memory images of those responses of others which were in answer to like actions. Thus the child can think about his conduct as good or bad only as he reacts to his own acts in the remembered words of his parents.   (1913/1964:146)

Within this kind of perspective, social knowledge becomes transmitted to the child's memory store, thus becoming implanted in the child. This knowledge is then used at later dates as a resource which is taken into account in deciding on lines of action. The knowledge potentially has trans-situational application – it can be of relevance to a variety of particular occasions – but clearly it is not of relevance to all situations. So, the child will also have recognition procedures to make the requisite identifications, to decide on matters such as what are 'like actions'. These will enable her to discriminate types of situation for which different orders of knowledge are pertinent. Within this perspective what we need to investigate is how the transmission and transfer of knowledge takes place and how that knowledge becomes internalized within the child's mind.

This kind of imagery has an obvious plausibility in that it is clear that human beings do amass a large store of knowledge which can come to have a bearing on the ways in which we deal with other people. Furthermore, various research findings on children are broadly consistent with, and illustrative of, this way of thinking about these matters. Let me cite some examples.

First, recent work on memory processes at around the age of two shows that by this time the child is capable of storing quite complex patterns (Bauer and Thal 1990; Nelson 1993). These memories can focus around particular events, or types of event, which have taken place in the past, or they can revolve around standard patterns of activity of which the child is aware. This knowledge, sometimes referred to as 'script' knowledge, thus potentially shapes the child's thinking and actions along lines consistent with the social milieus in which she is being brought up. Also consistent with these points is the fact that at around the age of two the child engages in forms of pretence which can involve her in reproducing patterns of action (e.g. shopkeeping) which are loosely modelled on patterns of activity with which she is familiar. This further documents the existence of such script knowledge in the child's mind.

Second, some work on children's early requesting suggests precise ways in which knowledge relevant to making requests comes to be transmitted to the child. In their account of requesting after the age of about 18 months, which is heavily influenced by speech act analysis, Bruner, Roy and Ratner (1982:106–10) note that the reasons used by parents to reject certain requests often amount to 'lessons' for the child in how to go about requesting. For example, when a parent rejects a request by saying 'You're able to get that yourself', the child is being instructed to take into account, more generally, a precept like 'do not ask for objects that you are able to obtain on your own'. They argue that in this way parents convey information relating to a number of such precepts. The clear implication is that such 'lessons' provide the child with a stock of knowledge, a trans-situational knowledge base, which subsequently serves to guide her conduct. It is through the construction of this base that the child's behaviour comes to be shaped into patterns which are more congruent with those of the adult.

Third, social linguistic studies of language use by children show that the child's selection of particular sentence constructions is sometimes correlated with the category of person to whom she is speaking (Becker 1982; Gordon and Ervin-Tripp 1984). For example, when making requests of a younger child, imperatives are more likely to be selected than when speaking to the father. This suggests not only that the child is capable of taking her recipient into account, but that she is taking such knowledge into account consistently across a range of specific occasions. In organizing her actions with regard to the specific identities of those with whom she is interacting, it can then be claimed that the child is thereby taking into account trans-situational knowledge concerning the type of person with which she is dealing.

Although these various strands of research are diverse, and uneven with regard to how far the claims they make receive empirical support, they nevertheless further articulate the imagery which I identified in the earlier quotation from Mead. First, the child derives knowledge from her immediate environment. Second, this knowledge is stored so as to become available in the long term. Third, this knowledge is drawn on in a variety of specific occasions, thus it has a trans-situational application. Fourth, and by implication, changes in these respects are a function of changes in the knowledge store. Interestingly, such research is often strong on establishing the existence of a knowledge store, but much weaker on how exactly the child draws elements into it, and how exactly it informs any particular act. Nevertheless, its imagery remains potent and I will be coming back to these lines of argument at various times within this book, particularly to the script theorists and the social linguistic findings. In general, although I am sympathetic to various critiques of this orientation,[4] I shall not want to claim that these bodies of research are ill founded, nor to exclude the possibility that the child has some kind of access to the type of knowledge in question. However, I shall argue that an account of shared understandings which focuses on the child's grasp of sequential knowledge offers a more compelling vision of how the child first accesses and makes use of social knowledge. I shall now give a preliminary synopsis of this account.

The sequential position

Instead of seeing the young child's actions as shaped and constrained by an emerging, general knowledge store, I shall argue that the critical knowledge on which she is drawing is intimately linked with the particular sequence of action in which she is engaged. In the course of participating in sequences of action the child develops a capacity to take into account what I shall call *understandings* which have arisen either from events earlier in the same sequence of talk or from ones occurring in a sequence in the relatively recent past. These understandings are quite simple phenomena, perhaps so simple from an adult point of view as barely to merit detailed attention. Here is an instance: the parent agrees to lift the child out of her high-chair, but then other talk ensues which delays this; on the completion of this talk the child then tells the parent to lift her out through the use of an imperative, **Lift out dad**. What I hope to demonstrate, among other things, is that by choosing to use an imperative the child takes account of the earlier agreement as to the appropriateness of this course of action, that in various ways her conduct is sensitive to the existence of such understandings. I shall argue that, by the age of two, the child is routinely engaged in lines of action which attend to understandings of this kind, and that such an attentiveness shapes many features of the child's behaviour at this age. In general, these understandings appear to have three important properties: they are local, public and moral.

[4] A recent book which collects together various critical themes is Chaiklin and Lave (1993). For example, Lave, addressing the appropriateness of terms like *transmission, transfer* and *internalization* as apt descriptors for the circulation of knowledge in society, suggests that they face 'the difficulty that they imply *uniformity* of knowledge. They do not acknowledge the fundamental imprint of interested parties, multiple activities, and different goals and circumstances, on what constitutes "knowing" on a given occasion or across a multitude of interrelated events. These terms imply that humans engage first and foremost in the reproduction of given knowledge rather than in the production of knowledgeability as a flexible process of engagement with the world' (pp. 12–13).

First, they are *local* in that their nature and force are only intelligible in the light of specific events which have taken place in the recent past. By this I mean that the child, at the end of her second year of life, seems to tailor aspects of her conduct to specific events which have recently taken place. The more direct evidence pertaining to this claim is presented mainly in chapters 3 and 4, and relates principally to the child's request behaviour. There I show that the type of linguistic design which the child uses to make her request is sensitive to the kind of understanding which has been specifically established earlier in the sequence of interaction in question, and that the child also recognizes, implicitly, the existence of such local understandings in other ways. In these respects there are various tensions with the kinds of script based accounts which I have mentioned above. According to my account what is required of the child at this age is the flexibility to operate on the basis of relevant local understandings, whereas script based ideas would suggest that competent forms of involvement on the part of the child are a function of the 'fit' between trans-situational script knowledge and the particulars of the given occasion. These tensions, and limitations attached to script based accounts in these respects, are brought out at various points within chapters 2, 3 and 4.

Second, these understandings are *public* in that they are informed by what has overtly taken place in the talk. In many of the sequences examined in chapters 3 and 4, for example, we find evidence of the parent agreeing with the child as to the feasibility of some course of action, and the child's subsequent actions appear to be fitted to the nature of these agreements. Contrary to this one might have supposed that the child's actions might be guided by private, idiosyncratic or inaccessible understandings as to how sequences of action might unfold; but this does not appear to be so. There is certainly evidence of child behaviour which parents find bizarre on the recordings which are analysed, but one of the most interesting findings, reported in chapter 4, is that in such cases there is also good evidence to suppose that the child, in acting as she does, is displaying close attention to overt agreements which have earlier been established. This attentiveness on the part of the child to what has been overtly agreed is a crucial feature because, more normally, it is in this way that her understandings can be recognized as having an order of compatibility with those of the parent; it is through these means that the child comes to articulate an awareness of shared understandings. One of the child's achievements, therefore, is coming to recognize, at around the age of two, that such public events as agreement have a special salience for the subsequent design of her conduct.

Third, these understandings have a *moral* quality. This becomes especially evident through the ways in which the child acts when these understandings are breached by her co-participant, a matter that is addressed most directly in chapter 4. Here a relatively small number of fraught incidents are examined which take place around the middle of the child's third year. These incidents have, from an adult point of view, certain paradoxical features. The adult is trying to assist the child in some way, to implement that which the child wants, but the child's reactions are ones of extreme distress. The reactions are, perhaps, typical forms of the behaviour which people refer to when they speak of the 'terrible twos'. Examination of these incidents reveals that a common feature which they share is an infraction by the parent of local understandings which are recognizable as having been established earlier in the sequences in question. In reacting in the ways in which she does to these parental misdemeanours, the child treats the sequential understandings which inform them as having moral properties, implications for what *ought* to take place; and, by the same token, these incidents also demonstrate ways in which these understandings play a central role in the organization and distribution of certain forms of emotional behaviour and social conflict at this age.

My argument will be that these local understandings are central to the young child's emerging grasp of the world of everyday life in which her linguistic behaviour is situated. Through recognizing their existence, the child's sensitivity to the 'context' in which she acts undergoes an enormous developmental step. Prior to being able to take understandings into account the child has various sequential skills, and she also has the capacity to recognize, and become creatively involved in, relatively routinized sequences of events, such as certain games. An overview of these preceding skills is presented in chapter 2; but recognizing that courses of action are contingent in systematic ways on locally arrived-at understandings constitutes a new departure, one which gives a privileged status to that which has taken place in preceding discourse. Action is now constructed in the light of, and is always contingent upon, locally prevailing, and sequentially based, understandings. In these ways, for the child, the sequential context comes to be the bearer of a new order of information, information which permits more finely tuned forms of calibration with the views of her co-participant. The child's actions can now become contextualized along lines which are commensurate, in precise ways, with the understandings which prevail in the local culture to which she is being exposed.

Links with psychology

As yet this discussion has not touched on what I think of as the mainstream work in cognitive developmental psychology which has had much to say about children in the age range under investigation. Here I am referring especially to the lines of research which have emerged from the work of Piaget and his co-workers, research that I refer to in chapter 6 as the 'cognitivist tradition', and which I discuss there in greatest detail. If we pose to this tradition the kind of question with which I began this chapter – how does cultural awareness become incorporated into the child's conduct? – the kind of answer we are likely to get is as follows. The nature of this incorporation will depend heavily on the child's level of information-processing capacity. There are now well-known stages in the development of these capacities. For example, Piaget (for an overview see Flavell 1963: chapter 3) and others (such as Leslie 1987) have identified, at around 18 months, the onset of an ability to work with true mental representations of objects and actions; most obviously this is suggested by the emergence at that time of pretence and other deferred forms of imitation. This capacity, therefore, will permit and constrain those forms of cultural sensibility which we can find in the child's behaviour at that age. Immediately subsequent to this age, a period to which Piaget himself paid relatively little attention, we find that the child gradually develops a capacity to take into account the desires and beliefs of other people, so that by about 3½ years old the child can recognize that other people can act on the basis of what the child knows to be false beliefs. Again, it could be argued, the crucial constraint on what it is possible for the child to know about the shape of the knowledge in her surrounding culture will be her stage of development in what is called her 'theory of mind' (see, for example, Wellman 1990).

Such a crude summary does little justice to the systematic, and often highly ingenious, empirical work which underpins this perspective. It seems fairly clear too that many of the transitions in capability which are being identified in this research are robust and generic to children of this age. What is much less clearcut are the developmental mechanisms which bring about the changes in question. For Piaget, and many others subsequently, these hinge around the processes of accommodation and assimilation, on the child coming across inadequacies in operating with the conceptual apparatus available to her, and modifying it in the light of her practical experience. In this regard, however, there has been relatively little empirical examination of the practical workings of accommodation and assimilation, let alone any careful exploration of how they might manifest themselves in the child's interactional dealings with other people – though Piaget himself speculated that the child's disagreements with other people as to understandings of events could form a routine site for accommodation.[5]

The sequentially based account which I have previously outlined, and which will form the focus of subsequent chapters, potentially offers a different kind of mechanism through which developmental change takes place. Instead of focusing on internal representations my focus will be on those public understandings which come to inform the child's ongoing lines of action. And instead of disagreement and internal cognitive conflict being the pivotal motors of change, as they are for Piaget, it is agreement, in my account, which is probably the more significant. Within the sequences I shall be examining, we routinely find the child to be constructing her later lines of action so as to be compatible with understandings which have been publicly agreed, or in other ways to be taking such understandings into account. Making use of these sequential connections offers the child a training and familiarity with the skills involved in taking account of the interactional alignments of other people. For the child, gaining access to the minds of other people is thus simplified at this early stage of development by the fact that the information which she is drawing on in this regard is public; it is information which has been overtly encoded within prior interaction. Furthermore, as we shall see in chapter 6, the availability of such procedures to the child simultaneously solves what continues to be a major problem for the 'theory of mind' position – the problem being that for a child to act appropriately she must have more than the capacity to make inferences about other people's minds, she needs to be able to make specific inferences which are apt for the particular occasion in question. Within the perspective I am offering this cannot be a 'problem' for the child because the ways in which she takes account of

---

[5] My discussion here risks exaggerating the significance of what I call 'cognitivism' at the expense of alternative theoretical traditions which have emerged within developmental psychology, notably that arising from the writings of Vygotsky (1962). I shall have more to say about these in chapter 6, but for the moment I note that, although many of Vygotsky's precepts for investigating the emergence of consciousness require him logically to give primacy to the organization of activities in social interaction, in practice his theoretical analyses usually pivot around the investigation of word meaning and entail giving an analytic primacy to the child's emerging cognitive categories. These limitations of his work are now well known – for an overview see Wertsch (1985: chapter 7) and the remarks in Forrester (1992:37–43). Subsequent work in the Russian tradition (see Wertsch *ibid.*) and by Bruner (1983) does much more to forefront the role of interactional organization in the emergence of children's skills.

other people's understandings are always tied to the specifics of what has transpired on any given occasion.

My purpose in drawing out these tensions, both here, in a preliminary way, and in the remainder of the book, is not to lay out an alternative theory of mental development. My principal aim, all along, is to spell out the ways in which conversational sequences appear to work: the main thrust of the analysis is an interactional one rather than one designed to explore how the child's mind works. Nevertheless, in the course of this it becomes apparent that certain kinds of mental mechanism are required of the child in order for her to participate in interaction in the ways in which she does. One of my further aims, therefore, is to sketch out, as clearly as I can, the kinds of mechanism which seem to be suggested by what my analysis reveals about the workings of these interaction processes. Therefore, teasing out these connections, together with their implications for existing models of the child's thinking processes, also comes to be a theme of the book; indeed, this is why the 'development of mind' figures in its title. So, I shall now indicate, again in a preliminary way, some of the implications which my analyses suggest for the workings of the child's psychological processes.

The key general question in this respect is what psychological processes are required of, and afforded to, the child in the course of monitoring talk for the state of local understanding that obtains, and in then constructing some related next line of action? Some of these processes can be briefly mentioned here. First, and most obviously, there are implications for the workings of memory. If the mind needs to recall sequences from the immediate past, in order to identify locally operative understandings which have been reached, then a premium is placed on relatively short-term memory. By contrast with script theory, which lays emphasis on long-term memory for the storage of relevant cultural configurations, my analysis implies that acuity in short-term memory is at the heart of the child's grasp of knowledge which is in some sense shared with her parents. Second, the potential connectedness of the child's action to what has taken place earlier also implies that the unit of time which can routinely come to have a bearing on the construction of lines of action is extended backwards, though not a long way backwards. If earlier understandings can become relevant to later action then it is insufficient for the child just to monitor the prior turn of talk: there is also an incentive to attend to ways in which a prior turn connects with earlier events, an incentive to monitor and track the talk in the light of that which has preceded it. Third, because the child is continually constructing and evaluating alignments in relation to prior sequential understandings then judgements of consistency and inconsistency in relation to earlier understandings are implicated. These, in turn, may facilitate the employment, by the child, of embryonic logical reasoning skills. Fourth, because the child is often constructing her action so as to accord with understandings which take the form of publicly stated preferences on the part of her co-interactant, then the child is developing a working capacity in taking into account knowledge of other people's minds. In all these spheres it seems to me that the availability and use of what I have called understandings must significantly shape and enable relevant cognitive procedures.

Request activity

The capacity to request that other people do things is of central significance to the communicative armoury of the young child. The reach gesture, accompanied by a consistent type of vocalization, which Dore, Franklin, Miller and Ramer (1976) refer to as a phonetically consistent form, is one of the child's main developmental accomplishments shortly after the age of 9 months, and it is clear that the principal use to which this is put is that of requesting. From then onwards request activity makes up a sizeable proportion of the young child's spontaneous speech output. In his study of a large number of children Wells (1985:228), for example, found that at the age of 30 months about 30 per cent of all child utterances were ones in which the child was trying to gain control over the present or future behaviour of someone present.

It is also clear that normally, in the course of her second year of life, a variety of linguistic devices are gradually incorporated into the child's repertoire for making requests. This much is reflected in the various taxonomies which have been developed to describe the semantic and pragmatic variation which exists in early child language (for example, Halliday 1975, Greenfield and Smith 1976; Ingram 1989 contains a useful overview of such work); and, after the age of 2, further devices for requesting become evident within the child's repertoire, notably, in English, question forms such as 'Can you do x?' once the child is capable of mastering subject–auxiliary inversion. Further taxonomies have been developed for this later period which capture the principal techniques available to the child for making requests. These various devices are amply illustrated in the body of this book. Chapter 2, for example, contains an overview of requesting as it develops from about 12 months to 2 years of age.

One line of critique of this taxonomic work has been concerned with the degree of commensurateness which exists between the analytic descriptions of types of linguistic design which are offered within these taxonomies and the child's own understandings as to these matters (see, for example, Francis 1979). For example, if, as seems to be the case, the child, by the end of her second year, can employ different linguistic devices at different times for making a request for the same thing then what is to be the basis for claiming that these different devices have, for the child, systematically different interactional properties? Clearly, this is a significant issue if our aim is to build accounts of child action which incorporate those parameters which are actually relevant to the child in the ongoing organization of her conduct. One obvious way to pursue this matter is to examine the specific sequences of action in which request devices are contained in order to see if they offer clues to the part these devices play, for the child, in the interaction in question. The main observations and arguments of this book emerge out of this type of inspection of particular sequences. The initial discovery which served to shape the direction of subsequent analysis hinged on observations about the circumstances in which the child used imperative constructions, constructions which appear to be usable by most English-speaking children by around the age of two.

Not all imperative constructions are used by the child to exercise control over other people; for example, both Piaget and Vygotsky drew attention to the ways in which they can be used as a sort of accompaniment to activities which the child is undertaking on her own.[6] But it emerged that those which do target the actions of others largely appear to have a distinctive form of connectedness to understandings which have been reached in prior interaction, either the same interaction sequence or one which has taken place in the recent past. This distinctiveness is evident through the fact that the standard alternative linguistic devices used for making requests at this age (e.g. 'I want x') do not appear to be connected to parallel forms of local understanding. The documentation of these arguments, together with their various implications, is contained within chapter 3 of this book.

If these arguments are correct then the possibility arises that the emer-

---

[6] Of course, Piaget and Vygotsky had quite different ideas as to the nature and developmental trajectory of such speech. For Piaget it was one of the hallmarks of egocentrism, whereas for Vygotsky it represented a form of self-regulation which was the precursor to the emergence of more mature forms of inner thought. See Wertsch (1985:108–28) for a useful acccount of these matters.

gence of the different linguistic devices for making requests is linked to their capacity to encode or index differential forms of understanding. My most systematic attempts to examine this possibility are to be found in chapter 5, where I compare the circumstances in which two new linguistic devices for making requests are used: 'Can you do x?' and 'Shall we do x?' In the corpus of data examined these appear from about the middle of the child's third year onwards. Their content and use pattern are compared with those of request designs used previously, and, in the light of this, continuities and discontinuities are established with regard to how the child deploys the request designs which are available to her. Specifically, 'Can you do x?' questions appear to be used where the child has no sequential basis for expecting parental compliance, and there is some evidence which suggests that in this regard they take over the role that, at an earlier age, was fulfilled through the use of certain imperatives. 'Shall we do x?' questions are first used in circumstances where there has been an agreement between the child and her interactional partner to engage in some kind of joint action, and these questions represent a new way of coding this 'jointness' at a later point within the sequence. It is argued that in these ways the adoption of these new kinds of question represents an interactional differentiation of the request domain which is linked in various ways to the child's capacity to operate with sequential understandings.

Insofar as this book is concerned with the development of requesting it has, therefore, a rather particular perspective on this process. In a way, the central phenomenon being addressed is why children come so early to adopt such a wide variety of devices for making requests. If, as the analysis suggests, there is a detectable link between these devices and various types of understanding, then these understandings must form a key ingredient for any account which seeks to come to terms with this early diversity in the use of request devices. In the light of my findings, alternative accounts framed in terms of the notion of 'politeness' are discussed in chapter 6, and various weaknesses in them are identified.

The general stance of these arguments comes to be a constructivist one in that strong 'internal' pressures for the child to introduce changes into her request repertoire are identified. Once she is capable of recognizing the salience of local understandings then there are various incentives for her to differentiate the nature of those understandings through her request selection. These incentives are not principally to be found in the instruction and guidance of parents, even though the child's orientation to local understandings permits an order of sensitivity to, and calibration with, the concerns of the local parental culture. They are, instead, best considered as internal emergent properties of the communicative system with which the child is operating. This system contains internal tensions and an internal momentum which fosters further request differentiation; and, because this is so, this type of account, by implication, offers a perspective on the bases which could have informed the elaboration and development of language in the request domain within the evolution of the human species, though this aspect is little more than hinted at in the course of the arguments which are developed in this book.

Mode of analysis

The principal arguments to be developed arise out of the detailed examination of particular sequences of interaction which occur when a child makes requests to one or other of her parents. The phrase 'arise out of' is to be taken quite literally here. These transactions were not approached with some pre-formed idea, or theory, as to the key parameters which could be expected to unfold. Certain phenomena were taken as starting points for analysis. For example, given the widespread and cross-cultural incidence of imperative constructions at the ages in question it seemed appropriate to subject these, as a set, to careful analysis. But the question of what, if any, status these linguistic constructions had as a set, and that of the direction in which their analysis should lead, was treated as problematic, as a matter that was to be decided on the basis of the various distributional features to be found within the exchanges in which such constructions were employed.

A variety of research traditions within the study of children also contain systematic analyses of interaction processes (see McTear 1985 for an overview) and, where appropriate, reference to such work is made in subsequent chapters. The perspective which informs my own analysis is that tradition of micro-sociology which has emerged from the writings of Garfinkel (1967) and Goffman (1959, 1971), and specifically the body of knowledge known as conversation analysis, initially articulated in the writings of Sacks (1992) and Schegloff (1968). What this tradition brings sharply into focus is the question of how people's conduct is shaped by their interactional concerns – how we reveal to each other our understandings as to the knowledge, concerns and interests of our co-participants in interaction; how we manage regular contingencies in interaction, such as turn-taking, repair and conversational closure, which require of us and our fellows an element of interpersonal co-ordination; the ways in which different types of activity, such as agreement and disagreement, telling stories, teasing and such like, are handled; how we display to others the distinctive nature of the setting and context in which our interaction is housed.[7]

In all this what distinguishes conversation analysis from other approaches which have examined like matters is an insistence on their analysis through the case by case investigation of the local orders of detail which pertain to the interactions under examination. It is through this type of investigation that relevant phenomena are identified for analysis, and it is from these details that the evidence which supports the analysis needs to be derived. This latter aspect is a crucial one. The analyst needs to demonstrate ways in which the people in the interaction in question display understandings which are consistent with those being claimed in the analysis. Identifying these 'ways' as they are evident within the interaction itself is, therefore, central to the proof procedures of conversation analysis (Wootton 1989).

Constructing analyses of particular stretches of interaction in which very young children are involved poses special problems. The competences which they possess and the kinds of grasp which they have of encounters are likely to be different in significant ways from those of the adult, and thereby more impervious to analysis. Furthermore, between the ages of 18 and 36 months these parameters are also undergoing rapid change, perhaps the most rapid change of any stage of people's lives. To my mind, these considerations make careful inductive analysis all the more important.[8] Our resources for achieving this, however, are more limited than they are when analysing the talk of adults. In particular, we have to be especially cautious as to the weight we place on understandings made of the child's

---

[7] For those unfamiliar with conversation analysis, the descriptions offered in Drew (1994) or Heritage (1984: chapter 8) constitute sound introductions; for a more linguistically based account see Levinson (1983). Discussion of important methodological issues is often embedded within such texts, though more overt consideration of such matters can be found in Sacks (1984), Wootton (1989) and Heritage (1995). For a discussion of the connections between the work of Goffman and conversation analysis see Schegloff (1988). Although the writings of Sacks (1992), dating from the mid 1960s to the early 1970s, are mainly available in lecture form they continue, nevertheless, to be seminal for these and many other matters.

[8] In an earlier monograph on the language use of one child of a similar age Halliday considered, and rejected, the possibility of pursuing an inductive tack. He rejected it because:

by the time the child is, say, aged 2½, we will no longer be able to give any kind of significant general account of his uses of language. By this time, like the adult, he already uses language for so many different purposes that if we try to list them we shall simply get an endless catalogue; or rather we shall get a whole series of catalogues with no

talk by adults, such as parents, who are interacting with her (Howe 1981).
Quite frequently, as becomes clear in subsequent chapters, it is evident on
close inspection that adult understandings are incommensurate with those
of the child. In fact, from an early age, as is emphasized in chapter 2, one
of the child's achievements is to develop various techniques for rectifying
and repairing such occurrences.

There are no simple methodological precepts for coming to terms with
these problems, and in the analysis of some sequences they may be insu-
perable. Such intractable occasions do not figure prominently in the analyses which I report, though the reader will often find, within subsequent
chapters, reference to lesser epistemological insecurities which bear on my
claims. There is no way in which the analysis of talk can be cleansed of
insecurity, but that does not mean that this kind of enquiry is necessarily
a free-for-all in which all we can do is sit around and trade interpretations.
The achievement of conversation analysis has been to demonstrate that,
by proceeding in an imaginative and careful manner, taking especially into
account all the relevant behavioural details of each occasion, it is possible
to come to terms with these insecurities in ways which permit the analyst
to identify procedures that people appear to employ in their joint interaction. The vestiges of insecurity do not appear to prevent this, so, in the end,
maybe they do not matter. The critical point is that in minimizing such
problems the analyst has to give special attention to those forms of behaviour through which, *on each and every occasion*, the child displays her
understanding of events. It is this kind of situated information which is

reason for preferring one over another. We have to find some other more theoretical
basis for matching the observations about language use with some theoretical construct
of a functional nature. (1975:16)

The theoretical constructs that he then chose were ones derived from his own theories concerning the functional make-up of sentences and the sociological ideas of Bernstein, ones
which clearly formed a powerful lens through which he viewed his data. To my mind, there
are equal dangers and difficulties involved in shaping analyses according to one's ideas
about what properties a language has, difficulties which Sacks repeatedly brings out in his
lectures (for example, see the comments on Weinreich in Sacks 1992:I, 428–34). Minimally,
this postpones the task of exploring how commensurate these ideas are with the organized
ways that members of society use in the construction of their lines of conduct. It is the
latter to which I seek to give primacy, 'language' being of interest only insofar as it is
systematically and artfully employed in the assembly of recognizable lines of conduct. If
my arguments are compelling they will serve to demonstrate further that taking the inductive route does not necessarily have the consequences that Halliday feared. Indeed, taking
this route allows us, among other things, to specify in more precise ways how it comes to
be possible for the child to develop those forms of contextual awareness which Halliday
and others have identified as being of such central significance to the ways in which we
speak.

being drawn on in my analyses and it is this which is given special prominence in the transcripts around which my arguments are developed.

The transcripts which I provide in subsequent chapters contain a level of detail which, within both conversation analysis and other approaches to the analysis of interaction (such as Ochs and Schieffelin 1979), has been shown to be potentially of significance to people in the ways in which they go about understanding what other people are saying and doing. The conventions which are used in these transcripts, based on those devised by Gail Jefferson, are shown below:

? ,	these mark the pitch contour on the last 'beat' of the preceding words: '?' indicates rising pitch; ',' indicates level pitch. Where no such marker is used the pitch is a falling one.
::	sound sustension.
___	underlining denotes stress on those syllables.
AND	capital letters denote high amplitude.
–	as in 'jus-', marks a sound cut-off.
[	marks points of overlap, usually speech overlap; it can also denote a simultaneous start by two speakers. Small square brackets are used to enclose phonetic script within the transcripts.
=	denotes no gap between speech on either side of the symbol.
( )	single brackets either indicate untranscribed words or, where words are inside the brackets, enclose words of which the transcriber is uncertain.
(( ))	double brackets enclose information about what is taking place which is not formally incorporated into the transcript.
(.)	short but noticeable pauses of under half a second; longer pauses are timed, e.g. (1.3).
rh/lh	right hand/left hand.
.hh/hh	audible inbreath/audible outbreath.

Superscript alphabetic characters which appear in transcripts (e.g. [A]) denote the positions in which accompanying photographic reproductions were made.

At the beginning of each extract there are three pieces of information. The first (e.g. 2.1) gives the chapter in which the extract occurs and then a number denoting the numerical positioning of the extract relative to others within this chapter (i.e. chapter 2, first extract, in this case). The second gives the age of the child in years and months (e.g. 1;7). The third, and least relevant for the reader's purposes, is a tape position identification number (e.g. /1:33:10).

The level of detail provided in the transcriptions of particular episodes is a result of two main considerations. First, it has to be such that the critical evidence which does, or could, bear on the arguments being made about the extract is included. Ideally, this should also permit the reader to assess, independently, the adequacy of these arguments. Second, it has to be readily intelligible to the standard reader. For the latter reason it has been decided to include phonetic detail only where absolutely necessary, even though some work has demonstrated that the organization of phonetic detail can have an important bearing on people's understandings of conversational activities (e.g. Local and Kelly 1986). The level of detail is, therefore, something of a compromise, but it should be stressed that the analyses which have been undertaken were always based on repeated inspection of the original video recordings, not on the transcripts. It is unlikely, therefore, that relevant orders of detail have been overlooked in the analysis even though I may not always have been successful in doing justice to such detail within the transcripts.

The procedure of analysis which I have described above has a number of implications with regard to how my arguments are presented. As the analyses were approached inductively, not with a view to testing or evaluating particular perspectives or theories about the child, the principal data analysis chapters, chapters 3 to 5, are organized so as to reflect this. In each of these chapters, discussion of relevant related research is, in the main, delayed until the end of the chapter, where it is considered in the light of the findings which have emerged from my analyses. A second implication of my approach is the prominence given to the analysis of conversation extracts on a case by case basis rather than numerical frequency patterns. In sociology such case by case analysis is sometimes loosely referred to as a qualitative approach, as though it lacks the rigour and generalizability of investigative techniques whose proof procedures centre around statistical analysis. But the key methodological issue for any investigator must be to find the strongest forms of evidence which pertain to the domain of analysis in question. If interactional processes constitute our domain of enquiry, and if our aim is to identify those procedures which people use, and which are oriented to by them as real, then the key evidence pertaining to this must arise out of the ways in which people display such an orientation. This kind of evidence is contained within, and only documentable out of, particular stretches of interaction.

The issue of generalizability, however, remains an important one as the reader may wonder how far the extracts chosen are representative of the child's more general behaviour. This matter is handled in various ways in subsequent chapters. Chapters 4 and 5 contain discussion and analysis of either all or virtually all relevant instances within the data corpus which are clearcut instances of the phenomena being addressed, so here there is no real issue of data selectivity. In chapter 3, which reports analysis of the child's use of imperatives and certain other request designs, the reader will find various kinds of information pertaining to the claims being made. Here, the analysis of transcripts is supplemented by frequency calculations which relate to aspects pertaining to this analysis, and there is also detailed attention to occurrences which run off in ways deviant from the majority. In this manner I hope to present both a rounded picture of the child's relevant behaviour at the ages in question, and one which is rigorously grounded in the analysis of interactional detail.

A final implication of proceeding in the inductive manner which I employ here is the burden which it places on the reader. If the detail relating to particular episodes of interaction matters, then an appreciation of that detail is also necessary for developing a sense of the shape and adequacy of the analysis. I recognize that this places heavy demands on the reader, and I have tried to alleviate this by writing the text so that it is not strictly necessary for the reader to work, independently, through the actual sequence of events as it unfolds in the transcript in question. I have also tried to limit the number of episodes discussed to digestable proportions. Nevertheless, the text, especially in chapters 3 to 5, does require a capacity and willingness to enter into the detailed workings of specific occasions.

The child and the recordings

The subject of this study is my daughter, Amy. From 10 months of age onwards video-recordings were made of her development by her mother and myself. Initially, they were about two hours long and were made at about 2-month intervals; in fact, some of those made between the ages of 12 and 19 months are drawn on in chapter 2 of this book, where relevant details of Amy's early language development are also provided. From the age of 24 months onwards, however, the length of the recordings was increased, mainly because we wanted to ensure that they contained a fuller cross-section of the child's communicative behaviour in a variety of domestic situations. From then onwards the time periods between the recordings were also gradually increased. The recordings which form the principal focus of this study, in chapters 3 to 5, took place between the ages of 25 and 37 months, and they are listed below:

Age	Minutes of recording
25 months 25 days	240
27 months 7 days	180
29 months 25 days	180
33 months 8 days	180
37 months 21 days	240

All the recordings were made at home, either inside the house or in the backyard which was Amy's main external play area. They were made with a tripod-mounted camera which was usually left in a fixed position during recording periods. Stretches of interaction lasting about 20–25 minutes were recorded, so the recording at any one age is made up of a series of such stretches. The recording was carried out over a period of 1 or 2 days and was designed to represent a range of domestic activities in which Amy was normally involved, such as mealtimes, playing with her toys and getting dressed. At the time of making the recordings we had no specific ideas as to the kinds of child behaviour that might be explored through the use of this data base, but as a result of a long-standing interest in childrens' requests I was concerned to ensure that the kinds of context in which these were known to occur, such as mealtimes, were adequately represented on the recordings.

As Amy had no brothers or sisters living at home, and as the recordings do not, on the whole, include her play with friends, the principal participants are Amy, her mother and myself. At the ages in question, Amy's time was split between involvements in a day nursery on some half-days during each week, involvements with a carer who came to the house for part of most days and involvements with us, her parents. So, although the recordings we have made are extensive they do not provide a picture of these other two main domains of Amy's life at this time.

Working with a data base of this kind, which is limited to just one child, offers various advantages and disadvantages. Because the recordings at any one time are fairly extensive we can be reasonably sure that they contain a representative range of the communicative skills which were then available to the child. And the fact that the recordings contain such a large number of instances of the key request behaviour which is under investigation adds a robustness to those generalizations which appear to hold across these various instances. Furthermore, for certain of the themes to be explored, notably the developmental trajectories which I trace in chapter 5, it is difficult to imagine how the relevant continuities and discontinuities between behaviours at different ages could be identified, let alone analysed, without a data corpus which, for any given child, is as extensive as this one. In this sense, the available recordings create special opportunities for the exploration of developmental patterns.

The main disadvantage of focusing so heavily on one child is that of being unsure how far the results are generalizable to other children, and how far the procedures and processes being identified are truly generic ones for children of this age. This problem is somewhat exacerbated by the relative absence in the literature of other studies which address comparable issues at the level of detail that proves to be important in the present study (though see Gerhardt (1990, 1991) for similar use of sequential evidence for the construction of arguments about the semantics and pragmatics of certain request forms). This paucity often renders impossible the direct comparison of my findings with those of other investigators. To overcome these problems I have deployed a number of strategies. Where possible I indicate any wider evidence which suggests that the forms of behaviour being addressed are characteristic of children of this age; I also explore, especially in chapter 6, how far my results are compatible with the findings of different types of investigation which have dealt with young childrens' request behaviour; and, usually at the end of each chapter and again in chapter 6, I identify ways in which my findings mesh with other lines of child investigation, with work on emotions, morality and cognition for example, again in order to explicate the relationship between my findings and these broader research traditions. So, although this is principally just a study of one child, I hope to articulate the findings in such a way as to make apparent their wider potential significance.

Context, intersubjectivity and understandings

From about the age of 9 months the child's understanding of the world becomes increasingly calibrated with the local culture to which she is exposed. She becomes familiar with everyday objects and their various uses, capable of grasping what is said to her when this talk is supported by non-verbal and contextual clues, and she develops the facility to initiate lines of conduct with those around her in ways that give her a degree of control over that which takes place in her immediate environment. During her second year of life important further developments take place, ones to be described in the next chapter. As well as making advances with regard to her levels of linguistic production and comprehension the child also develops the facility to attempt rectification and repair on occasions in which her communicative intentions have been misunderstood. This is a critical skill, as Schegloff (1991b), and perhaps Hamlyn (1983), have argued. It is only through having a procedure for rectifying such misunderstandings that the child can potentially discriminate for others those occasions on which she has been adequately understood from those on which this is not the case: it is the availability of what Schegloff has called 'third position repair', the ability to display that someone has just misunderstood what you last said, that permits the child to differentiate states of mutual understanding which obtain.

The process of building a version of the world which is tuned to that of the parent eventually involves the child in more than the act of engaging in third position repair. What also emerges in the later part of the child's second year of life is the capacity to recognize that other people are acting on understandings, and it is through becoming able to act on such recognitions, normally in ways designed to be consistent with them, that a new order of intersubjectivity is made possible for the child. In effect, her actions can then come to embody understandings which she has derived from prior interaction, understandings which, as was mentioned earlier, have the properties of being local, public and moral. Tracing the emergence of the capacity to recognize such understandings is another major line of enquiry in the next chapter. There I shall examine the range of evidence in the literature which relates to the emergence of contextual understanding as it is displayed in the child's conduct with other people during her second year of life. Within this material, and in my own recordings, what I find most striking is the capacity of children, at or shortly after 18 months of age, to articulate such understandings overtly as negative statements, statements designed to reiterate prohibitions and the like, but ones which are essentially designed to be agreed with by the parent. For me this is the earliest sign of the child having the capacity to operate with the forms of sequential understanding which come to inform her conduct in her third year of life, the forms which I then go on to identify more thoroughly and extensively in chapters 3 to 5.

Before getting down to business let me make a final cautionary comment about my use of the term *understanding*. What I shall be claiming is that the child has ways through which she displays that she recognizes the existence of such understandings, and it is these ways, and the *kinds* of understanding implied by these ways, which are at the forefront of my concerns. While the fact that these ways come to be available to the child is important, as is the fact that their existence permits a more delicate attunement between her version of the world and that of her parents, it is not being claimed that these understandings represent, in some perfectly co-ordinated way, beliefs which are, in fact, jointly shared by both the child and the parent. Even in adult interaction, sophisticated analysis, from Goffman onwards, suggests that such a vision of shared understanding would not necessarily be appropriate.[9] In the child–parent encounters to be examined we shall see that an orientation to such understandings on the part of the child can generate conflict as much as consensus. And even where consensus appears to reign supreme – where, for example, the parent appears willing to go along with what the child wants her to do – that willingness might arise from recognizing simply that the child has a legitimate basis for expecting her to do this thing rather than from a desire on the parent's part to do the thing. What an orientation to public understandings brings into play is a discourse which takes heed of what has previously been said – it is a discourse in which the child can sometimes rely on what has been said to warrant what she does next. To claim that the child and the parent both take heed of, and pay respect to, that which is, or has been, accountably present in the talk is quite a different claim to one which formulates intersubjectivity in terms which hinge around the idea of two minds thinking in like manner. What the child acquires, and what the subsequent analyses seek to trace, is a capacity to identify, and give special regard to, stances which have been taken by her interactional partner. It is in taking such stances into

[9] In the opening pages of his first book Goffman describes the state of play that exists between people in encounters as a working consensus: he writes 'Together the participants contribute to a single over-all definition of the situation which involves not so much a real agreement as to what exists but rather a real agreement as to whose claims concerning what issues will be temporarily honoured' (1959:9–10). Throughout Garfinkel's writing, and in the work of Schutz (1962) on which Garfinkel, in part, initially drew, there is also a recognition and documentation of the importance of shared social practices as the critical vehicle through which we assemble some mutually recognizable and intelligible sense of social occasions (for a useful account see Heritage 1984). Clearly, these practices, together with those to which Goffman alludes, require of people a psychological make-up that permits their operation. But they do not require of people that they necessarily think about a situation in the same way, even when in apparent agreement and harmony. Participating in interaction imposes disciplines on us, thought is a free area; thus the potential for disassociation comes to be an integral feature of our ordinary dealings with each other.

account that the child is taking a major step towards recognizing the existence of a realm of social reality which is, in some sense, independent of herself; a step into the realm of what Durkheim may have been referring to when he spoke of collective representations.

2

Requesting at 12–24 months: an overview

At about 9 months of age children make heavy use of manual gestures when attempting to communicate with other people. Two such gestures which come to the fore at that time, the reach and the point, appear to be in use among all normal children of this age. Although the hand configurations characteristic of these two gestures can be found among younger children it is only then, at about 9 months, that they are constructed as symbolic, communicative acts.[1] In the case of reaching, for example, whereas earlier forms of this gesture were associated with attempts by the child to grasp an object we now find many occasions on which reaches are performed in a non-effortful way. Furthermore, on these same occasions we can find the child sustaining the reach in a fixed position. Usually such manual acts are accompanied by vocalizations (Bruner, Roy and Ratner 1982; Masur 1983:101–2). The sounds that children produce at this age are not normally recognizable versions of adult words. Sometimes technically known as 'protowords', these sounds are usually idiosyncratic to particular children; but, for any given child, they have systematic and distinctive links with gestures which the child produces. For example, the child studied by Halliday (1975) consistently used the sound [nã] with his reach gestures at this age, the child studied by Carter (1978) used [m]-initial monosyllables, while Amy, our subject in this book, used [ʔəɐ̈ʔə]. It is the co-occurrence of these various features, these ways in which gestures are performed together with their accompanying vocalizations, which suggests that for the child these gesture/sound combinations represent a new, symbolic way of engaging in communicative activity with those around her.

A key feature of these new gesture/sound combinations, from the

---

[1] Relevant research relating to pointing can be found in Hannan (1987); see also, on pointing, Murphy (1978), Zinober and Martlew (1985a) and Butterworth and Grover (1988).

child's point of view, is that they are designed so as to extract a response from the other party in the interaction (Griffiths 1985:93). This is documented in a number of ways. The most important of these is the fact that if the child does not obtain a response from the person she is addressing then she can employ a follow-up turn in pursuit of her sequential objective. Where, for example, she does not obtain a response, she can re-do the vocalization which was used in her initial gesture/sound combination, often whilst maintaining her gesture in position. From about 12 months onwards her interest in eliciting a response through these acts is also conveyed in other ways, notably by gazing towards the person she is addressing, either during the initial production of a gesture/sound combination, or during some subsequent attempt to elicit a response. In general terms, it seems plain enough that the child's communicative skills at this age allow her to engage in a variety of initiating communicative acts, and that these are designed with expectation of a response from her recipient.

So far I have mentioned one contingency which the child may be faced with after producing an initial gesture/sound combination, namely non-response on the part of the person she is addressing. This, however, is only one of several sequential possibilities with which she can be confronted. The other party, who, from now on, for convenience only, I will refer to as the parent,[2] may attempt to clarify with the child what it is that she wants. In her study of 3 children between the ages of 12 and 18 months Golinkoff found that on average 49 per cent of their initiating gesture/sound combinations were followed by some display of comprehension problem on the part of the adult (1986:466; see also Bruner et al. 1982:101–4). These displays can prompt various kinds of negotiation about the nature of what it is that the child wants. A further contingency that can confront the child is one in which the parent, wilfully or otherwise, misunderstands the nature of her communicative

---

[2] Clearly, the child is capable of interacting with people other than parents at this age. For example, in many cultures it has been the responsibility of elder female children to play a major role in the care of the young (Whiting and Edwards 1988). Whether, when and in what ways the child of this age treats a parent distinctively is thus an interesting empirical question, but one which is largely unaddressed in the literature. The caution I display in the text is meant to index such matters, matters which have been of central relevance to the writings of conversation analysts on adults (Schegloff 1991a). Preferably, I would choose the more neutral term *recipient*, or some such, to avoid any implication that the processes being discussed, both here and later in the book, are in some way specific to the child's dealings with her parents. Sometimes I do use the term 'recipient' but, as the parent is the main co-interactant discussed in the book, and as the term 'parent' may be more digestible than 'recipient', I normally throw caution to the wind.

intention. For example, when the child wants the parent to pass object x to her, the parent may pass object y (Wootton 1994). Evidently, during the early part of her second year of life, the child is placed in the position of having to navigate these various sequential contingencies and, in so doing, to construct further actions in pursuit of her objective. In the course of this her initial sequential expectation will guide and inform her judgements as to the adequacy or otherwise of the parental response with which she is confronted.[3]

Between 12 and 18 months the child increasingly resorts to alternative techniques in order to further her communicative objectives. Pointing gestures, for example, originally not found in activities such as requests for object transfer, quickly come to be usable in various such activities; and once she is able to use recognizable words then these can come to play a part in her navigation procedures. In #2.1, for example, Amy (A) makes an initial request with a version of her request protoword together with a point. Her mother (M; F denotes father) passes her an object that she does not appear to want, a saucer. That this not what she was wanting is partly conveyed through the comportment of her right hand (see lines 4–9), and partly through her absence of immediate interest in making some use of the saucer.[4] In addition, it is conveyed by the fact that, at line 11, she re-requests by pointing again and producing a version of 'cup daddy', to indicate that it is my cup that she is wanting rather than her mother's saucer.

[3] A further potential by-product for the child of being able to construct initial acts which have a sequential expectation attached to them is that it enables a discrimination to take place between different orders of immediately subsequent parental behaviour. Specifically, it becomes possible to make a distinction between forms of parental behaviour which are *attempting* to satisfy the child's sequential expectation, forms which are in some cases successful and in other cases less so, and forms of behaviour which are quite unrelated to the request. By the latter I am thinking of various kinds of occasion, but the most extreme would be those on which, after the child has made a request, the recipient turns to speak to someone else on unrelated matters. One investigable issue, not addressed in the literature to my knowledge, is the way in which the child comes to display an orientation to these distinctions.

[4] This display of not wanting an object, both in this and other such cases in request sequences at this age, is complicated because, in such sequences, the child displays a willingness to take objects even though they are not the ones she is seeking, e.g. in #2.1 there is every suggestion that the child would have taken hold of the saucer if her mother had placed it in her hand. Interestingly, the mother does not do this. Although she moves it initially on a trajectory towards the hand she finds a basis for then choosing to change her mind and place it on the table. The fact that the mother, also, can find a basis for the child to be not wishing to take the saucer is, of course, consistent with the analysis that I am offering of the child's behaviour here. For much fuller discussion of this and comparable cases see Wootton (1994).

2.1 1;7/232

Both parents sit at the dining table with a cup and saucer in front of each of them; Amy sits in her high-chair next to her mother. When the mother puts her cup down the child requests that it be passed to her; the cup, without the saucer, is given to her and she holds this in her lh; she briefly looks inside it and then makes a further request:

1	A:	[ʔəʔhʔəːʔ] ((+ rh point in the direction of F's cup and M's
2		saucer, which are on the same line of vision for her))
3		(.)
4	M:	And the saucer you want as well ((in the course of saying
5		this M moves the saucer towards A: A opens her rh, as
6		though willing to take it, but does not move it towards the
7		saucer: M puts the saucer on A's tray rather than in her
8		hand: as soon as it is clear to A that M is going to do this
9		she bunches the fingers of her rh ready to point))
10		(.)
11	A:	[ʔʌʔʌ] cu' dadee ((+ rh point at F's cup + gaze at cup))
12		(.)
13	M:	Daddy's cup ((M reaches for F's cup to pass to A))

In some such sequences it remains unclear whether the child ever succeeds in achieving what she wants.[5] But in most, as in #2.1, after some toing-and-froing the child is successful. These periods of toing-and-froing provide the child with experience in dealing with sequences embedded between an initiating child act and the eventual appropriately fitted response to that act. Embedded sequences can take various forms, but await detailed technical description in the context of child–parent talk at this age. In #2.1 the parent's incorrect pass of the saucer becomes the first turn of such a sequence by virtue of the child's declining to take it (though see fn. 4). In #2.6 (p. 49) another kind of embedded sequence is initiated by the mother's **Mm::?** at line 4. In further cases, in request sequences, insertions can be initiated with adult queries like 'Do you want x?' subsequent to a child initiation. The child's grasp and control of such

---

[5] There is a possible example of this kind of phenomenon in that part of #2.2 in which the child does not appear to be requesting. At lines 1 and 4 she seems to be asking her mother about what is under the lid of the sand tray. Neither turn receives an appropriately fitted reply, and the child then appears to abandon her enquiry. Abandoning such sequences is an important way of coping with demonstrable and continuing lack of grasp on the part of the parent.

sequences is somewhat variable at this age. In #2.6, at lines 5–6, Amy manages to clarify the nature of what it is that she wants principally through non-verbal means. But Zukow, Reilly and Greenfield (1982) have shown that the child's comprehension of turns such as 'Do you want x?' is heavily dependent on matters such as whether the parent is clearly showing, or otherwise indicating, that which is being referred to. Even where the parent does succeed in identifying what it is that the child wants she often makes no affirmative response. In effect, she is more adept at rectifying inappropriate parental actions than she is in affirming appropriate ones. Nevertheless, what is clear is that by the age of 18 months the child is capable of drawing on both linguistic and non-verbal resources in the course of clarifying her communicative intent.

The child's sequential expectation attached to an initial gesture/sound combination can, therefore, inform and have a bearing not just on the immediate parental response but also on the trajectory of extended subsequent sequences, and more particularly on the construction of the child's actions within those sequences. Furthermore, it is the satisfaction of this sequential expectation that appears to play a central role in whether or not the child manages to achieve recognizable states of mutual, common understanding with the parent. In the case of requests for the transfer of objects, for example, it is the child's acceptance of the object being proffered by the parent, or, more precisely, the *way* in which the child accepts it, that constitutes grounds for the parent to suppose that the nature of the child's initial request has been adequately divined. The sense of intersubjective alignment is an outcome of the way in which the child deals with any response that the parent makes. The fact that the child has available to her ways of displaying a parental response to be either adequate or inadequate means that intersubjective alignment is a matter that the child can attend to, in an ongoing fashion. And the existence of the sequential expectation creates both the template and the interactional incentive for engaging in these forms of attentiveness. These considerations obtain in *all* sequences which are initiated by the kinds of gesture/sound combinations that I have been discussing so far.

Request indicating devices

It is because many of the child's early gesture/sound combinations are designed to elicit responses from her recipient that some, such as Carter (1978), have used the term 'request' to cover a wide range of actions by the child at this age. For example, when a child of 12 months uses a sustained point along with her protoword associated with reference, she expects the parent minimally to look at what she is pointing at. An act is required of the parent in response to this initiation, and to this extent the initiation is a request of sorts. In this brief overview of requesting prior to 2 years of age, however, I want to confine my remarks to a narrower domain of request-like actions. The requests between the ages of 2 and 3, those that form the core concerns of this book, are ones in which the child is trying to enlist some form of assistance from the parent. Her interest there is in things like obtaining objects and getting the parent to help her in solving problems; it is the precursors to this type of request that we need to identify. In this section I will briefly describe some of the main changes in the verbal and non-verbal composition of these acts before 2 years of age, and in the next section I will discuss the principal forms of knowledge which appear to inform their production.

Between the ages of about 12 and 18 months there are quite a variety of request techniques, even within the more delimited range of such actions with which we are concerned. In general, the techniques seem to be differentiated according to the type of interactional business which they are used to deal with. Certain of these techniques seem idiosyncratic to quite specific types of interactional occasion. For example, particular words can be combined with particular types of gesture, as when the child uses the word 'up' in combination with a raising of her arms so as to request that she be picked up (Lock 1978); or, in what Bruner *et al.* (1982) refer to as 'requests for joint role enactment', the child may draw the parent's attention to what she wants the parent to do by holding, showing or touching relevant things in the immediate environment:

> The child may bounce on the adult's knee to request 'Ride a Cock Horse', take the microphone to father to offer him a turn at talking into it, or touch the radiator and guide the observer's hand to it to share the feel of its warmth.   (1982:110)

Bruner *et al.* go on to note that although vocalizations can occur in this type of case they have 'neither the stereotypy nor the insistence' found in other requests. In other words the devices used to convey such requests are relatively idiosyncratic to the lines of action they are attempting to get underway.

In contrast, certain routine interactional tasks attract much more stereotypy in their design. The best example of this is the request for object transfer, instances in which the child wants some object that the parent is either holding or in a position to obtain for her. This is a routine enough situation because, even though the child may now be mobile, many objects that she may be interested in obtaining are, intentionally or inadvertently, located in positions out of her reach. The gesture/sound combination consisting of a reach and request protoword, that I have already mentioned, represents the child's earliest request device designed to deal with this contingency. Although this interactional circumstance may diminish in significance, relative to those occasioning other request devices, in the period up to 24 months (e.g. Haselkorn 1981; Bruner *et al.* 1982), it nevertheless continues to be a significant site for requests even beyond 24 months, and the signals contained within the device undergo important changes. Quite early on, at 12 months in the case of my own daughter, we find that pointing rather than reaching can be used in conjunction with the object transfer request protoword. Such referential concerns are further exhibited once the child starts using recognizable words, normally at or around 16 months. These can then come to be incorporated into this request device, though often, in the initial stages, as in #2.1 (line 11), they supplement rather than replace the request protoword. Once the child is able to use other words such as 'more', a word often among the first 50 words acquired, then this can serve as the vocal element for requesting a variety of different objects, without naming them. This word is also useful in a number of other contexts, such as the aforementioned 'requests for joint role enactment', as it can serve as a vehicle for getting the parent to do something without having to spell out what it is that should be done. Quite quickly this word becomes combined with other words, to become a typical example of the child's early two-word combinations. Amy's first certain uses of such a combination occur on our recordings at 21 months, in constructions like **more bread**.

Before the second birthday further major changes will have occurred which have implications for children's requests in a variety of different interactional circumstances. By then the gestures that were so integral a part of early request design are much less apparent. Although the open-handed reach and pointing can still occur, they appear to serve more specific interactional functions that, at these later ages, have yet to be fully described (though see Masur 1983 and Zinober and Martlew 1985a, 1985b). For some time most children will have been using action words such as 'chase', 'sit', 'up' and 'down' (the latter in their verb-like action senses), agent identification words like 'mummy' and object words like 'bread' and 'cup'. Indeed, by 20 months their general vocabulary is likely to exceed 50 words. Such words, alone or in combination, may still be used to make requests, but before 24 months certain linguistic designs come to have a favoured status for the child in this regard. Often, for example, the verb 'want' now comes to be widely used. At 23 months Amy was using constructions like 'I want x' in a variety of contexts (see, for example, line 1 of #2.7), although a more frequently used design for her was 'I like x', as in **I like more, I like daddy's** and **Like 'at sweets up there**. These designs have the property of being more generally usable than many earlier request designs; they can be used to instigate a range of request-like business, such as enlisting help from an adult and suggesting a line of action as well as requesting the transfer of some object. One implication of this is that the child is now clearly in the position of being capable of building her request design for any given thing in a number of different ways. For example, in the case of requesting more food at 23 months she could, and does, say **more** or **I want more** or **I like more** or she may just name the food that she wants. In the next section I will in part discuss work which argues that alternative ways of requesting for any given thing may be available to the child even earlier than this. For the moment, however, the point for emphasis is that, by the time of her second birthday, the child has a number of widely used request designs to select from when enacting any particular request.

In this section I have not discussed all the various circumstances and forms of child request between 12 and 24 months. Several fairly comprehensive accounts of these matters exist, though there is much debate concerning the most appropriate ways of describing and classifying such actions both at the single- and multiple-word stages of development.[6] Some of these debates need not concern us, but some have a relevance to my task in the next section, which is to take stock of the kinds of knowledge which appear to inform request design from about 12 months onwards. In the course of this I shall be amplifying somewhat on aspects of the brief overview that I have presented above as well as documenting some aspects that have as yet received no attention.

Knowledge that informs requesting

One of the main arguments in this book will be that from about 2 years onwards children take account of understandings that have been arrived at in earlier talk. That this is so can be deduced from the ways in which these understandings come to inform the organization of request behaviour.

---

[6] A useful overview of these matters is contained in Ingram (1989: chapters 6 and 7).

Documenting this case and its various implications is a matter that is of concern to later chapters. At the moment I want to identify the kinds of knowledge that researchers have located as potentially of relevance to the design of requests in the period between 12 and 24 months. In doing this I hope to contextualize the later chapters and to identify early signs of the child's use of sequential knowledge which prefigure the phenomena which are the focus of my later discussion.

Conceptual underpinnings of words

Perhaps the largest body of work concerned with children's knowledge at 12–24 months has been concerned with the semantic and conceptual underpinnings that inform the child's use of single words or combinations of words. Various research traditions have addressed these issues, of which three will be mentioned here. First is research concerned with the ways in which the child attaches meaning to particular words. It is well known, for example, that the child aged between about 18 and 24 months appears, by comparison with her later usage, either to underextend or overextend the referents to which she applies some words. These types of phenomena have become the focus for debate as to the relative merits of rival theories about word meaning, the principal current contenders being feature theory and prototype theory (Ingram 1989: chapter 8). As far as I can tell this research has little direct bearing on the child's request behaviour. Second is that body of work which has sought to identify sets of semantic relations that underlie the variety of multi-word utterances that children come to be capable of constructing in the second half of their second year of life. For example, it has been shown that in children's two-word combinations the possessor/possession relation is likely to be one such underlying semantic relation, realized by utterances such as 'mummy chair', 'daddy sock', etc. A relatively small set of such relations appears to be common to children of this age learning a variety of languages (see Ingram 1989: section 7.3 for a useful overview). Third are those attempts to connect theories of cognitive development with the child's emerging language. The most influential cognitive theory in this respect has been that of Piaget who has quite specific claims to make about alterations in children's thought processes during the period 12–18 months. For example, for him, fully developed object permanence and the capacity for mental representation only emerge at about 15 months, and writers such as Bloom have identified this as a necessary precondition for the rapid expansion in children's vocabulary that is usually evident after about 18 months (Bloom 1973; Bloom, Lifter and Broughton 1985).

This kind of work has done much to specify the kind of grasp that children have of those words that they use, especially when comprehension studies are taken alongside those of children's production; and such studies can have quite direct implications for child request behaviour. For example, it is of great interest that children begin to use their object request device mainly by requesting objects that are in sight, often ones that the parent is actually holding. Only later, at about 14–15 months, does the child begin to make requests for absent objects, ones not in sight – that is at about the time that Piagetian theory would suggest the onset of fully fledged object permanence (Bruner et al. 1982). But, usually it is more difficult to make connections between the concerns of these studies and the child's organization of her interactional practices. Take the work on the possessor/possession semantic relation as an example. The fact that the child has some grasp of this notion seems fairly clear both from this work and from research which has explored how young children negotiate the ownership of objects with their peers (Ross and Conant 1992:171–4). The question remains, however, as to what kinds of understanding the child has about possession. By this I am referring to the various social understandings and conventions which cluster around occasions on which possession is a matter of concern. For example, the notion of ownership can confer various entitlements – entitlements to be asked for things that 'belong' to you, entitlements to ask for things back when others have been allowed to use them, entitlements to have a say in the ways in which others are using them; similarly there can be corresponding obligations when the object in question does not belong to you. And in the latter case we can also come to recognize distinctions between things that are likely to belong to someone and things that belong to no-one or to anyone at all.[7] These matters are somewhat marginal to the linguistic concerns of those who are interested in identifying the semantic primitives which inform the range of early word combinations of which children are capable. They are fairly central, however, for the question of how the child's request behaviour is organized with respect to what she knows about possessions and relationships of possession. The child's grasp of matters relating to possession at this age is rather different from our own. For example, in the early months of her second year one can request to look at something which a child is

---

[7] My points here lean on suggestive discussion by Sacks (1992:I, 384–8) concerning the ways in which we, as adults, can orient to social understandings concerning possession.

holding, only to find that as soon as the object has been passed over to you she immediately wants it back again – even when you thought you had made it plain that you only wanted to look at the object briefly and temporarily. It is also clear that there is important cross-cultural variability in practices relating to possession (see especially, Schieffelin 1990:134, 178), though what is less clear is the precise age when children display some order of control over these practices. However, these points suggest that discovering what it is that children understand about possession, especially through the manner in which they act, is an important research objective. It is unfortunate, therefore, that rather little is known about these things (though see Ross and Conant 1992).

Although, therefore, there are sometimes links to be made between requesting and traditions of research which have focused on representations and representational procedures underlying language, these links are usually subject to the kinds of difficulty just mentioned. By virtue of abstracting properties of language from contexts of use, and leaving unanalysed the roles which such language plays in those contexts of use, we are given little more than hints as to the nature of such knowledge and how it informs the child's ongoing verbal and non-verbal conduct.

Scripts

A second body of research that claims to describe knowledge that the child brings with her to social action is that concerned with *scripts*. Nelson (Nelson and Gruendel 1981) first explored the possibility that through participation and observation children build up event representations, scripts concerning the canonical ways in which familiar events proceed. Such a possibility is important for my overall arguments in this book in that this suggests that the child's actions may in some way be guided, in any given stretch of action, by a trans-contextual and pre-existing sense of a normal order of events. If this is so then any given child act, at least in some circumstances, may be organized by reference to such an event template. Research which explores the child's grasp of scripts in the 12- to 24-month age range has mainly explored this by examining the child's capacity to recall different types of event. Both experimental (e.g. Bauer and Thal 1990) and naturalistic (e.g. Nelson 1989, 1993) research suggests that, particularly towards the end of this period, the child does have the capacity to memorize orderings of events, and a fairly robust sense of the ordering of certain familiar events. For example, where a familiar event is presented to the 21-month-old child with its constituents in a scrambled order the child will often unscramble it into its familiar pattern in the course of reproducing it (Bauer and Thal 1990). From this research there seems little doubt that the child coming up to 2 years old has the capacity to retain within her memory some kind of knowledge about the canonical organizations of various events in which she has been involved.

The question remains as to what part such script-like knowledge might play in the child's productive ongoing behaviour, in the context of activities like requesting. Here it seems to me that the relevant evidence is somewhat unclear and fragmentary. Bruner *et al.*'s (1982) discussion of the development of two children is the one that has most explicitly addressed this kind of possibility. They note that, when requesting objects that she cannot see, the child will gesture in the direction of the canonical location in which such a thing is to be found, thus implying a knowledge of the typical whereabouts of objects with which she is familiar. Furthermore, they argue that in the third phase of development of what they call 'requests for supportive action' – requests in which the child attempts to enlist the parent's assistance in the enactment of an activity – the child's strategies of 'successive guidance' of the parent presuppose the existence of scripts. In these cases, which did not appear before 22 months, where the child needs parental assistance, say, to obtain an object, she breaks down the requested actions into two or more steps. For example, she first gets the parent's attention, then encourages her to move towards the vicinity in which the relevant object is to be found, and only then, when the parent is appropriately positioned, makes the actual request for the object.

The best evidence for the influence of scripts on child activity would come from studies which identified these scripts independently of the lines of conduct to which they were supposedly related. No such studies exist to my knowledge, nor is there any overall account of the main script-like knowledge that children of this age might possess. So we are left in the position of, first, recognizing that children do probably have some order of control over event-like representations of the kind denoted by scripts, but, second, having little clear idea as to the role that these understandings come to play in the ongoing design of conduct. The potential significance of script-like knowledge in accounting for the child's request behaviour will be touched on at several points in this book. The principal weakness of the notion arises from an observation that has already been made, namely that by the later part of her second year of life the child can employ several ways of making requests for any given thing to any given person. If this is so then it is difficult to see how scripts *per se* can play a part in accounting for the nature of this request differentiation – which is to say that scripts are weak with regard to their capacity to explicate variation in the detailed nature of the child's conduct.[8]

The principle of informativeness

Within the age range of 18–24 months the question of why the child selects one way of designing an action rather than another has been most explicitly addressed in research associated with Greenfield (Greenfield and Zukow 1978; Greenfield, Reilly, Leaper and Baker 1985; see also Miller 1979). This is concerned with the verbal, rather than non-verbal, features of action design. In broad terms it is argued that in choosing a word the child presupposes certain knowledge, knowledge which is, in effect, redundant. The kind of knowledge which is treated in this way is that representing constant features of the child's immediate environment. The words which the child actually chooses to use draw attention to non-constant features of the environment, to things that are variable and changeable in the local context in question. So, for example, according to what Greenfield calls this 'principle of informativeness' we might normally expect a child, when making a request of her mother at the one-word stage of development, to focus in her choice of word on what it is that she wants her mother to *do* rather than on the fact that she wants *her* to do it. Her mother is a relatively constant request recipient, whereas the particular object or act being requested is a more variable element. So, when a child wants her mother to pass her a cup we might normally expect the child to say 'cup' rather than 'mummy'.

To claim, in such circumstances as those described above, that the child lexically presupposes an agent like 'mummy' is in various ways controversial among researchers who have attempted to make links between the child's grasp of grammatical structure in her one- and two-word speech (see Ingram 1989:240–5 for a useful summary discussion). More central to my concerns here, however, is the role of the child's non-verbal behaviour. While it is the case that, at the one-word stage, the child does tend to lexicalize, for example, the request object or action, rather than the request recipient, it is also the case that the child has alternative ways available to

---

[8] For further difficulties with the notion of script, from various disciplinary perspectives, see Holland, Holyoak, Nisbett and Thagard (1986:12–14), A. Clark (1989:27–31), Forrester (1992:19–20) and Toren (1993).

her for identifying her request recipient. For example, after about 12 months of age I have already noted that she systematically uses gaze at her recipient as a communicative device, and other aspects such as body positioning can also make clear at whom a request is directed. Such practices display an ongoing orientation to her current recipient even though that concern may not normally be encoded in word selection. In fact, Greenfield and her colleagues explicitly recognize that what they are addressing is lexical design rather than pragmatic design: 'The "implicit" elements are, however, generally explicit from the point of view of the pragmatic component for they are expressed by means of non-verbal communication' (Greenfield *et al.* 1985:251). By focusing exclusively on what is lexicalized, therefore, this approach is of limited relevance to any consideration of developmental changes in the overall design of request actions.

Greenfield and her co-workers propose a complex set of rules that inform the implicit word selections which take place at this age whenever the child speaks (see especially Greenfield and Zukow 1978). In general terms, these claim that the child takes account of such matters as who is to carry out an action, who possesses an object, the constancy of an object or an action in any given situation, etc. These considerations have been shown to have a relevance to what the child says at both her one-word and two-word stages of language development, though their significance after the two-word stage is less researched. There are potential logical difficulties in using naturalistic data as a basis for these claims because it is difficult to assess independently the rules of informativeness and the child's verbal behaviour which supposedly attends to, and evidences the existence of, such rules (Pea 1979); but from both experimental and naturalistic studies it seems quite likely that the child can take account of such matters when making a lexical selection, and in this sense Greenfield's approach identifies parameters of social action which any analysis certainly needs to consider. A difficulty I have, however, is the emphasis placed in Greenfield's account on what the child immediately *perceives* in the situation, on the constancy or non-constancy of people, objects or actions in this respect. What this underplays, specifically with regard to lexical selection, is an emerging sensitivity to the sequential positioning of talk on the part of the child. For example, in #2.1 the child employs two means of requesting the saucer. First, at line 1, she uses a point gesture together with a version of her request protoword. Then, at line 11, after being passed what for her was the wrong thing, she points again whilst saying **cu' dadee**, in conjunction with another version of her request protoword. This could mean 'I want daddy's cup' or 'I want daddy to pass me the cup.' For my purposes we do not need to weigh up the merits of each alternative. Either way, the possibility arises here that the second technique that the child uses to locate the saucer is specifically sensitive to the fact that her recipient has initially failed to identify what she is wanting. The words **cu' dadee** may be selected to handle the specific type of interactional contingency that has arisen. This in turn suggests that the nature of such contingencies may systematically exercise an influence on the child's lexical selections contained within them. Although this specific type of contingency, one in which the parent passes the child an incorrect object, may not be especially frequent, we have already noted that a large proportion of sequences initiated by the child at around, say, 18 months, are ones in which some form of further negotiation and discussion takes place as to the child's communicative intention (Golinkoff 1986). So, in all these cases the child will be constructing a next turn in a sequence in the light of what has just taken place. Although such sequential considerations play an important part in Greenfield's account of syntactic changes between the child's one- and two-word speech (Greenfield *et al.* 1985), their potential modifications of the 'principle of informativeness' seem, to me, underplayed.[9]

The child's attention to the local sequential history of an occasion can also take other forms. Consider #2.7 (p. 51), and the matter of how the child uses the terms 'please' and 'thankyou'. Presumably the child's selection of **Please** at line 5 is influenced by the sequential position of F's **What do you sa:y?**, which occurs immediately after a child request, **Want 'at**. If F's question had occurred in a different sequential position, namely when the requested object was actually being passed to the child, then the child could have replied with the word 'thankyou'. In these ways it is clear that the child of this age can take sequential position into account when making lexical selections. I now want to argue that other forms of understanding based on prior sequences of action can also come to be acknowledged within the child's talk, and that an important facet of development during the second half of the child's second year of life is the way in which such

[9] The child's attention to the local sequential history of an occasion can also take other forms. I have already noted that at this age a word that is frequently found in the child's vocabulary is 'more'. Once this is used to express recurrence – when using it, rather than, say, an object name – the child is acknowledging that what is being asked for now is equivalent in some way to what has been given or asked for before, perhaps as a result of some prior request. The selection of this word is therefore contingent on, and a means of displaying, the child's awareness of such sequential considerations.

understandings undergo transformation. It is these kinds of understanding to which I now turn.

Privileged access and negative understandings

Between 12 and 24 months the child increasingly recognizes that her conduct is subject to social constraints of various kinds. One way in which this becomes apparent is through ways in which she makes it evident that the consent of the parent is required for certain lines of action to proceed. In a sense, the very fact that the child can engage in requests for objects at all from about 12 months onwards, rather than just taking the object in question, is evidence of this. In this regard Bruner *et al.* make the following observation:

> When the child requests an object held by another, and it is within his reach, he does not seize it straightaway. He makes a 'formal' request, extending his hand *towards* the object first. Only one instance of an outright grab was recorded (at 11 months) when the desired object was held by another infant. This suggests, in effect, that the child in this early period already recognizes request as a means of altering possession.   (1982:98)

To some extent this is, of course, oversimplified. The child, both in the early and later parts of this period, can simply take an object that a co-participant is holding. For example, I have already noted (pp. 36–7) the intriguing phenomenon of the child (at around 14 months) immediately taking back an object that she has just allowed someone else to hold: distinctive sequential formations of this kind seem to matter to the child from a very early age.[10] In most cases, however, she does not simply take things from other people, which suggests that the child's actions are increasingly informed by a capacity to differentiate occasions where 'takes' are in some way warranted from those in which they are not. Implied in all this is a growing awareness that other people can exercise certain forms of control over the child's courses of action. Initially, say at 12 months, such a recognition may, in the case of object requests, be limited to a recognition that by virtue of holding an object the other party may have what Edwards (1978) has called a 'privileged access' to that object (see also Ross and Conant 1992:172). Such a recognition, when taken together with local circumstances, may lead the child, on the whole, to treat objects held by persons differently from objects that lie on surfaces within her reach. I say 'may'

---

[10] For discussion of some of the social laminations involved in object transfer behaviour involving young children see R. A. Clark (1978) and Wootton (1991).

because systematic studies of this kind of phenomenon have not been carried out. What is clear enough, however, is that the domain of privileged access is significantly altered during the course of the child's second year.

Privileged access is broadened in the sense that the child comes to recognize that the parent is to be treated as having control over things not just by virtue of holding them but by virtue of further kinds of consideration. By 23 months, for example, Amy can employ forms of request initiation which appear to check with the parent on whether or not a line of action that she is intent on is permissible. In #2.2 at line 6 she says **O:n the::re?** when she is standing next to her sand tray, an utterance that her mother interprets as an enquiry related to an interest in standing in the sand tray, and as unconnected to the immediately preceding line of talk. Such an interpretation also seems consistent with the child's understanding in that early in the course of her mother's reply Amy moves to crawl on to the sand tray. In short, the domain of control that the child can treat her co-participant as having over her actions is extended so as to include not just cases in which the co-participant has privileged access, but also those in which the co-participant has other forms of entitlement to exercise control over the child's lines of action.

Privileged access also becomes more complicated during this period. Focus for a moment on those instances in which the child's co-participant

2.2 1;11/1:1:34

Amy runs out of the house into the yard where her sand tray is positioned close to the door. Her mother is standing close-by. The tray has its plastic cover on top of it:

1 A: Wha:t's in tha:t ((pointing to tray))

2 M: Watching tha:t=watching wha:t, ((i.e. mishearing what A
3   says))

4 A: ((now by the tray)) Wha:t's in tha:t
5   (.7)
6 A: O:n the::re? ((+brief gesture to the tray, and gazes at M))

7 M: D'you want to sta:nd on the:re=I think its allright if you
8   do::=I'm not su:re ((A starts to gear up for climbing on
9   top of the tray at the word 'stand'))

---

is treated differentially on the basis of their possession of an object, the earlier paradigmatic case of privileged access. Several investigators suggest that during this time period the notion of possession that the child operates with undergoes significant alteration (Carter 1975; Greenfield and Smith 1976). Broadly, it is claimed that it moves from a position in which objects are associated with people, simply by virtue of their having a perceived consistent association, to one in which a sense of 'belonging to' seems to inform the child's actions. Even so, by 18 months the child has still got far to go in mastering the various language games and understandings that can be bound to notions of possession. For example, although she may be prepared, sometimes only with encouragement, to ask for something on the understanding that it 'belongs' to someone else, the understanding that the object in question should be returned to its owner may still be a remote one.

2.3 From Edwards (1978:79): child aged 24 months 3 weeks

Child reaches for her mother's glasses on top of the television set:

M: Off. Leave them alone Helen

H: ((pulls back, and pointing at glasses says)) Mummy glasses

---

Edwards (1978:79) has argued that by about 18 months, the child's understandings concerning possession are increasingly shaped by the local conventions and beliefs of those in her immediate milieu. One way in which this is made manifest is through the child's own articulation of such understandings, often in prohibitional contexts. In #2.3, Edwards gives an example from his own daughter at 24 months. It is interesting that, here, Helen formulates the possessive relationship, **Mummy glasses**, in positive terms. Prior to this time, from roughly 18 months onwards, the child appears to articulate much of the conventional knowledge that she is acquiring in negative terms, and the ways in which she does this have an importance for the rest of this book as well as this chapter. The kind of phenomenon I have in mind here has been noticed by a number of previous observers of children (see Pea 1980 for an overview), but perhaps receives best treatment in Pea's own work (1978, 1980). An early example from the recordings of Amy is #2.4. Here, when she says **Nuh:::,** at line 8, Amy is identifying a further place, the top of my cup, in which it is not suitable for the lid that she is holding to be placed. In doing this she is picking another place similar to that which has just been prohibited by her mother, and she is displaying her understanding that the prohibition that was applicable to that first location is also applicable to this location. In this, and other analogous instances, the response from the parent is to agree with the child: my **No: not for daddy's cup no its just for your cup**, at line 11, in no way treats Amy's action as arising from a concern on her part to put the lid on my cup – intonationally it is constructed as an agreement with the claim that Amy is making.

2.4 1;7/44:06

Amy stands by her mother, who is sitting on the sofa. M has her own cup and saucer resting on her stomach, and A's drinking cup is on M's knee. Father is also sitting nearby. A has taken off the lid of her own drinking cup and makes to put it on top of M's cup:

```
1    M:    No I don't want it to go  in the::re  ((smiley voice))
                                    ⌈
2    F:                             ⌊No not in the:re Amy
3                          (.)  ((A withdraws lid))
4    M:    ⌈(        )
           ⌊
5    F:    Not in mummy's cup
6                     (4.3)  ((A looks at the lid and bites it))
7    F:    Its just for your cup

8    A:    Nuh:::= ((+ brief shake of head + point gesture, with the
9          hand that still holds the lid, in the direction of F's cup,
10         about three feet away from her))

11   F:    No: not for daddy's cup no its just for your cup
```

Now this is just one of a number of ways in which children may display an awareness of prohibitions. A further way, in fact the one that most interests Pea, is the child's employment of self-prohibition statements in the process of carrying out some course of action. From as young as 9 months the child can appear to check on the reaction of an adult to what she is doing, and by 18 months one can usually find instances in which the child will appear to check herself, perhaps by saying 'No', when engaging in some self-contained course of action. Pea argues, in Vygotskyan vein, that what is happening here is a transmutation process, one in which the child's knowledge of external prohibitions comes to be an internal standard used to guide her own ongoing conduct. For this reason such self-prohibitions have also attracted interest from more psychoanalytic investigators concerned with the emergence of conscience and superego (Emde, Johnson and Easterbrooks 1990).

What is of special interest, and developmentally new, in instances like #2.4, however, is the way in which the child publicly recapitulates the nature of understandings which have been arrived at. The key child turn there, described in lines 8–10, is constructed as a communicative act vis-à-vis the assembled company; it is designed to display for those present an understanding which the child has derived from the earlier part of the sequence. Unlike the self-prohibitions above it is not stated for its relevance to some line of action that the child is now about to embark on. And, partly because it is detached from such concerns, it stands as a type of utterance that the child need not have made at all. It is, if you like, just a statement about mutual, shared knowledge. And as it stands as warranted by the earlier understanding then it expects corroboration, agreement of sorts, from those who are present; indeed, parental agreement is the response that such turns normally get (as in this case, at line 11). In reproducing such understandings, therefore, the child is publicly entering into the security of a joint, mutually agreed-on world of understanding with the parent.

There are two further observations to be made about the articulation of these understandings by the child. The first is that by 23 months there is evidence, within the recordings of Amy, of their being producable at times which are more remote from the sequences in which these understandings were first jointly negotiated in interaction. In #2.5, for instance, Amy says **Cant take 'at do:wn** (line 13) accompanied by a brief hand gesture, shake of the head and gaze towards a high shelf on which there is a wooden parrot on a stand. In saying this she is articulating, in a more fully lexicalized way than at earlier times, an agreed-on joint understanding, that this object is not one that can be brought down for her to play with. This understanding does not emanate from the immediately prior interaction sequence, which has involved her in various activities related to building towers. Nor indeed has this topic occurred in an earlier part of the recording in question. Nevertheless, we know that this matter had been discussed at an earlier date with the child, and what seems clear enough is that **Cant take 'at do:wn** indexes that understanding. So, in saying this, the child can rely not just on herself having this understanding, but also on that understanding being available to those to whom she is speaking. Within the data that we have for Amy such remote negative understandings, as in #2.5, probably occurred later than those which were tied to particular sequences, as in #2.4, and it would be of great interest if that ordering turned out to be a systematic one for children of this age. More careful naturalistic studies of this kind of phenomenon are obviously needed in this regard. For our purposes here, however, the key point is that by 23 months there are clear cases of this child being able to display trans-sequence understandings through her production of these negative statements.

2.5 1;11/47:00

Amy sits in the middle of the room playing with her bricks. Her father is lying on the floor close-by, and her mother is sitting on the nearby sofa. M and F are talking together about an aspect of Amy's speech:

1	F:	I don't know I haven't really thought about it ⌐have you? ((to
2		M, turning to look at M at end of the turn))
3	M:	⌐((brief laugh))
4		(2.5)
5	A:	I'm making a big towe::r=
6	M:	=We::ll that's good isn't it? ((to A))
7		(1.4)
8	F:	I would think to us it would be quite lo:ng ⌐actually? ((to M))
9	M:	⌐Mm: : ye: : s ((to
10		F; A stopped playing with bricks, looking in M's direction))
11		(1.2)
12	M:	Yeah ((to F))
13	A:	Can't take 'at do:wn ((+shake of head and brief open-handed
14		gesture towards high shelf behind M and F))
15	M:	No you can't take that down because its fixed isn't it (.)
16		mummy fixed it up,

((there is subsequent talk which confirms that what A was referring to was the wooden parrot attached to a perch, which is on the shelf; A does not ask for it to be taken down))

The second further observation to be made about these negative statements is that although they occur principally in what have been called prohibitional contexts, situations in which parents have placed some form of
limitation on courses of action open to the child, they are not strictly
confined to such contexts. Extract 2.6 illustrates another way in which they
can arise in the context of requesting, though in this case what the child
articulates is an understanding about a course of action that arises out of
her own earlier stated preference rather than one articulated by the parent.
The child's concerns in this extract, at 19 months, centre around the toast
that she is eating at breakfast time – more specifically, with what is to be
spread on it. After initially asking for marmalade, prior to the transcript
beginning, she makes it patently clear that she does not like this, by passing
the toast back to her mother. The honeyed toast which she is then given
proves much more agreeable. About 5 minutes later, when the transcript
begins, she gestures towards the honey and asks for **M-mo::re**, and then
again, at lines 5–6, gesturally indicating her toast. It seems fairly clear that
she wants more honey on her toast, and, although her mother's vocal
response to all this (lines 7–8) looks somewhat equivocal, the fact that her
mother reaches for and picks up the honey jar is perfectly visible to the
child by the beginning of line 12. It is then that the child produces her negative vocalization, **N:uhuhuh**, together with her headshakes and point
towards the marmalade jar. As in some of the previous extracts, this statement indexes an understanding that is parasitic on an earlier sequence. In
this case, though, it is the child's own earlier display of her dispreference
for the marmalade, rather than an adult display of dispreference, which
forms the basis for her subsequent negative statement.[11]

Between 12 and 24 months of age, therefore, there seem to be consider-
able alterations with regard to the knowledge which the child takes into
account both when making requests and when not making them. In the
account above special emphasis has been placed on the latter situation.
From about the middle of this year onwards the child is capable of identifying, explicitly, courses of action on which it is inappropriate to embark.
She does this by drawing on understandings which have arisen in earlier
sequential positions, and the way in which she does this, by presenting negative statements for corroboration by the parent, displays a recognition on
her part that these understandings are *shared*, known in common. In

---

[11] In his discussion of these matters Edwards (1978:76) identifies other types of constraint
which the child can also come to recognize through such negative statements, notably phys-
ical constraints.

2.6 1;7/1:44:10

Amy, her mother and father are sitting at the table eating breakfast. About 5 minutes before the incident below Amy was given some marmalade on toast, after making a request for this. Shortly after starting to eat this toast she hands it back to her mother, next to her, making it clear she does not like it. She is then given some toast with honey on it, which she proceeds to start eating in the meantime. Talk around other topics also takes place before the following occurs:

```
1   A:   M- mo::re ((+rh point to honey jar + gaze switch to M, who
2        is drinking from her cup))
3                        (.7)
4   M:   Mm::? ((looks at A))

5   A:   (   ) ((+looks at toast she is holding in her lh, and touches
6        it with her rh))

7   M:   D'you want some mo:re on there? ((+ putting her cup
8        down))
9                        (1.5)
10  M:   Wc:ll we'll have to see: ((+ reaches for the honey jar, which
11       she has picked up before A's next turn))

12  A:   N:uhuhuh ((+ point to marmalade jar + 3 shakes of her
13       head))

14  M:   No:: we won't have any marmalade on it we'll have some
15       honey on it?
```

---

effect, she is recognizing, perhaps for the first time, that action can be grounded in such understandings. In the middle of the year her own actions may not always be securely related to these understandings. It is well known, for example, that at that time the child may sometimes approach and touch an object shortly after she has given some sign to the parent which appears to recognize the negative connotations of so doing (Emde *et al.* 1990). Notwithstanding such details there seems little doubt that by the end of her second year the child has access to new and distinctive forms of shared understanding.

The form of requests

One way in which child requests are marked out as special kinds of event in early child–parent interaction, even in the second year of life, is through the selective attention that parents give to the form in which they are made, to the choice of words used by the child. Most obviously, in English and American cultures, this revolves around the inclusion or exclusion of the word 'please' (Gleason, Perlmann and Greif 1984). Nelson (1973), for example, found that the words 'please' and 'thankyou' were among the first fifty words acquired in 38 per cent of the children that she studied. In other cultures, such as the Kaluli studied by Schieffelin (1990), young children are given explicit instruction as to how to say things to other people, and, there also, requests, though not only requests, appear to be a prime target for such coaching. In order for such coaching to take place, in all societies, the child clearly has to have a grasp of the procedures through which the coaching is done. Among the Kaluli this usually involves the child in copying the model that is presented to her, following what Schieffelin describes as the 'elema' routine. Among western children this more often seems to involve the parent in identifying an inadequacy in the way in which the child has formulated a request. After a child request the parent initiates some form of request for repair, and the child is then given the opportunity to engage in repair. Extract 2.7 contains an example of this. Two general points can be made about such repair procedures. First, for them to operate successfully they require the child to recognize that they occur at a specific place in a type of sequence. They do not, however, require the child to have any general social knowledge as to when and where to use a word like 'please', nor do they aim to instil such knowledge. All that is required of the child is the capacity to recognize that her request is formatted in a deficient way, and, at the most, to recall that the word 'please' is a remedy for that order of deficiency. No guidance is given by the parent to the child as to when, or with whom, the word should be included in a request, so the child is not being overtly expected to grasp, or have grasped, a principled procedure for distinguishing those occasions when such a word is necessary from the large majority in which, evidently, it is not. Secondly, for the child to recognize that her request is deficient she is required to have a grasp of the workings of this repair procedure, to recognize that words like **What do you sa:y?**, used in #2.7, in this sequential position, are identifying some kind of deficiency in the prior turn.

By her second birthday, therefore, the child has a strange mixture of

2.7 1;11/35:38

Amy and her father are eating together at the table, Amy in her high-chair. After F has put some spoonfuls of food into Amy's mouth Amy points to some of the food on F's plate and says:

1	A:	Want 'at ((pointing at F's food))
2		(.7)
3	F:	What do you sa:y? ((already moving his hand towards the
4		food))
5	A:	Please
6	F:	Very good

---

competences with regard to her use of the word 'please'. She may, occasionally, employ the term when making a request, but more often it is likely to be elicited in the context of adult repair. At least, this is the pattern in our recordings of Amy prior to two years of age, though her use of the term both then and when just two years old was very infrequent. After the age of two, in quasi-experimental work, when required to ask for something more 'nicely' the child may sometimes do more than just add the word 'please' (Bates and Silvern 1977); but on Amy's recordings both before and immediately after the age of two this is not the case. As in #2.7 (line 5) she just uses the word 'please' in her repair turn, rather than, say, repeating or altering any of the words used in her initial request (e.g., 'Want 'at please'). In addition, the child appears to be given little or no explicit guidance as to when and where to use the term 'please'. Although she has a capacity to make 'politeness' repairs, and although, perhaps as a result of this, she has some awareness of the fact that some ways of asking for things are more socially approved than others, it remains unclear as to whether terms such as 'please' have any further interactional significance for the child of this age. For the parent it seems clear enough, especially from comparisons between cultures where terms like *please* and *thankyou* are used differently (for example, Apte 1974), that in requiring children to say 'please' and 'thankyou' parents are encouraging their children to treat the co-operation of the parent as potentially non-presumable, as not something that the child can treat as an open cheque.

Summary

The account that I have given of requesting during the period between 12 and 24 months has attempted to place the child's ongoing actual behaviour centre-stage. A core feature of this behaviour is the emergence of child initiating actions, at about 9 months, which exercise systematic forms of control over immediately subsequent events. In seeking a fitted response to her request the child often has to navigate a variety of contingencies that can arise. In doing this she gains an expertise in implementing her communicative intentions over a series of turns. And in order to do this she has to develop various skills with regard to different kinds of parental response. Parents may, for example, respond incorrectly or seek further clarification, so there is an incentive for the child to develop repair techniques which can deal with these various exigencies. Similarly, she must learn to deal with the repair elicitations used by adults in the context of politeness repair. Much remains to be discovered about the child's grasp of the detailed workings of repair procedures, though some headway has been made in this regard (for example, Golinkoff 1986; Tarplee 1993; Wootton 1994).

The web of interactional practices that clusters around request sequences can also be considered for the ways in which it is informed by knowledge of the world. To formulate this point in this way risks implying that the child's knowledge is built up in some separate fashion from those practical lines of action in which she is engaged. Most theoretical positions and their associated bodies of empirical work (e.g. the Piagetian one) would reject such a model. Whatever the status of those mental representations possessed by the child at this age, and of the child's procedures for processing them, their sites of formation, renewal and reconstruction lie within ongoing action and interaction processes. I have briefly discussed three types of knowledge that have been heavily focused on in the age range 12–24 months. First, semantic knowledge which differentiates, say, types of two-word utterance; second, script-like knowledge which takes the form of event representations; third, perceptual knowledge which gives a salience and significance to particular features of the situation in which the child finds herself. In some ways there are interesting connections to be made between this work and the child's construction of her request activity. Potentially, this is most true of Greenfield's work on the 'principle of informativeness', though here I have argued that sequential dimensions of the child's conduct need fuller consideration and incorporation, especially as these sequential considerations appear to be ubiquitous to those occasions on which requesting takes place. The other approaches do not appear to offer any account of the systematic bases which the child uses when selecting one way, rather than another, of enacting a request. This would seem to be a fairly central issue for the study of request behaviour, and it is a complex one because, towards the end of this age range, it is evident that the child can employ any of a number of devices for making any given request.

An important developmental transition occurs when the child does not just know something but knows that what she knows is commensurate with what someone else knows. Once the latter is recognized as a possibility by the child then a new world of shared knowledge, shared cultural understandings, comes to be possible. Through certain negative statements, which were discussed in a later part of this chapter, the child comes to articulate understandings concerning lines of action that are compatible with those of her co-participants. The fact that these statements have their interactional home in certain sequential positions, and in certain types of sequence, suggests that they, and the forms of knowledge which they embody, have a logical connection with quite specific forms of interaction. Their connection with action, however, and more specifically with requesting, is a negative one rather than a positive one. In making these negative statements the child is formulating grounds for *not* engaging in certain kinds of act. In saying, in #2.5, that the parrot is not to come down from the shelf, Amy specifically implies that requesting it would not be an appropriate line of action to follow. These statements, therefore, are pertinent to the important question of how the child identifies certain things as non-requestables, but the issue remains as to when and how the child's new-found capacity for identifying shared forms of understanding comes to inform what she *does* rather than what she does not. This is a matter that is of central concern to the next chapter, but before moving into that discussion I want to present a brief picture of Amy's request skills at the end of the period that I have been discussing in this chapter.

The child at 23 months

Some information about Amy's development prior to 24 months has already been provided in earlier sections of this chapter. Like most children, her main spurt in the emergence of a productive language occurred after 18 months of age. Between then and 20 months her recognizable vocabulary increased from about 10 to about 60 words; after then it increased so fast that our attempts to monitor and keep pace with it seemed barely adequate. However, what is material to the subsequent discussion is the more specific question of how she managed to make requests, and in order to convey this I will attempt to give an overview of the linguistic designs that Amy employed to this end on the last set of recordings we made prior to those that form my focus in subsequent chapters.

Two hours of recordings were made when Amy was 23 months of age, and in these she makes use of a variety of devices for making requests. Although no single linguistic design is outstanding from the rest in terms of frequency the one which she uses most frequently is 'I like x', as in **I like more** and **I like mushroom**. When requesting objects several additional designs are also available to her. She can use 'I want x' constructions, as in **I want more**, or ones involving the verb 'have', as in **I have that**, or imperative constructions like **Get more that**. Simpler formats that were popular on earlier recordings are also still in use on occasion, such as **More** on its own, or **Another one**. Some of these designs are also used in requests which more explicitly seek some form of action on the part of the parent. **Have that bean**, for example, is glossable in context as 'You have this bean.' Imperative-like designs are also used, as in **Take that down**, but more often explicit requests to the adult to do some action take forms which, though akin to imperatives, are more syntactically ambiguous – **Daddy sit down there**, for example, could equally well be a precursor to formats like 'You sit down there', formats which she quickly adopts in the coming months. Other less conventionalized ways of asking the parent to do something are also employable. For example, **I get out** is usable to indicate to the parent that she wishes to be lifted out of her high-chair, and there is also one instance of **Need to get out** in this context.

In general, it is important to note that utterances with the kinds of surface form that I have indicated above may not always be serving as requests to get the other party to perform some action. Many of these forms are also used by the child as though addressed to herself in the course of engaging in some line of conduct. This point applies particularly to imperatives, which occur more frequently in this latter context, as in **Put it in there** and **Make a ( )**. It is at this age, 23 months, that, for this child, such explicit self-guidance of her own activities seems to be at its zenith. From here on this is much less evident in her talk; this seems consistent with the observations and claims of Vygotsky (1962; see also Wertsch

1985:chapter 4) that the child's capacity to guide her actions externally lays the foundation for her subsequent capacity to organize them internally, as thought.

The surface forms of request-like utterances can also be misleading in other ways at this age. For example, **Daddy take (   ) shoes off** looks like a request to me to perform some action, but it is accompanied by Amy actually beginning to take my shoes off, and in context appears glossable as 'I'll take daddy's shoes off.' In addition, several of the surface forms that have been mentioned can now, with distinctive intonation, also be used as questions by the child. **Want another one mummy?** and **Like some?** are two examples: more rarely, other forms of question, such as **O:n the::re?** in #2.2, can also be used to further some course of child action. At this age the child has not mastered the construction of formal yes/no-answer questions (e.g. 'Can I do/have x?'), but she is able to use a limited range of Wh questions, such as **What's that?**; however, none of these are used as vehicles for making the kinds of request that I shall be concerned with.

A final domain of request-like activity at this age that should be mentioned is the oppositional one, utterances which usually attempt to restore a situation to the preceding *status quo*, or to prevent the continuation of another person's action. Injunctions, such as **No (.) no that one**, form part of the child's repertoire in this respect; other linguistic designs which are usable are variants of those already mentioned, such as **Go away** and **Don't like it**. At this age, however, oppositional utterances of this kind do not figure prominently in the interaction we recorded. More frequent are ones like **I don't like it**, which indicate that she herself does not want to do something that others are expecting her to do, such as eat the food with which she has been provided, or wear clothes in which she is being dressed.

So, we now move into the substance of the analysis, which takes off with the child early in her third year of life. Just as she has to find ways of finding out about *our* world so we will need to try and penetrate her world in order to discover something of its practices and precepts. In this respect, the ethnographic enterprise of uncovering that which is distinctive to her world is never far from our concerns. What we will find is that as her language use is deeply embedded in sequential and social formations, then the careful examination of its use offers a special kind of route into discovering that which is distinctive about the sensibilities of a child of this age.

3

Imperatives and sequential knowledge

One kind of linguistic design which is used to perform requests is the imperative construction – orders and injunctions such as 'Go away', 'Leave him alone' and 'Don't do that.' By the age of two most English-speaking children are capable of using this construction, and equivalent kinds of construction are reported as being in the repertoire of children of this age in other cultures (for example, Schieffelin 1990: chapter 7). Even where the imperative is syntactically more difficult to produce, as in Italian, children still seem to acquire the requisite skills by about the age of 2;4, and before that age they manage to use linguistic forms which are functionally similar in that they are also designed as orders or injunctions (Bates 1976: chapter 8).

From the age at which such imperatives are first used the child also has alternative ways available to her for making requests.[1] In the case of Amy, who first made extensive use of imperatives in her recordings at 2;1, some of these alternatives are used quite infrequently. Examples of these would

[1] The reader will note that, both here and elsewhere, I am leery of providing a stipulative definition as to what I am taking to be 'requests'. To some extent this is warranted by the fact that I shall be principally focusing on certain linguistic designs which have seemed both to me and to other investigators to have a canonical association with requesting. But in chapter 2, and in the present chapter, I note that even for this limited range of designs this association by no means holds across all instances of their use. Such definitional matters are clearly central, and difficult, ones for analyses which place heavy emphasis on forms of evidence revealed in frequency tabulations. Within my mode of analysis whether, and in what ways, utterances appear to have some request-like intent is a matter that cannot be decided by prior definition; it is always something that analysis needs to attend to on a case by case basis, an outcome of engaging in analysis rather than something that can be resolved by analytic pre-specification. Furthermore, at the end of the day it seems to me unlikely that we can rigorously and usefully differentiate, through the definitions employed in some analytic language, a domain of child activity that consists of 'requesting'. Hopefully, this lack of what, in some quarters, might be viewed as 'precision' will be compensated for by greater forms of precision when it comes to showing, and evidencing, those generic procedures to which the child attends within my data.

be constructions involving the verb phrase 'have to do x' (as in **Mummy have to get the medicine now** and **Mummy have to put it**); simple namings of the thing desired by the child (as in **A little bit of that cheese**) which, in context, can function as requests; and problem descriptions (such as **That one won't stand up properly**). However, at 2;1 there are two further linguistic designs which are also being used with about the same frequency as imperatives in order to make requests (see Table 5.1, p. 143). First, 'I like x' (as in **I like some medicine on it**) and second, 'I want x' (as in **I want it here daddy**). Usually, these latter two designs do not overtly specify the action that the child wants her parent to engage in. **I like some medicine on it**, for example, omits overt reference to the necessary (parental) actions of fetching the medicine and putting it on the child's body (compare 'Put some medicine on'). Occasionally, however, these forms, like imperatives, can be more explicit in this respect. **Want eat it**, for example, in context, can mean 'I want you to eat it', and **I like sit down mummy** can mean 'I'd like you to sit down mummy.' At this age Amy does not normally insert 'you' and 'to' so as to make constructions like 'Want (you to) eat it', so **Want eat it** is her closest approximation.

The picture at 2;1, then, is one of the child having a wide array of techniques available to her for steering into desired channels of action the conduct of those with whom she is in contact. When she uses an imperative to ask her parent to do something she is, in effect, selecting this design from a range of others that could, in principle, have been usable by her. In the course of the early part of this third year there is every suggestion that imperatives continue to play a prominent role in children's requesting. In Amy's case, while they make up about 24 per cent of all her requests at 2;1, by 2;5 they have become the most popular design, making up about 47 per cent of her requests (see Table 5.1, p. 143). In a study of eleven 2½-year-olds speaking mainly with an adult who was unrelated to the child, but with the parent present, Newcombe and Zaslow (1981) found that just over half the children's requests were imperatives. And by all accounts such imperatives are likely to be even more prominent in such children's speech to other children of a similar or younger age (Dunn and Kendrick 1982).

In this chapter I shall be focusing mainly on imperatives, and I shall be attempting to identify some of the ways in which Amy uses them during the three sets of recordings made between 2;1 and 2;5. In particular, I shall focus on the sequential relationship that exists between them and understandings which have been established earlier in the interaction. The fact that there is a systematic connection to be found in this respect suggests that when she is using imperatives at this age she is relying on earlier forms of interactional understanding, that such understandings now constitute relevant grounds for the child's organization of her own conduct. These grounds permit the child to use imperatives in different circumstances. Sometimes she uses them when she knows that the parent will be opposed to that for which she is asking. Elsewhere, they can be used in the opposite circumstances, ones in which the child has grounds for believing that what she is asking the parent to do will *not* be a contentious matter. A further aspect of the argument will involve showing that in these latter circumstances non-imperative request forms are used relatively rarely. The important implication of this is that, when selecting between the principal request forms which are available to her, a relevant consideration, for the child, routinely, is the kind of local interactional understanding that obtains. These understandings now form contexts which shape the child's ongoing lines of action, and are thus integral to the developmental process through which the child's actions can come to be recognizably contextualized.[2]

In making these arguments my principal empirical focus will be on the child's use of imperatives. The analysis by no means takes in *all* the imperatives used by the child on these recordings. Sometimes, for example, she uses imperative designs when enacting the self-guiding speech that various other writers, from Piaget and Vygotsky onwards, have drawn to our attention.[3] My focus, then, is just on imperatives which are used by the child so as to channel and direct the behaviour of a recipient. Their use falls into two domains, each of which will be separately discussed in the early parts of the chapter. In one of these, which I call 'offence sequences', the child treats her recipient as at fault in some way. This may be because her recipient has committed, is committing, or appears to be about to commit, an offence. Imperatives represent one kind of linguistic design that the child can employ in dealing with these circumstances. The domain I shall deal with first, however, consists of the large residual set where no such offence appears to be at issue, 'non-offence sequences'. After discussing these two domains I shall go on to make some comparisons with the child's use of alternative request designs, and finally I shall draw out some of the implications and corollaries of these empirical patterns.

---

[2] The importance of contextualization for the analysis of linguistic conduct has been brought out in a number of research traditions. See especially Gumperz (1982), Schegloff (1991a), and, for a somewhat uneven overview, Figueroa (1994: chapter 5).

[3] These kinds of imperative are excluded from Table 5.1 on page 143.

Next-step connections in non-offence sequences

In this section I shall show how the child's use of this subset of her imperatives is largely associated with circumstances which are conducive to their having a non-contentious character. These circumstances take a number of different interactional forms, and for most of this section I shall be describing some of the more important of these. What these forms share, though, is that they contain events which create a basis for the child to suppose that the action proposed by the imperative will not be out of line, or discordant, with lines of action being envisaged by the other party. My argument will be that imperatives are distinct by virtue of habitually arising out of, and having this intimate connection with, interactional circumstances of this kind.

For the sake of exposition I shall now separate out two types of interactional circumstance. In the first, the events that connect with the child's imperative take place earlier in the same sequence in which the imperative itself occurs. In the second, relevant events take place at some point prior to the immediate sequence; these earlier events nevertheless impinge on, and constitute a relevant context for, the construction of the subsequent imperative.

Same-sequence connections

For the most part the same-sequence connections which inform Amy's use of imperatives relate to understandings which have been overtly stated in the immediately preceding talk, and it is with these that this section will be principally concerned; but perhaps at their crudest level such understandings can be detected by the child purely in non-verbal ways, on the basis of the shape of an unfolding activity. In such cases, as in #3.1, the child can use an imperative to tell the parent to perform an action which she can identify as being compatible with the next step of the unfolding activity sequence. So, in #3.1, the child can see that her mother is walking towards the sofa, holding a cup of coffee. It is also possible that her mother is looking towards a potential sitting position, and that this fact is available to the child who is monitoring her mother's movement at this point (prior to Plate A in #3.1); unfortunately, this only remains a possibility as the mother's face is out of camera. The child's imperative, **S:i:t he::re** (line 1), directs her mother to one of the possible locations on the sofa in which to perform the next phase of the visibly unfolding activity sequence: sitting down. In this case, then, what

3.1 2;3/I 40:03

Amy stands by the sofa, a chocolate biscuit in one hand and her drinking
cup in the other. She watches her mother as the latter walks into the
room and then, out of camera, puts something on the nearby table. Then
her mother moves towards the sofa, cup of coffee in hand:

1	A:	S̞:i:t^A he::re, ((as she says this she taps the place on the sofa
2		where she wants her mother to sit close to her; and she
3		also sits down on her small stool which is right beside
4		her))
5	F:	ᴸVery lucky to get biscuits= ((an ironic remark, addressed
6		to both A and M))
7	M:	=Mm ((to A)) (.) An outrageous suggestion that we dont
8		have biscuits in this house? ((latter part addresses F's ironic
9		remark; as she says this M moves some material from the
10		spot on the sofa that A has indicated, in preparation to sit
11		there))

Plate A

---

the parent is being told to do is potentially compatible with the next step of
the activity in which the parent is engaging.

Much more frequently, however, the imperative has connections with
overt details of the talk in the immediately preceding sequence. Inspection
of these details often reveals them to contain understandings that have
connections with the child's subsequent use of the imperative. The imperative, in effect, instructs the parent to perform an action that is compatible
with the understanding that has just been reached. Here I present two

3.2 2;1/5665

Amy and her father sit by a jigsaw that is being dismantled. However, the immediately prior topics concern the noises that different animals make and F taking his glasses off; the talk below initiates a return to jigsaw matters:

1	A:	Like an: .hh like another one daddy? ((after the first two
2		words she briefly looks towards the table and then
3		positions her face so as to be looking more directly into F's
4		face))

5	F:	Yes please Amy
6		(.)
7:	F:	⌐Yes

8	A:	└ Jus: put^A it on the:re daddy ((from the word put onwards
9		she points to the chair))
10		(.9)
11	F:	Alright then ((reaches for jigsaw piece))

Plate A

---

examples of this kind of phenomenon, the second, #3.3, being a more complex case than the first, #3.2.

In #3.2 the imperative is **Jus: put it on the:re daddy** (line 8). Immediately prior to this Amy has established that I want to engage in some form of action with another piece of the jigsaw. She asks **Like another one daddy?**, and, importantly, I confirm that I do, by saying **Yes please Amy**. As we are now in the process of dismantling the jigsaw the relevant next action is for a piece of the jigsaw to be moved on to the nearby chair, alongside three other pieces that have already been moved there. My further **Yes**, which overlaps with Amy's **Jus:**, together with the absence of any hand movement on my part, and the inclusion of the word **please** in my initial reply, display an expectation on my part that the first step in this movement of the jigsaw piece to the chair will be for Amy to pick a piece up and pass it to me, for me to then put it on the chair. But, leaving aside this differing under-standing on the part of the two participants, what seems clear enough is that the child's imperative, **Jus: put it on the:re daddy**, is compatible with the understanding that has just been arrived at in the interaction. That understanding consists of my having made it clear that I do want a piece of the jigsaw to be transferred to the chair. Amy's imperative is broadly in line with this understanding.

Extract 3.3 is more complex in that here the imperatives instruct the parent towards the means of achieving an objective. Nevertheless, prior to their occurrence there is again clear evidence that the objective is accept-able to the parent; and because the actions which are required by the imper-atives are recognizable as steps towards the attainment of the objective they are, therefore, compatible with the objective.

In #3.3 the two relevant imperatives are **And put that paper down in the (room)** (line 4) and **And get some chalks (.) there for you** (line 14). Amy's intervening utterance, which is probably **And (save hh them in a minute)** (line 10), will not be addressed here. From the initial exchange in #3.3 it is clear that the child's recipient is keen on engaging in chalking and that Amy herself is also agreeable to this. This then, parental chalking, is what I have referred to as the 'objective' that is acceptable to the parent. Given that the parent is holding a magazine (Plate A), without any chalks in her hand, the instructions contained in the imperatives are patently designed to prepare the child's recipient for engagement in the activity of chalking. They are steps towards the objective that has been agreed; indeed, this connectedness to that earlier agreement is marked here by the use of the word **And** that pre-fixes both these imperatives. That earlier agreement creates an environment in which the child can presume a willingness on the part of her recipient to go along with the lines of action being proposed in the imperatives. Further evidence concerning the details of the child's hand movements is also con-sistent with these claims. Of particular interest in this respect is what begins to happen when Amy says the word **room** (line 4). She then turns her head away from the direction of the floor towards the magazine that her mother is still holding. Then she brings her left hand towards the magazine and opens the hand in preparation for taking hold of it (Plate B). In fact, she never actually does take hold of it because at the same moment her mother begins to move it towards the floor. Nevertheless, Amy's hand then shadows this movement, all of which suggests that at this point she was going to take the magazine from her mother's hand, had the mother not taken steps to release it. This suggests, then, that when the child says **And put that paper down in the (room)** she is displaying some basis for feeling entitled to remove the paper from the parent's grasp. The obvious basis for such an entitlement is the fact that the parent has just made plain her preparedness to engage in the alternative activity of chalking.

In extracts 3.1–3.3 I have shown how imperative use can be connected to understandings that have arisen out of the preceding sequence. Specifically, they are used to further lines of action which are compatible with that which has been implicitly or explicitly agreed by the other party, the child's recipient. There are several further points to make about these sequences, which I will return to later. For example, one reason I have included extracts 3.2 and 3.3 is that the sequences which precede the imperatives are initiated by child enquiries – **Like another one daddy?** (line 1) in #3.2 and **Want some chalks?** (line 1) in #3.3. Sequences containing such enquiries are not the only ones which display the orderliness described above, but I shall argue later that the location of such enquiries in these sequences does have a special analytic interest. At this stage, however, I turn to examining imperatives which are informed by sequences of action occurring prior to those which contain the imperative.

Earlier-sequence connections

Many of the child's imperatives at this age could not be connected to earlier turns of the sequences in which they occur because they themselves are sequence initial items. They are not 'part of' some ongoing sequence, but rather initiate some new line of talk. For example, whilst in her high-chair at the meal table, in her recordings at 2;1, Amy suddenly says to me **Lift out dad**; this occurs immediately after she has been involved in having ointment put on her gums, and other activities involving medicines. It is a clear topical departure from the immediately preceding talk.

Faced with this kind of instance it might be attractive to reconcile it with my prior discussion by drawing on the notion of 'scripts'. By this age it is clear that children can have a sense of the typical patterns that actions may take in any particular setting: scripts (see p. 38). So, Amy might be expected to know that having a meal normally consists of sitting in her high-chair, eating her meal and then leaving her chair at the end. As she might also expect such knowledge to be available to her parents, this type

3.3 2;5/III 35:58

About 10 seconds earlier Amy's mother, at Amy's request, has resumed her seating position close to the chalk board. M continues to look at a magazine that she is holding:

```
1   A:    Want some chalks?A
2               (.7)
3   M:    Can I do some chalking now?

4   A:    Yeh (.) And put that paper down in the (room) ((gesturing
5         to floor with her left arm))
6               (.6)

7   M:    JustBdown here? ((moving paper to floor as she says this))

8   A:    Yeh

9   M:    O⌐kay

10  A:    └And (save hh ⌐them in a minute) ((getting seated in her
11        chair as she says│ this))

12  M:                     └No:w

13  M:    Okay=

14  A:    =And get some chalks (.) there for you  ((passing box to M
15        as she says this))

16  M:    Can I have this one here? ((picking up and showing A a
17        chalk here))

18  A:    Yeh? (.)  Now I want some? ((taking box  back from M as
19        she says this))
```

Plate A   Plate B

---

of request could be connected to, and compatible with, what she takes to be mutual knowledge.

In chapter 2 I have already, however, outlined reasons for treating such arguments as less than helpful. I do not, of course, want to deny that the child has access to knowledge of a script-like kind, nor even that when a child has finished her meal, she might expect to leave the table. But, at the very least, the notion of script leaves unexplicated the basis upon which the child selects one way of enacting the script rather than another. When leaving the table the child can employ quite different utterance designs in order to take matters further. At 2;1, for example, there are also instances of Amy saying **Wanna go down** and **Like get out now** as ways of asking to get down from the table. Appeal to scripts, therefore, leaves undiscriminated the character of the work being achieved by particular utterance and interactional formats in accomplishing the given activity.

If we examine the distribution of topic initial imperatives in non-offence sequences what we usually find is that there are connections between the line of action being furthered by these imperatives and understandings that have been established in sequences that have taken place somewhat earlier. Here I shall begin my illustration of this by looking more closely at the occasion, presented in #3.4, on which Amy makes the utterance to which I have already referred, namely **Lift out dad**.

What we find is that, prior to the discussion of medicine and gum ointment that immediately preceded this imperative, there was a discussion about Amy leaving the table. I ask Amy, after checking whether she wants more to eat, whether or not she now wants to get down from the table (line 6). She answers in the affirmative, but then her mother's utterance **Right I**

3.4 2;1/4524

Amy and her father sit at the table, mother standing close-by out of
camera. A has just been playing with F, giving him bread that she knows
he doesn't want. Then F says:

1   F: Would you like any more to eat?

2   M: D'you ⌐want any more

3   A: ⌊ No:

4   F: No ((confirmatory in intonation))

5   M: No?=

6   F: =D'you want to get down now,

7   A: Yes^A=

8   M: Mm: right I think its probably medicine time again now

.
.
((56 secs))
.
.

((M is now out of room and gum ointment put away; A, standing in her
high-chair, then gives F another medicine box; F puts it to the other end
of the table and says:))

9   F: Thats for mummy isnt it to do your eyes ((to A))

10   M: Well I think I generally let her do more things so then she
11   assumes that in other ways she can= ((to F, linking back to
12   earlier talk))

13   A: =Lift out^B⌐dad, ((as she says this A begins to climb up on to
14   the tray │ of her high-chair))
                       │
15   F: ⌊Mm ((to M))

16   M: Do more= ((to F, completes M's prior turn))

17   F: Okay ((to A; raises his arms to lift her out of the chair))

Plate A   Plate B

---

think its probably medicine time again now (line 8) introduces a series of actions relating to medical matters, a series in which Amy is only too happy to partake as she had a great fondness for consuming the gum ointment in question. When she eventually says **Lift out dad** (line 13) this is in a position where the intervening medical matters have reached a completion point, and one in which she is also able to rely on the earlier understanding, between herself and myself, that the time is now opportune for her to leave the table. So, her imperative is again compatible with an earlier understanding, albeit one arising from an earlier sequence. Also, as in #3.3, one can note how her accompanying non-verbal behaviour also displays, and further documents, the unproblematicness of her expectation here: as she says **Lift out dad** she has already begun to climb out of her chair on to the top of the adjacent table (Plate B).

I shall also briefly present here two further instances – extracts 3.5 and 3.6 – of a similar kind of phenomenon, the second being in certain ways different to extracts 3.4 and 3.5.

In #3.5 we again find an imperative connected to an understanding that has been arrived at in the earlier interaction. In this extract, which takes place by the same chalking board as #3.3 above, the imperative is **Put it on his (.7) Paws** (lines 12 and 16). In saying this the child is asking her mother to put the chalk, which the mother is currently holding, into the puppet dog's paw so that the child, who has her own hand inside the puppet, can then 'make' the puppet do some chalking on the board. The relevant history goes back about a minute before this imperative. Then, the mother had been holding the dog, with a piece of chalk in the dog's paw, doing drawings on the board. Amy, unimpressed by the dog's performance, says **I'd better help him...cos he's not very good at doing it** (lines 1 and 4). She prepares to do this but quickly becomes diverted by a piece of chalk that

3.5 2;5/III 18:50

The mother is sitting by the chalking board with the puppet dog on one of her hands. Using this same hand she has done a drawing on the board now Amy addresses what the 'dog' has done:

1   A: I'd better help him=

2   M: =Yes ⌐ I think you'd better help him

3   A: ⌊ Cos he's is-

4   A: Cos he's not very good at doing it=

5   M: =No ⌐ he's not

6   A: ⌊ LOOK one dropped, ((pointing to a chalk on the
7   floor))

                        ·
                     ·
                 (45 seconds)
                     ·

((after cleaning up a mark A returns to a kneeling position on her chair, facing the board. She then turns to M, stretching out her arm expecting to take the dog. A takes the dog from M's hand))

8   M: No:w ⌐then^A

9   A: ⌊ ( ) help ((quiet, reaching for the dog as she says this.
10   Then A and M move dog to board))
11   (1.0)
12   A: ( ) chalking ((quiet))=Put it on^B his ((A turns to M during
13   these words; M moves 'it', the chalk, forward to the dog's
14   paw after the word 'it'))
15   (.7)
16   A: Paws (and then),

Plate A   Plate B

has fallen on the floor, and with wiping off the carpet a mark that she thinks it has made. So, on the occasion of Amy later saying **Put it on his (.7) paws** there is an understanding that Amy is going to take over the manipulation of the dog, an understanding that dates back to the earlier discussion. **Put it on his (.7) paws** instructs her mother to perform an action that is consistent with that earlier understanding. Indeed, in this case we also find detailed evidence which suggests that the parent is also orienting to such an understanding. She, the parent, begins to move the chalk towards the puppet after Amy's words **Put it** but before the words **his paws** – that is before Amy states where the chalk is to be put (Plate B).

One type of same-sequence connection that was not discussed in the prior section obtains where the child asks the parent to perform again an action that the parent has just completed. For example, on one occasion when I complete reading a story to Amy on the recordings at 2;3 she immediately says to me **Read another one**. In the face of no signs of opposition to such a request prior to making it, the child's request is situated in a position where the fact that a line of action has just been engaged in by the parent can form a basis for her treating it as re-performable. At 2;3 there are also a number of occasions on which parallel incidents take place where the child's behaviour is linkable to what has taken place in earlier sequences. In these cases the child, using an imperative, asks the parent to engage in an action similar or identical to an action that the parent has engaged in with the child at an earlier point in the recording. In the intervening time there has been no suggestion that the parent is unwilling to resume or perform again the earlier activity, and the possibility arises that, even though there has been no explicit understanding that the activity will take place again, the fact that the parent has been willing to engage

Initially, Amy and her father are discussing the picture/story in the book
that F is showing to A:

1 F: Where are the rabbits going now

2 A: Tea party ((F then turns the page of the book))
3   (1.8)
4 A: I want to^A make a farmyard wi' you, ((simultaneously
5   reaching for toy animals nearby. Then F closes book and
6   puts it down))

7 F: Allright

.
.
                    (11 seconds)
.
.

8   F: How much of the tape is there left,   ((to M))

9   M: I dont know=

10 F: =Can you tell ((to M))
11   (12.2)
12 M: I would say we've ⌐ done about half of it ((to F))
          ⌊
13 A: ⌊ Read 'at-^B(.) 'At ⌐'to::r .hh rabbit
14   hu::tch ((to F))   ⌊

15 F: ⌊ Mm: ((to M))

Plate A   Plate B

in the activity before is taken as a basis for its being expectable that the parent will undertake the activity again. Extract 3.6 is one such incident. Here, the imperative **Read 'at- (.) 'At 'to::r .hh rabbit hu::tch** (lines 13–14)[4] (i.e. 'Read that story about the rabbit hutch') occurs about 30 seconds after the book has been closed. The book had not been closed as a result of any decision that no more reading was to take place. Rather, its closing had been occasioned by a switch of interest on Amy's part to making farms (line 4). So, when she says **Read 'at- (.) 'At 'to::r .hh rabbit hu::tch** she has no basis for supposing the adult to be unwilling to resume the activity, which in turn creates the possibility that the nature of the prior parental involvement in the activity is taken, by the child, as a basis for treating its resumption as unproblematic.

About 85 per cent of Amy's imperatives in non-offence sequences on the 3 recordings between the ages of 2;1 and 2;5 have either same-sequence or earlier-sequence connections of the kind that I have been documenting through extracts 3.1–3.6. In general, therefore, there is ample evidence of the kind that I have been using to suggest that when selecting an imperative, the child usually has a basis for supposing that what she is requiring the parent to do is not incompatible with understandings which have been arrived at in the recent past. The remaining 15 per cent include some which are obdurate to analysis, but within this figure there is a group which definitely do not appear to be embedded in such understandings. Occasionally, Amy says things to us like **Get some chalks out of there for me** where no prior basis seems to have been established for such a line of action being congruent with our interests. This minority comes to be important for arguments developed in chapter 5. There we will find that it is this minority which disappears from the child's use of these non-offence imperatives during the course of her third year, and this matter turns out to have important implications for understanding certain new request forms which emerge at that time; but this is to anticipate. Between the ages of 2;1 and 2;5 the large majority of these non-offence imperatives are embedded in sequential understandings of the kind to which I have been alluding.

---

[4] The disfluency within this turn of the child's may in part be bound up with the difficulty of the construction which she is attempting, but the fact that it is produced in overlap with line 12 may also be of relevance. For example, her recycling of the word 'at, after cutting off her first attempt at the word and then pausing fractionally, resembles closely one of the ways in which adults can handle overlap positions. On these matters among adults see Schegloff (1987); see Peskett and Wootton (1985) for a discussion of related issues among developmentally younger children.

Imperatives and understandings in offence sequences

There is a wealth of evidence, both from Amy's recordings and from other studies, of the child developing a capacity to articulate concerns about the allowability and appropriateness of conduct well before the age of 2 (Edwards 1978; Pea 1980; Emde *et al.* 1990). Indeed, in chapter 2 special emphasis was placed on the emergence, after 18 months, of certain negative constructions, constructions which appear to document the child's awareness that certain actions have a non-allowable status. For example, in #2.5 (p. 47), at age 1;11, Amy gestured towards a wooden parrot on a shelf and, while shaking her head, said **Cant take 'at do:wn**. In doing this she was alluding to an earlier understanding that had been reached about the said parrot. Initially, as is probably true in this instance, the child's interest in non-allowable matters seems to focus around her own lines of action, what *she* may or may not do, but by the age of 2;1 this interest in what is allowable and non-allowable extends to the actions of others, as well as her own.

The child's interest in offences can arise in a variety of interactional circumstances. The other party, a parent or whoever, can be recognized as being about to commit an untoward act, as already in the course of committing one or as already having committed one. The child has a wide range of ways for dealing with such eventualities. She may resort to her newly acquired deontic language in order to convey her awareness of obligation and necessity. Here I am referring especially to constructions involving the phrases 'have to' and 'supposed to', as in **Mummy have to put it, Mummy supposed (to) eat it** and **I supposed (to) have it**, all of which occurred at 2;1 on the recordings of Amy, and which are reported as occurring at about this age in analyses of other English-speaking children (Stephany 1986). Much more often, she simply uses the injunction **No**, or formats like **Not too much daddy**. One of the most common types of format for dealing with such events, however, is an imperative. These imperatives are, in certain respects, unlike those discussed in the prior section. We saw there, in non-offence sequences, that imperatives are often connected to earlier forms of understanding, understandings where, broadly, the child has a basis for supposing that what she wants the parent to do is congruent with what she knows of the preference and understanding of the parent. This is not usually the case in offence sequences. For example, when Amy says to me, at 2;3, **Put me down** when I am lifting her, uninvited, high up into the air, what she is asking me to do is clearly in opposition to the line of action I am currently adopting. Imperatives, when used in offence sequences, are, then, usually proposing courses of action which are at odds with what it is the other person looks likely to do, what they are doing or what they have done. They seem to run counter to what evidence the child has available to her concerning the parent's preferred line of action.

By the ages in question here, 2;1–2;5, it is possible for certain imperatives that deal with offences to refer to broader trans-contextual understandings that bear on the particular event in question. In such circumstances the understanding being drawn on is not specific to the sequence preceding the use of the imperative, but rather draws on the child's growing awareness of the general relevance of certain behavioural precepts to a variety of particular interactional contexts. The most obvious examples of such imperatives are ones which associate themselves with overt interactional rules. At 2;3, for example, Amy says to me at the mealtable **Don't lick that knife daddy** (.) **'pposed to cut it up**. The topic of licking knives or the more general one of manners in eating had not been discussed earlier on this recording, so in advising me that the knife is for cutting things up, not for licking (the action that I had just indulged in), the child is here drawing on more general understandings about the organization of one's conduct when eating. Another similar case would be **Say thankyou when you get it** (.) **Not please**, said to her mother at 2;5 shortly after her mother had used the word 'please' when about to receive an object being passed to her. Again, no related understanding had been overtly touched on in prior interaction in the immediate past.

Much more often, however, imperatives that deal with offences do draw on understandings that connect with events in the prior interaction sequence. On each of the three recordings on which we are drawing in this chapter there are, for example, several instances in which the word 'back' accompanies an imperative, as in **No put it back there**. Such cases usually involve the child requesting that a person return, or, as in this case, an object be returned, to an original location. In such cases the warrant for the return does not usually hang on the fact that the location for return is that in which the person or object is normally to be found. It hangs on the fact that this location has a particular, local significance within the sequence in question. In the case above, for example, involving the words **No put it back there**, the 'there' being referred to is simply the place where the object happened to be prior to the parent picking it up. It is not a place in which it could be said that this object had any sort of canonical location. Therefore, in saying **No put it back there,** the child is drawing on a local understanding as to the original location of the object, and displaying that understanding as warranting the imperative that is being used.

Certain of these offence-related imperatives have a more overt connection with understandings that have been established earlier in the interaction. To this extent they have parallels with the sequences that were examined in the prior section. It is these cases which I now want to illustrate in more detail. In the first of them, #3.7, the connection is with an understanding which has just been arrived at within this same sequence, whilst in #3.8 the relevant understanding that is being drawn on occurs in an earlier sequence.

In #3.7 Amy is again at her chalk board, this time standing on her chair. She drops the chalk that she is holding and her mother immediately moves her right hand to pick it up. At about the time when the mother's hand reaches the chalk Amy begins to say **I'll pick it u:p** (line 1), but her mother nevertheless picks up the chalk and proffers it to Amy. Amy's response, which contains the imperative in which we are interested, is **No leave it on the floo:r** (line 4). Her subsequent actions make it clear that she does not, for example, want the chalk left on the floor for good, but that she wants it left on the floor so that she, the child, can pick it up, rather than her mother. In this way she organizes her actions with reference to the original statement of her intention, **I'll pick it u:p.** This statement is treated as having primacy over the parent's subsequent offer, and it is the connection and compatibility between this statement and her imperative that appears to lay the basis for this primacy. Once again, as with several of the examples I dealt with in the last section, the child reveals non-verbally her understanding of the non-problematic nature of what she is requiring the parent to do. As she says the word **leave** in line 4 she pushes the parent's hand away with her left hand, thus rendering her rejection of the proffer entirely unequivocal (see Plate B). Presumably, what forms the ground for this action, as well as the imperative itself, is her stated intention to pick the object up herself.

Extract 3.7 is of particular interest because with her imperative, the child is rejecting an offer of assistance from the parent. Such offers of assistance quite often occasion acceptance on the child's part – they are not forms of action to which the expected form of response will be a rejection. The rejection, in this instance, cannot be understood, then, simply in terms

3.7 2;5/III 10:40

Amy's mother has just been asked by the child to wipe a circle off the
chalking board with a cloth. As A points to that which she wants wiped
off she drops her chalk which she is holding in that same hand. Her
mother makes to pick up the chalk as the child watches her:

1	A:	I'll^A pick it u:p ((but M continues to pick it up and then
2		proffers it to the child))
3		(.)
4	A:	No leave^B it on the floo:r ((A pushes M's hand away at the
5		beginning of this turn; by mid-turn it is clear that M is
6		putting the chalk back on the floor))
7		(.)
8	M:	OK ((quiet)) (.) Now which part am I pick- ⌐which part am
9		I (working on)
10	A:	∟ I want to get
11		o:ff, ((as A says this she gestures towards the box of chalks
12		which is on the chair she is standing on, impeding her
13		descent from the chair; by the time she next speaks the box
14		is already being moved by her mother))
15		(.)
16	A:	Quick,

((after another brief exchange about where her mother can draw on the
board the child picks up the chalk from the floor and resumes her
original position on her chair))

Plate A   Plate B

of its being a standard type of response to an offer. It takes its appropriateness specifically from its association with the child's earlier statement of intent, **I'll pick it u:p**; it is this understanding that informs and explains the unusual nature of what it is that the child is doing here when she says **No leave it on the floo:r**. By virtue of having publicly said **I'll pick it u:p** to the parent, the child can rely on the parent as having monitored that this is the child's preference. So when the child says **No leave it on the floo:r**, the child can also rely on the parent being able to connect the imperative to her earlier public statement. In short, the understanding that informs the child's imperative is an overt, public one, one available to the parent as well as to herself.

In #3.8, when Amy is aged 2;1, the relevant imperative is her **Dont do it again: daddy** (line 17). This occurs in the same jigsaw situation that was discussed earlier in connection with #3.2. What occasions this rebuke, and the further forms of censure which follow it, is my taking a piece of the jigsaw from the board in front of us and moving it on to the nearby chair. The understanding that informs what is taking place here occurred about 30 seconds earlier in the interaction. At that point I asked if I was to put the jigsaw pieces on the chair (**D'you want me to put them on there** [line 1]), to which I was given the answer **N:o:t** (line 4). There is subsequently a rather childish discussion about who is the silliest person in the house, in which Amy and I end up in agreement that her mother is the biggest of all the **silly billys**. It is on the termination of this discussion that I move a piece of the jigsaw on to the chair (lines 12–14). There is every indication that my movement of this piece of the jigsaw is designed as provocative and teasing. It is carried out very quickly, with no reference to, or acknowledgement of, matters bearing on the allowability of this action, when Amy is in a position to see what is taking place and with a smile on my face (Plate A). It is patently a deliberate flouting of the understanding that had been arrived at earlier, an act the significance of which was to be derived from its relation to that earlier understanding. The nature of Amy's reaction to this act also suggests that it is informed by that same earlier understanding. Of particular note here is the scale of the rebuke (lines 15, 17, 22 and 25), which is inconsistent with the possibility that the child is treating this movement of the jigsaw piece as a one-off infraction, unrelated to events which had preceded it. Furthermore, the child also uses the word **again** in the imperative, which may implicate relevant happenings in the past as well as an orientation towards the future. It seems self-evident that in this sequence the use of the imperative by the child, as well as the provocative act by myself, are constructed in the light of the understanding arrived at in the earlier sequence.[5]

Alternative request designs

The argument so far is that Amy's use of imperatives often displays forms of connectedness to understandings that have been reached in prior inter- action, and that their use is informed by such understandings. I now want to suggest that the affinity that imperatives have with this type of sequen- tial connectedness is, in certain respects, a distinctive one; that other ways of handling request-type activities do not, at the ages in question, link back to prior understandings in the ways that imperatives often do. If I can show that these alternative request actions are routinely employed in a *different* interactional environment from imperatives then that will have important implications for the argument. It will suggest that whenever the child makes a request, whenever in effect she makes a selection from those request designs which are available to her, then at least one kind of consideration that informs that selection will be the presence or absence of the kinds of sequential understanding which the analysis so far has been seeking to document.

In order to develop this argument I need to contrast the child's use of imperatives with alternatively usable request-like actions. This task is made slightly more complex because the alternative actions that are avail- able to the child in the two types of situation with which I have been dealing – offence-related and non-offence-related sequences – can be somewhat different. In offence situations, when confronted by the prospect or actuality of adult delinquency the child can employ various turn types as a way of intervening in events. For example, in one incident to which I have fleetingly referred, the child, after seeing me lick my knife at the mealtable, said to me **Don't lick that knife daddy (.) 'pposed to cut it up.** Shortly afterwards, when she thinks that she can see signs of me being

---

[5] Extract 3.8 illustrates one kind of interactional activity which is made possible by the child's grasp of understandings. As she can now be relied on to have grasped such under- standings then the adult can employ forms of humour, such as that found here, which rely on this fact through attempting to subvert them. As far as I can tell, parallel usages of understandings for the creation of humour are not employed by adults in the first 18 months of the child's life. For example, the forms of creativity in the peekaboo game, as identified by Bruner and Sherwood (1976), essentially rely on the child forming expecta- tions, which can then be thwarted by the adult, on the basis of earlier *perceivable* patterns. The relevant expectations are not ones which are mediated through understandings estab- lished in the discourse, as is the case in #3.8.

Amy and her father are transferring pieces of a jigsaw from a board on to
a nearby chair. The last topic was on another matter. F re-opens the
activity by picking up a piece of the jigsaw and saying:

1	F:	D'you want me to put them on there, ((holding a piece of the
2		jigsaw in a mid-air static position))
3		(2.2)
4	A:	N:o:t ((also shakes her head and makes to take the piece
5		from F's hand))

| 6 | F: | No: you're going to put them on there are you ((F lets A |
| 7 | | take the piece from his hand in the course of this turn)) |

((30 secs omitted, involving talk between F and A about who is the
silliest person: see text))

| 8 | F: | She's the biggest of a:ll the silly billys ((A here starts to pick |
| 9 | | up a jigsaw piece from the board)) |

10	A:	Yes ((then A puts the piece on the chair))
11		(((.) between last turn and F's next action))
12		((F picks up a piece of the jigsaw and loudly places it down
13		on the chair,^{A} a smile on his face; looks at A, who is
14		looking at the piece on the chair))

15	A:	No:, ((and shakes her head))
16		(1.1)
17	A:	((Turns to look at F)) Dont^B do it again: daddy, ((sharply
18		lifts and drops her left arm at Dont; does a weak hit to F's
19		shoulder with her right arm at again; moves both her arms to
20		either side of F's head at daddy; all somewhat playful))

| 21 | F: | I'm sorry Amy, |

| 22 | A: | Ye- your a naughty daddy, ((A's face almost touching F's |
| 23 | | here)) |

| 24 | F: | Oh= |

| 25 | A: | =Go away ((still low key - no pushing away or agonized |
| 26 | | intonation)) |

Plate A   Plate B

about to engage in a further act of this self-same kind she simply says **Eh!**, rather loudly, in the form of a warning. This operates as a warning partly because it reminds me of what the child has just said, it relies on that earlier sequential understanding. When analysed, it turns out that, in addition to imperatives, many other turn types employed by the child in offence sequences, such as warnings like the one to which I have just referred, connect with, and amount to particular ways of dealing with, understandings which have their basis in earlier sequential events. In such offence situations, therefore, there is less of a case to be made that imperatives are *distinctively* associated with the presence of such understandings in comparison with other types of turn construction. Rather, imperatives, together with a variety of other turn types, represent particular ways of handling the interactional contingencies associated with such understandings. Although it would still be possible to demonstrate the generic significance of such sequential understandings to these offence sequences, this line of analysis will not be developed here.[6] Instead, I shall compare the use of imperatives to that of other requests in non-offence sequences. These data show more clearly how request selection is contingent on particular forms of sequential understanding.

In non-offence sequences we found that most, though not all, imperatives were used in certain types of circumstance. Their use was associated with occasions on which earlier events had occurred which had connections with the later use of the imperative. Specifically, when the child uses

---

[6] For work within conversation analysis which explores in more detail some of the dynamics of such offence sequences involving children, though not children of this age, the reader could consult Maynard (1985), Wootton (1986), Schegloff (1989) and Goodwin (1990). See also Shantz (1987) for a useful overview of related research.

the imperative she often has a basis for supposing that what she is asking the parent to do is compatible with an earlier understanding. This order of connectedness was demonstrated with regard both to understandings which had emerged from within the same sequence as that in which the imperative occurs (extracts 3.1–3.3), and to those which had arisen out of earlier sequences (#3.5). When we examine the distribution of the other main linguistic designs used for making requests at this age a different pattern emerges. Between the ages of 2;1 and 2;5 there are 3 such alternative designs in frequent use on these recordings – 'I like x', 'I want x' and 'You do x' (Table 5.1, p. 143). The principal observation to be made here is that in non-offence sequences the large majority of these, about 95 per cent, *are not used in sequential positions analogous to those which seem most characteristic of imperative use.* They do not generally occur in positions where the child has a sequential basis for supposing that what she is asking for is compatible with the understanding of her recipient.

Within the 5 per cent which seem to constitute the exceptions to this pattern, the ones which bear resemblance to the pattern of imperative use, the majority occur in interactional circumstances analogous to #3.6. These are ones in which the child asks the parent to do again something that the parent has done before, in the recent past, where there has been no suggestion of the parent being unwilling to perform that action again. In #3.6 we found that the child could employ an imperative to request a repeat performance of the earlier activity. There, Amy asked me to read another story, the story about the rabbit hutch, shortly after a prior story-reading session had ended. Alternative request designs can, however, be drawn upon by the child in comparable circumstances. In one such, Amy's mother is playing a 'Hickory Dickory Dock' game with her. She makes her fingers walk along Amy's arm and then on to the top of her head, saying the early words of the rhyme as she does so. Amy's garbled attempt to complete the words of the rhyme, as her mother's hand returns down the arm (to the words 'the mouse ran down'), occasions much mirth. There is subsequently no suggestion of her mother being unwilling to play the game again, but instead of using an imperative to request the repeat performance, as we found Amy doing in #3.6, she says **I want it again**. This, and other instances, instructs us to recognize that when the child is requesting such repeat performances it is possible for her to handle this contingency in a variety of ways. In doing this the child is, in a sense, displaying differential analyses of the nature of the contingency that obtains. But I will, however, reserve further consideration of the implications of such deviant cases until the end of this section.

Instead of being used in the sequential positions most characteristic of imperatives, the three principal alternative request designs are employed mainly in two interactional slots. The first, and most pervasive in terms of frequency patterns, is as *a first* way of broaching a request with the parent. This can be illustrated by looking at an extract which takes place in circumstances analogous to those discussed earlier in #3.4, when Amy was wanting to get out of her chair. In connection with that extract I mentioned that at 2;1 Amy also made requests to leave her high-chair by saying **Wanna go down** and **Like get out now**. There seems little doubt here that these requests, like **Lift out dad**, also have as their objective that the parent should assist her to get out of the chair: she was not able to get down on her own! Extract 3.9 contains the **Like get out now** instance. Whereas in #3.4 there had been prior discussion which related to the matter of whether or not it was appropriate for the child to leave the chair, containing agreement to the prospect of her getting out, in #3.9 no prior discussion of any kind has taken place. This is the first time, in the context of this mealtime, that this matter has been raised. The child's first **Like get out now** (line 1) in #3.9, therefore, illustrates the predominant way in which she uses the three principal alternative request designs available to her, as a way of initially broaching the matter with the parent. Although imperatives can occasionally be used in this way, as I have noted, this is not the use with which they are most often associated in non-offence sequences.

The second interactional slot in which the child regularly employs request designs other than the imperative is where the parent has already given some indication that he or she is unwilling to grant such a request. As it happens there is also an example of this in #3.9. My initial reply to the child's **Like get out now – Get out now? But you haven't finished your apple –** is hardly a propitious one, and my next turn, **Finish your apple first** (line 5), even less so. In the face of each of these signs of reservation on the part of the parent, that is in sequential positions in which the child has a basis for supposing the parent to be opposed in some way to her proposed line of action, the child persists with her request by re-adopting the 'Like' request format (lines 3 and 6).[7] Imperatives are rarely used to engage in re-

---

[7] Re-requesting for something that the parent is initially unwilling to grant is most often enacted with the 'I want x' design by Amy rather than 'I like x.' See Wootton (1981b) for parallel patterns among four-year-old children. Here, and elsewhere in the text, I do not address the issue of whether or not there are systematic differences between the ways in which the child employs 'I want x', 'I like x' and 'You do x' formats. From provisional analyses which have been carried out it seems likely to be the case that there are such differences, but, as I see it, this issue is peripheral to the main arguments developed in this book. For relevant discussion and analyses of such matters see Gerhardt (1991).

3.9 2;1/4479

Amy, in her chair at the table, has just been asking for some orange, and
told that we do not have any. She then turns down an offer of some
banana, and after eating two bits of apple on her tray begins to climb out
of her seat. As she does this she says:

1   A: Like get out^A now ((still in process of lifting herself up))

2   F: Get out now?=But you haven't finished your apple

3   A: (But) like get out, ((by end of this turn she is in a crouched
4   position with her feet on the seat of her chair))

5   F: Finish your apple first

6   A: Like get out^B no:w, ((kneeling on seat by the end of this turn
7   and looking directly at F))

8   F: Can't you finish those pieces of apple first

9   A: No::::::::::: ((starts high pitch and gradually descends in
10   song-like intonation; as she says this she remains stilled,
11   looking steadily slightly away from F))

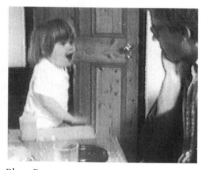

Plate A   Plate B

---

requesting work in the face of parental opposition. In fact in non-offence
sequences they are, as previously noted, generally used where the child has
a basis for supposing parental compliance. Again, however, on a small
number of occasions there are cases which deviate from this pattern. For

example, on one such at 2;5 (presented as #5.3 on p. 154) I am wanting Amy to put her toys away at bedtime. She replies by saying **No**, and follows this up by saying **Play with them** several times in response to my protestations, this being a request not just for her to play with them but me also.

These various deviant cases to which I have been alluding in this section seem to me most important. They suggest that at this age the child, when selecting her request design in non-offence sequences, is not doing this on the basis of there being, for her, a one-to-one mapping between a type of request, such as an imperative, and a particular kind of interactional scenario. When, for example, the child wishes to pursue a request in the face of parental opposition she may select various request forms with which to do this, or, for that matter, other devices. It seems likely to be the case that these various devices, by virtue of having distinctive properties, also have the capacity to convey differential displays of the child's understanding of the nature of the interactional contingency in which she finds herself. So there are ways in which it is grossly simplifying to speak, as I have done, about interactional positions in which 'the child wishes to pursue a request in the face of parental opposition', especially if that is taken to imply that these positions are interactionally equivalent for the child. This point can be more concretely expressed by addressing one of the other interactional positions in which deviant cases have emerged. When requesting for a repeat performance of some action, where the parent has expressed no reservation about this, the child most often uses an imperative, as in #3.6. Sometimes, however, as in the 'Hickory Dickory Dock' example, an 'I want' request design can be employed for this purpose. Presumably, the employment of the latter may imply that, for the child, the repetition of the associated game was problematic in ways that did not apply to the repetition of the book reading in #3.6. If this is so, then the character of the interactional situation, from the child's point of view, would be analysably different in each case.[8]

[8] In #3.9 there are also non-verbal signs of the child expecting to have her request granted. Not only is she beginning to climb out of her chair when she makes her initial request at line 1, but she also continues to engage in such preparations during her second request. Whilst such accompanying non-verbal behaviour can occur with 'like x' requests, as in this case, it is much more consistently associated with imperatives, as in the comparable situation depicted in line 13 (Plate B) of #3.4, where the form that it takes appears to make stronger assumptions as to the request being granted. In #3.4 Amy does more than raise herself into a position from which she can be lifted, she actually begins to climb out of the chair on to the table. Extract 3.3 offers further evidence bearing on this contrast between non-verbal behaviour in imperative and in 'like' forms. There, at around line 5, we found Amy prepared to take the magazine from her mother's hand in the context of imperative use. There are no comparable cases in which 'like' requests are similarly associated with removing objects from the parent's hand. The various forms of non-verbal behaviour referred to above are rarely found with 'want' requests.

While these various observations about deviant cases, and their implications, seem to me important, nevertheless they do not undermine the principal claims that I have been making, both in this section, and in the earlier sections of this chapter. The kind of analysis I have offered does not claim to have an account of the workings of imperatives which explicates the interactional role that they play in all known positions within these request sequences. Whether, and in what ways, their less usual uses contribute to the scenes in which they play a part is a matter that others can take up. In fact in the last analysis my interest in imperatives, in their own right, is less important than the nature of the sequential understandings to which they seem to be related. In this respect two principal claims *are* being made. First, that, within a variety of sequences, there is a range of internal evidence, examined earlier in this chapter, that imperatives are connected with certain types of preceding understanding. Second, that other available request designs are not generally used in parallel circumstances, and that the circumstances where they *are* used are not ones in which imperatives are normally used. The crucial implication of this, it seems to me, is that in making a request selection the child is taking into account, routinely, though not in a deterministic fashion, the nature of the local sequential understanding that obtains.

Corollaries and implications

In the final section of this chapter I want to explore some of the implications of the main findings which have been reported above.

Connections and entitlements

The arguments about sequential connections that I have made so far have been largely expressed in cognitive terms. The main thrust of these claims has been that, in general, the course of action that the child, early in her third year of life, seeks to further through her use of an imperative is one that connects with, and is compatible with, an understanding that can be tracked back into the details of prior interaction. In non-offence sequences this understanding is one that the child can use as a basis for expecting her imperative to be in accord with the preferences of the other party. In offence sequences, whilst no such accord is necessarily implied, imperatives are, nevertheless, usually consistent with understandings which are identifiable as having been established by the child in prior interaction.

In constituting grounds for the selection of the imperative the earlier understanding also creates a type of justification for its use. The fact that these grounds exist creates a basis not just for the child to perform an imperative when she does, but also to feel entitled to do so. This is most obviously so in offence sequences, in instances like #3.7. There the fact that the child (line 1) initially states that she is going to pick up the chalk creates a warrantable basis for her then to tell her mother to leave it on the floor (line 4), a basis for opposing the line of conduct in which her mother engages. What seems to be occurring here, then, is that child actions, in having a connectedness to earlier forms of understanding, can implicitly also claim an entitlement to engage in such courses of action. These close associations between the entitled, and warrantable, nature of action and sequential connections are so important that the next chapter is largely devoted to their further exploration. There we shall find that our understanding of incidents which involve serious conflict between parent and child is deepened once we recognize that, on the basis of earlier sequential events, children of this age can entertain expectations that subsequent lines of action will unfold in a particular fashion. Where events do not unfold in expected ways, then the child can express her grievances in a forthright manner, this very forthrightness testifying to the fact that what has been thwarted is what the child felt entitled to expect. In these ways, sequential understandings come to have parameters which extend beyond the cognitive into the organization and expression of affect.

For the time being I just want to note that in talking about the entitled and warrantable character of action at this age we are touching on an important parameter of developmental change. A feature of adult talk to which several writers have drawn our attention is its *accountability* (see especially Garfinkel 1967). By this Garfinkel is referring to the fact that the interactional stances which we adopt, usually – though not of course exclusively – in our talk, emanate from, and are embedded in, human forms of reasoning. In a superficial sense this is documented through the ways in which we have recourse to 'good reasons' when called upon to explain or defend what we have done or said. In a broader sense, as other writers have also noted (Wittgenstein 1953; Winch 1958), to grasp the specific nature of a bit of human action is to identify that web of practice and reasoning which informs its composition. One thing that is taking place in childhood is an induction into this specifically human world of reasoning and intelligibility, the parameters of which are shaped by the kind of intersubjective order that language makes possible. In noting the importance of sequential understandings for the two-year-old we are noting ways through which shared understandings are coming to be treated by the child as being consequential for her own later lines of conduct. Once she is able to build her actions in the light of understandings that have been reached on earlier occasions then there has been a significant shift in the order of accountable reason that informs her conduct, one which also permits, in new ways, the child's actions to be informed by whatever distinctive set of understandings mark out the particular form of the human culture to which she is exposed.

Interest in the child's interactional partner

I have shown that, within what I have called non-offence sequences, the child is systematically sensitive to whether or not the person she is interacting with has, in the immediate or near sequential past, provided the child with grounds for supposing that he or she will be well disposed towards envisaged lines of conduct. In certain circumstances such information will not be available to the child, and in these circumstances one course of action that is employable by her is to use a non-imperative request design, such as 'I want x' or 'I like x.' Given the potential relevance of knowing the other party's preferences, however, another tack that is compatible with such an orientation to the grounds for action is for the child to seek such information where it is not available. Indeed, the existence of such an orientation creates an incentive for the child to ask such questions. In this respect what is interesting is that the child, from the age of 2;1, a time when she still has no formal syntactic control over the construction of yes/no questions, nevertheless can, as in #3.2, elicit such information from her recipient. In #3.2 Amy, referring to the jigsaw pieces, initially says **Like another one daddy?** before subsequently issuing her imperative, **Jus: put it on the:re daddy.** Similarly, in #3.3, Amy initiates the sequence by enquiring whether or not her mother wants the chalks, **Want some chalks?**, prior to her subsequent use of imperatives.

This interest in seeking such information is not confined to sequences in which imperatives are subsequently used. Extracts 3.10 and 3.11, both of which occur at the age of 2;1, illustrate other sequence trajectories which can accompany such questions. In #3.10 Amy says **Daddy ye like do it again?** (line 1) to establish whether or not I am prepared to engage, with her, in another round of cleaning the stool. This occurs in a position where it is already clear that Amy herself intends to engage in this activity. Her enquiry extracts from me a begrudging kind of acquiescence, one which treats that enquiry as amounting to at least an invitation, on Amy's part, for me to become involved, possibly even some form of request. Either way

3.10 2;1/4859

Amy has been cleaning a small stool using a piece of tissue as a cloth.
She decides she needs a new piece of tissue; after getting it, with F's
assistance, she says, out of camera shot, I is doing the bi ˙ob again, to
which F, also out of shot, replies <u>You've got to do that big job
again?=Gosh</u>. As Amy walks back to the stool she says to F:

```
1   A:    Daddy ye like do it^A again? ((standing by the stool, looking
2         at F))
3                          (.7)
4   F:    Do you want me to help you again, ((sitting down by the
5         stool in the course of saying this))

6   A:    Yes   ((then kneels down by stool))

7   F:    Mmmm   ((now lying on floor by stool))
```

Plate A

---

it is clear from this extract that the enquiry arises from an interest on Amy's
part in my participating in the activity and that, in these circumstances, no
further form of turn on Amy's part, such as an imperative, is necessarily
required to make this further evident. In #3.11 Amy's **Like sit do::wn** (line
4, intonationally a question) again clearly conveys an interest on Amy's
part in having me sit down. Again the device used to initiate this is simply
to ask if the recipient would like to do it.

It seems clear that, from the same age that the child uses non-offence-
related imperatives with any frequency (2;1), we also find that, in similar
situations, there are occasions on which she can find reason to seek
information about the preferences of her recipient. Given that non-offence

3.11 2;1/6768

Amy's mother has just got up from the table where she has been sitting
by Amy. Amy continues sitting in her high-chair at the table, eating a
boiled egg. She has a finger in the egg and is referring to this when she
speaks to F. F is standing about 4 feet from the table, out of camera:

```
1    A:    I'm putting my finger i:n .hh I'm putting my finger i:n
2          ((looking at F both here and subsequently))

3    F:    Are you::?

4    A:    ( ) Like sit do::wnᴬ
5                        (.6)
6    A:    Like sit do:::wn= ((F looms towards A in later part of this
7          turn))

8    F:    =No I wouldn't like to sit down I'm watching the rugby at the
9          moment (.) Mummy's going to sit with you in a
10         moment
```

Plate A

---

imperatives are organized by reference to overt evidence that the child has
about the preferences of her interactional partner, then one possibility is
that the child's use of enquiries at this same age similarly documents her
awareness that these self-same grounds have an ongoing relevance to anticipated lines of conduct. Indeed, if it is not tautological, it might be useful
to think of this awareness as forming a practical motivation for the child
to ask such questions. Whether this awareness is *first* made evident through
her use of imperatives or whether both these developments occur at

roughly the same time is not a matter that can be decided from my data base. What seems clear enough, however, is that an orientation to the relevance of other people's wishes and desires, in the form of these types of question, seems to go hand-in-hand with the emergence of a capacity to take such information into account when making her request selections.

Memory and cognitive architecture

A question that one can ask about any type of interactional sequence is - what is the kind of cognitive architecture that is necessary for such a sequence to work in the way that it does? If the child's behaviour is sensitive to understandings which have been arrived at earlier in the interaction then what implications does that have as to the kinds of mental processing required of the child? Clearly, one mental facility that is required is memory. Perhaps we normally talk as if, when using memory, we are engaging in acts of remembering, acts which involve us in a reflective search for something in our memory, self-conscious 'efforts after meaning' as Bartlett calls them (1932:20). Shotter reminds us, though, of 'the indefinitely many everyday occasions in which no such experience of referring to an "inner" image in order to remember occurs' (1990:122). And if such is true for adults then surely it is even more so for the child who, according to many, has yet (at, say, 2;1) even to acquire the capacity for mature reflective thought. This more mundane use of memory is required not just for those cases where the child's subsequent actions/requests rely on the recollection of earlier understandings, as seems to be the case when she employs imperatives; it is also only through using her memory to identify the absence of earlier understandings that the child can select appropriate alternative forms of request design.

What we need to get clear, then, is what kinds of implications our analyses have for the way in which memory works. Here the key point seems to be that, irrespective of whatever else is in the memory, the critical features which will have a direct bearing on action selection will normally relate to local understandings which have arisen in the course of the same sequence or an earlier sequence. If request selection can hang on the nature of those understandings then an incentive is created for memory to give priority to the storage and retrieval of such understandings. Memory is the handmaiden of pragmatics. If this is so then, in trade parlance, it is short-term rather than long-term memory where efficiency is most required at this age, a demanding kind of on-line efficiency which continually informs each and every request-like action.

All this is not to deny, of course, that long term, script-like, components of memory both exist and develop at or around the beginning of the child's third year of life (see pp. 37–8). Indeed, in the course of writing about offence related imperatives I noted the child's capacity to work with, and thus in some way memorize, general behavioural precepts such as politeness rules. Earlier, however, in connection with **Lift out dad** in #3.4, I have also argued that scripts *per se* leave undiscriminated the various ways in which it is possible for the child to enact any particular activity type. And the same point can equally be made about the child's use of behavioural precepts. The child can display an orientation to such precepts in a variety of ways – as was so in the case when I was first told not to lick my knife, then later warned through Amy's use of the word **Eh**. The precept itself obviously cannot account for such variable details of the child's behaviour. Therefore, although script-like knowledge must be continually fuelled and modified by the child's on-line experience, what bearing scripts have on the on-line design of conduct remains indefinite.[9]

An implication of my argument, therefore, is that it is necessary for the child to possess a mental apparatus which is efficient for the storage and access of local understandings. We have seen that a critical feature of these understandings is their public nature, which is to say that they are things that have been *explicitly* oriented to earlier in the interaction. For example, when, in #3.4, Amy says **Lift out dad** as a way of asking me to take her out of her high-chair, the understanding that informs the construction of this action – my earlier consent to the prospect of her leaving her chair – had been made overtly apparent in the interaction. In making a request selection, therefore, what memory must be sensitive to is not so much private memories of the past, earlier mental understandings that never became exposed within the interaction, but public ones: what has transpired on the interactional surface. Memory is, of course, free to turn its attentions to matters outside the public domain, but in doing this it must now always keep one ear open for understandings which can subsequently become germane. In this sense the key events, the ones to which memory is required to give privileged status, are now those which are publicly accountable.

[9] It seems to me that my arguments in this section are particularly compatible with one well-known phenomenon which researchers such as Nelson (1993) have re-drawn to our attention, namely childhood amnesia. This refers to the inability of both children and adults to remember particular incidents or even standard patterns of event in early childhood. If the memory of the child at this younger age is mainly concerned with local events, and much less with interconnections across events which, to the adult eye, seem to be similar, then there is little cognitive incentive for putting memory to work in order to extract and hold on to event representations in the long term.

Understandings of other people

When making request selections at this age what the child is implicitly doing is gaining experience and practice in identifying and dealing with not only her own understandings but also those of other people. This process is aided by the fact that the understandings in question are overt in ways which I have described above. In this regard what is called for is not so much the capacity to make inferences about what is in the minds of other people as a capacity to recall other people's publicly stated preferences, with the possibility of enquiring as to the nature of these preferences if such information is not available. In these ways the child builds up knowledge about the workings of other people's minds, and a practical sense of the connections between understandings about these matters and behaviour which is compatible and incompatible with them. The child can act in the light of the earlier stated preferences of her interactional partner, either in such a way as to be consistent with those preferences or so as to be inconsistent with them; in this chapter evidence has been presented which bears on both these types of situation. Perhaps the most vivid accounts of the latter are provided in the work of Dunn (for example 1988). She has amply demonstrated the capacity of children, early in their third year of life, to engage in the taunting and teasing of brothers or sisters. This suggests to her a capacity on their part, by that age, to exploit the knowledge that they have concerning the likes and dislikes of their siblings.

A matter of some importance in these respects is the sheer extent of request-type behaviour in the average speech corpus of children of this age, most of it initiated by the child. Wells (1985:228), for example, found that, within the large sample of children he studied, 30 per cent of all child utterances at the age of 30 months were ones in which the child was trying to gain control over the present or future behaviour of someone present. In the light of this the practice, and practising, of taking into account other people's preferences, to which I have just referred, is potentially of some developmental significance. Indeed, there could well be a connection between the radically reduced levels of request initiation that we find in certain groups of children and their much more limited capacity to make inferences regarding the mental states of other people. The obvious group that I have in mind here is children with autistic disorders. That these children have special impairments with regard to taking account of other people's beliefs is now well known (Frith 1989:chapter 10). What is also well known about these children is their radical avoidance of interactional contact with other people (McTear 1985: chapter 9; Loveland, Landry, Hughes, Hall and McEvoy 1988; Local and Wootton 1995). Where they do engage in such contact their expertise is most highly developed with regard to responding to other people's questions. Their overall levels of communicative speech initiation towards other people are very low by comparison with normal children.

In considering the interactional precursors and correlates of autism, one currently influential position highlights the significance of a delay in onset of a certain type of pointing behaviour among autistic children (Baron-Cohen 1991). This is not the pointing that a child can do in accompaniment to her requests, but that which is used simply to draw her recipient's attention to matters of shared interest in the world – the sort of pointing which is done, for example, when labelling pictures in books. The delay in this form of behaviour is taken to imply a reduced level of awareness of other people on the part of the autistic child. While there may be an element of truth in this,[10] it also seems to be the case, as I have noted above, that the interaction patterns of the autistic child are radically disturbed across the range of contexts in which normal children participate, including request contexts. In particular, if the child is engaging in little request initiation then there is going to be little scope for ever recognizing that conduct can be designed so as to take account of sequentially based understandings. If this site is, as I have argued, an important one for developing a working acquaintance with such understandings, then the pattern of interactional involvement displayed by the autistic child will have as its corollary a radically diminished acquaintance with the practice of taking other people's views into account. So, while there will almost certainly be neurological and early developmental predisposers to autism, ones which may well be causally distinctive to this condition, the specific bases for the impairment in taking account of the mental states of other people may lie in the relative absence of normal patterns of later behaviour. If it is through activities such as requesting that the normal child develops a working, practical skill in taking account of the preferences of other people, then it seems likely to be the lack of this interactional experience which could underpin the much diminished skills of the autistic child in this regard.

---

[10] At the stage of present research there seems to be a dearth of careful observational work on the initiation techniques of autistic children, which might serve to corroborate the suggestions from the mainly experimental work which relates to referential pointing.

As a final observation about autism one might say that these children demonstrate the difficulties that are incurred by having a mind which is principally structured in terms of scripts. Their mind is script-like in that these children have as their main preoccupation the reproduction of familiar routines, often of a non-verbal nature and often ones they like to carry out on their own. Their memory is put to work for the storage of these routines; indeed, even where these children can speak, their spontaneous talk often consists in large part of what is known as 'delayed echolalia', which means the repetition out loud of phrases which they have heard in the past, though not normally in such a way as to expect a response from other people who may be present (Prizant and Rydell 1984). Such phrases are also often used in a recurrent, stereotypical way. The displayed preoccupations of the memories of autistic children are, therefore, precisely with script-like knowledge; but this kind of knowledge only permits these children access to relatively crude forms of interactional involvement. And by having little incentive to engage in such involvement there is little opportunity to put their memory to work in handling the on-line business of interaction. That, to me, seems to be one way of describing the nature of their predicament.

Reflexivity, language and time

The notion of a sequentially based *understanding* has figured prominently in the analysis and discussion so far. I have chosen the term *understanding* rather than a term like 'representation' for particular reasons. In the study of children of this age the term 'representation' was used extensively by Piaget. He saw the emergence of the child's capacity to engage in thought which draws on representations, at or around 18 months of age, as freeing her from the spatio-temporal constraints of the sensorimotor period. The existence of these stable representations meant that they could form a filter between her and the here-and-now, their key property being that they had an enduring existence which extended beyond the here-and-now. And in these respects there is rather little important difference between the Piagetian and Vygotskyan traditions. The *understandings* which I am highlighting, though possibly predicated on some order of knowledge of the kind being alluded to through the notion of 'representations', are essentially bound up with the here-and-now, with what has been specifically agreed or claimed within prior interaction. In order to identify them and construct a related line of action the child must have the capacity and flexibility to attend to the specifics of occasions, and to treat those specifics as consequential, as mattering. The notion of an *understanding* is, therefore, highlighting a different domain of relevance to the child, the domain of that which is local to the particular occasion, and that which has been made public in that occasion.

The nature of the connection between a child request and the prior understanding is the matter I now want to address. One way of describing this connection would be to say, like Barthes (1957), that the child is displaying the capacity to use a sign (an imperative) to refer to another sign (the earlier interactional event). While there is some obvious truth in that, the Garfinkelian notion of reflexivity captures more accurately the nature of the connection in question (Garfinkel 1967). One way of making this point is to think of there being many such understandings which could potentially be arrived at in the course of the child's interaction with others, many happenings that *could* become relevant to later interaction. In practice, however, later talk only addresses some of these possibilities. When this happens, as in **Lift out dad** in #3.4, connections are made to earlier events, and those events are turned into signs of ongoing understandings, whereas other earlier events that remain unaddressed, unconnected-with, thereby never attain an equivalent status. At the same time, however, the later events, turns like **Lift out dad**, have the character that they do by virtue of their connectability to the happenings that have preceded them. Therefore, turns like **Lift out dad** achieve their status as embodying understandings by virtue of the mutual informing, the reflexive relationship, that interconnects the earlier and later events. In the last analysis, then, to say here that an understanding exists is to say no more, and no less, than that this order of reflexive connectability exists between these events.

The possession of a language is clearly an invaluable, possibly even a necessary, tool for such understandings to become embodied in action. Language offers a uniquely flexible basis for people to design their conduct in the light of recent sequential events. Instead of having to guess the interactional state of play by other means, once the child can exploit the signalling potential of language so as to gain a sense of understandings that obtain, and once she can organize her actions in the light of them, then she is in a position to adopt a much more sensitive and flexible positioning vis-à-vis those she deals with. Having said this, however, it is also important to stress that, in order for these sequential connections to work, all that is required of the language is that it be sufficiently precise, in the properties which it has, for the establishment of the reflexive relationships that are at the heart of these matters. In this respect, for example, any rigid mapping of semantic meanings to words would create numerous difficulties for the developing child. What is needed, and what she seems to have, is a lexicon with the capacity to be contextually nuanced and re-shaped. Take #3.3 as an example of this. There, Amy's mother agreed that she would like to do some 'chalking'. A question that could be asked is whether we could identify, for this child, a set of features which represent what is meant by the use of this term. These might, for example, involve holding a chalk, making marks on a board, and such like. In practice, however, in instances like #3.3, it seems possible for an indefinite range of actions to become viewed by the child as integral to the activity. In #3.3, she identifies her mother's holding of a magazine as incompatible with engagement in chalking; in other instances, for example, she suggests that her mother position herself closer to the board so as to be able to engage in the activity. In short, in context, the child can find any one of an indefinite variety of aspects to be pertinent and relevant to the engagement of someone in the activity of chalking. What the child needs to be capable of doing, in order to engage in sequences in the ways in which she does, is to *find* which of this indefinite range of local circumstances bears on what is entailed in an activity such as chalking.

If the arguments which I have made concerning the importance of recent sequential events for the child's design of her request behaviour are correct then this also has implications regarding the child's orientation to time. Perhaps the foundational work on time remains that of Piaget. Piaget's research focused especially on the period up to 18 months and developments after the age of 4. For him, the child of 18 months has grasped ways in which events can have a serial and temporal ordering. Eventually, well after the age of 4, the child will develop a *conceptual* grasp of such matters as temporal order of succession and temporal intervals. Piaget recognizes that between these times the child will learn, 'to anticipate successions on the practical plane (by localising them in the immediate present) or to take certain durations into account' (1969:257), but he himself did not investigate these matters. The observations which I have made precisely relate to this dark period. If it is the case that the child's behaviour is increasingly taking into account understandings which have been reached in prior interaction then what must also be routinely taking place is an extension backwards in time of that stretch of interaction which can become relevant to the child's present course of action. The temporal horizons pertinent to action, therefore, shift radically in this event. In effect, when she moves from about 16 months to 24 months of age, she exchanges the uncertainties of an interactional world which consists largely of a series of one-off exchanges for a world of sequential attentiveness which routinely requires her to monitor wider units of time. As a result, the type of time orientation, or 'time consciousness' as Husserl put it (1964), must undergo radical alteration. If so, this alteration must be intimately connected to the alteration in the nature of the child's practical activities over this period – more specifically to the altered relevance of sequential considerations in the child's organization of her conduct.

In this chapter I have drawn together a variety of evidence which suggests that by early in her third year of life the child is capable of taking sequential understandings into account. This has principally been done by demonstrating that these understandings have specific links with the use of imperatives. Because these links are much less demonstrable in her use of other request designs, this suggests that in making request selections the child routinely takes account of such understandings in systematic ways. It has also been argued that these understandings have implications for a variety of psychological processes such as memory, time awareness and knowledge of other people. To this extent these understandings seem, to me, to be potentially pivotal and generic for the explanation of a broad spectrum of the child's behaviour at this age. In this respect, one aspect which has been touched on is the child's capacity to recognize a moral dimension to conduct. This is the aspect which is to become the principal focus of my attention in the next chapter.

4

Distressing incidents

The phrase 'terrible twos' is often used in discussions of children of Amy's age to index the emotional turbulence which seems to be especially marked at this time. When Amy was aged 2;5 and 2;9 a small number of incidents took place on the recordings which bring this phrase to mind. For a parent these incidents are not pleasant ones to report or analyse. A feature they share in common is the level of distress displayed by the child; in the course of them she becomes angry and upset. One place in which such troubles can occur in request sequences among children of this age is where a child's request is rejected. Indeed, such occurrences are to be found on our recordings, and at a later point in this chapter I shall have more to say about them. But the intriguing thing about the incidents in question here is that rather than occurring in circumstances in which the parent is thwarting the child's desires, rejecting a request, they occur in ones where the parent is actually attempting to grant the request, or assist the child in some other way. For this reason they usually seemed perplexing from a parental point of view, even infuriating at times. It is these incidents which are the focus of my discussion in this chapter.

In general, my argument will be that any account of the way these incidents work will need to make reference to the sequential expectations which the child brings to them. To this extent this chapter explores, and contains further evidence for, claims about the centrality of sequential phenomena that were made in the previous chapter. In the course of this it will emerge that the seemingly bizarre behaviour of the child in these incidents – behaviour which is often, I think, described as 'spoilt' – has quite systematic foundations. It turns out that it is the spoiling behaviour of the parents which is the key to this, behaviour which creates contingencies which, for the child, admit only of non-conventional, emotionally distraught, remedy.

The incidents which will be analysed took place in two kinds of interactional circumstances, and these are accorded separate treatment in the following discussion. In the first ones to be discussed, the child asks the parent to do something. The parent then attempts to grant the request; but the granting's manner of execution leads to distress on the part of the child. In the second type of incident, the child says that *she* wants to obtain something, and becomes distressed when the parent displays a preparedness to obtain the thing for her; clearly her preference is to obtain it by herself.

Distressed reactions to request grantings

Let me briefly describe the kind of incident that is being referred to here with an actual example. The child is sitting with her mother away from the dining table; she makes it clear that she would like some honey and her mother agrees that she can have some. I fetch the honey from the table and pass it to the child, but she is upset at this and reacts strongly against it, saying that her mother is the one to get it, not me. This incident, and a further one, will be examined in more detail shortly. First of all, however, I want to consider the techniques that the child has available to her for rectifying responses to her request, such as this, which are flawed in some way. The fact that she has more mundane techniques available to her, ones which do not entail distressed reactions, makes all the more interesting the question of what prevents the use of these lower-key techniques in the distressing incidents which I will then go on to examine. Finally, I shall identify the properties of the sequences which are associated with these distressed reactions.

Third position repair

Once the child is capable of directing request-like communicative intentions to other people then one interactional contingency that can arise is that the response of the other party can be misfitted to the child's request. The other party may, deliberately or otherwise, perform an action that is not what the child wants. The child may, for example, be passed the wrong thing or find that a course of action on which the parent is embarking is in some other way incompatible with that which she envisages. If we speak of the child's initial request as the first position item, and the parent's response as being in second position, we can then inspect third position to see how the child deals with those occasions on which such a misfitted response occurs. In chapter 2 (pp. 28–30) we have seen that in third position the child has ways of dealing with such an eventuality from early in her second year of life. By the time she is aged 2;0, therefore, she has various techniques available to her for engaging in rectificational business.

Some of these techniques can be identified in #4.1, which took place when Amy was aged 2;1 Here, Amy's mother, seated between me and Amy, has just brought her own plate of food to the table. Amy's gesture together with her incomplete **I want some more- som- something** (line 6) make it evident that she wants something on her mother's plate, this forming the basis for my attempt to guess what she is wanting by then saying **A chip? (.) D'you want a chip?** (lines 9–10), and proffering a chip towards her. Amy, in third position, treats this interpretation of her turn as deficient. She does this by shaking her left arm whilst emitting two brief guttural, irritated sounds immediately followed by **Mummy (gan get)** (line 12), the latter being said with controlled, non-upset, voice quality – all done with her drinking cup in her mouth! So, this first technique of remedying the inapt response to her request consists of rejecting, in a fashion, the proposed request object and requesting again for that which she really wanted; all done in a relatively controlled manner. The parents' interpretation of all this is to infer that Amy wants her mother to give her a chip, rather than her father.

Amy's response to her mother's proffer of the chip, described in lines 18–25, is initially to treat it also as deficient. Whilst still drinking, she shakes her left hand as the chip approaches, and after her mother has put it on her tray she takes it and places it on the table, further away from herself and her tray. On this second occasion, therefore, the child displays non-verbal signs of rejection (the hand movement), and in other ways makes it clear that the object is not one for which she currently has a use. A further technique which is available to the child is illustrated by what happens next (lines 23–5). Instead of leaving the chip where it is she picks it up and develops an interest in it. That is, in spite of the request not having been responded to in a satisfactory way by her recipient(s) she may, nevertheless, go along with what they do, let their deficiency pass and develop an interest in that which the response of the other party has made available.[1] Finally, as a footnote to the present discussion, it is interesting to note what happens about three minutes after #4.1. Amy returns to the theme of the chips by saying **Mummy I like a little- I li- Mummy like to**

---

[1] Especially at younger ages than this it is possible for the child to react in this way to the *first* response made to her request. On such occasions, it is usually possible to tell when this is occurring as various non-verbal signs are given off which signal that what the child is being given is not what she was really after, even though she appears prepared to accept that which she is being offered.

4.1 2;1/4198

Amy, sitting in her chair at the table, has just been eating some bits of
cheese proffered to her by F on a knife. F puts the cheese away and
begins to eat his sandwich. Amy then pushes herself higher in her chair,
and says:

1   A: I want some,^{A}.hh= ((then puts out both her arms in a
2   gesture to the end of the table; vocally this turn is incomplete,
3   she was going on to say more))

4   F: =I want a drink? ((said in the process of him standing up))
5   (.9)
6   A: A- I want some more- som-, something ((in the early part of
7   this turn she points with her┌ rh, but in the later part she
8   picks up her drinking cup   │   with this same hand))
                                       │
9   F: └A chip?

10 F: D'you want a chip? ((then F proffers one of M's chips towards
11   A))

12 A: (   )^{B}Mummy (gan get) ((sharp horizontal movements
13   of her left hand in the first part of the turn, and by the end
14   of this part the chip is being taken back by F towards M's
15   plate))
16   (.)
17 F: ((quietly, to M)) Oh: mummy's got to get it

18   ((M picks up a chip and proffers it towards A, who continues
19   to drink from her cup in her right hand. A repeats the
20   earlier horizontal movements of her left hand, whereupon
21   M puts the chip down on A's tray. A then picks the chip up
22   from her tray and puts it on the table adjacent to the tray, an
23   act that generates chuckles from M. Then A picks the chip
24   up again and looks at it for several moments, after which
25   she takes a bite from it.))

Plate A   Plate B

pass the- I like- I (like) you to pass mummy's plate, an utterance that begins
by being addressed to her mother but ends by targeting me. Clearly Amy
is attempting, with some difficulty, to frame her request so as to avoid the
misunderstandings which have occurred previously, by specifying exactly
what she wants. It turns out that what she wants, and may have wanted all
along, is for her mother's plate to be passed to her so that she can take a
chip off herself!

It appears, therefore, that the child, at 2;1, can employ various techniques to rectify or otherwise deal with situations in which the parent
reacts in ways misfitted to her requests. Sometimes her techniques are more
overtly correctional in character than is the case in #4.1. In #4.2, for
example, the child indicates that she would like to make a jigsaw puzzle by
saying to me Like 'at jigsa:w again (line 3). My reaction is to agree to this,
but to try and steer her towards setting up the jigsaw in the middle of the
room rather than in the location – the corner of the room – where we had
been playing with it earlier in the day. As the corner of the room is out of
current camera shot, my unstated reason for acting like this is to arrange
things so that the subsequent action can be caught on film without changing the camera position. My restatement of my preferred location, And
then (.6) we'll do the jigsaw, (.8) over here (lines 19–21), is met with opposition by the child. She says (Oh) no no no 'pposed to do it .hh over .hh
HE::RE ( ) .hh 'upposed to- (lines 22–3), and continues, with eventual
success, to oppose my proposal.

Finally, it is important to emphasize that the child can also sometimes
react to misfitted actions in such a way as not to try and rectify them. For
example, in some circumstances, such as in #4.1, she can temporarily
abandon the pursuit of a request when the parent appears unable to grasp

4.2 2;1/4925

Amy and her father have just finished cleaning a small stool. A takes the stool to a corner of the room; F lies on the floor in the middle of the room. The later part of the sequence all takes place out of camera:

```
 1   A:    I li- I like 'at jigs(.hh)a::w again,

 2   F:    (  ⌐ -)
            │
 3   A:     └ Like 'at jigsa:w again?
 4                          (.)
 5   F:    'T jigsaw again,

 6   A:    Yes,
 7                       (1.0)
 8   F:    Okay,    ((then he starts to stand up))
 9                       (.9)
10   F:    Well let's do it a bit over here
11                       (1.0)
12   F:    Lets put um:::,

13                 (5.6) ((F moving things on floor  out of camera))

14   F:    Put those there

15   A:    ((quiet)) Yes
16                       (1.2)
17   F:    Like that
18                       (1.8)
19   F:    And then (.6) we'll do the jigsaw,
20                       (.8)
21   F:    Ov⌐ er here
            │
22   A:     └ (Oh) no no no 'pposed to do it .hh over .hh HE::RE (
23            ).hh 'upposed to-,

24   F:    Well I wd- wanted to do it over here,

25   A:    I want it .hh he::re daddy:=

26   F:    =Oh: (.8) Allright
```

what she is seeking, and in other circumstances she is capable of accepting the opposite of what she asks for, or of changing her mind about what it is that she wants. These various techniques are all part of the child's flexible response armoury which can be brought to bear in dealing with misfitted responses from the other party.

Distressed responses to request grantings

The point of looking at extracts 4.1 and 4.2 has been to illustrate some of the techniques which, even at 2;1, Amy has at her disposal for dealing with contingencies where the parent's response to her request is in some way deficient, from her point of view. Now I want to highlight how these techniques contrast with the ways in which she behaves in those sequences which have been termed distressing incidents. Stated in simple terms, the child's equivalent behaviour in these latter incidents seems much less flexible and much more extreme. Extract 4.3, for example, presents the honey incident that I briefly described earlier, the one in which Amy was not happy about my passing her a jar of honey that she had requested. Although her left arm movements accompanying **No: No: le:t mummy: ge:t i::t** (line 27) have similarities to the arm movements in #4.1, the co-occurring head turns and the agonized voice quality accompanying these words and those she speaks next, **NO:: NO::, Ge::t it fro:m the ta-, Ge:t it fro:m the ta:bl:e** (lines 32, 35 and 37), together with her attempts to push the honey away even when I have transferred it to her mother's hand (lines 32–3), all contribute to this sense of 'extremeness'. In #4.4 matters are even more clearcut. Here the flaw that the child is finding concerns the position in which her mother is sitting; after being asked to sit in one place, on a child's chair that is too small for her, her mother sits in another place, on the floor close by. This provokes an outburst of wrath on Amy's part. On first seeing her mother sitting in the 'wrong' position she shouts **NO: NO: NO::::::** etc (line 23) and goes into a stamping canter-like movement around the room before taking her mother's hand, saying **NO::::::::: (.) (GE::T U::P)** (lines 28 and 30) as she pulls at her to get up. Then her mother is told to **GO: AWA:::::Y** (line 33) and led out of the room.

The child's techniques for dealing with the deficiencies with which she is confronted in extracts 4.3 and 4.4 contrast markedly with those which we saw her using in #4.1. In #4.4, for example, she does not simply ask her mother to move to the correct seating position. This was the kind of solution to her chip problem that was attempted by Amy in #4.1, when she said

4.3 2;5/3755

Amy is sitting on her mother's knee, having her socks pulled on. They
have just been talking about a picture on the blackboard, and this is the
first mentioning of the honey in this sequence. Her father is sitting just
out of camera shot to the right, reading a newspaper:

1   A: I want- I wanta- Get me (a) honey

2   M: Get you the honey?=Well if you're going to have some honey
3   you're going to have to (.) have your hands washed properly
4   (.6)
5   M: Cos your hands are all messy
6   (1.0)
7   A: ⌈ (-)
            |
8   M: ⌊ All messy with chalk,

9   A: You get it for me,(.) Put it on the:re[A]for me, ((points to stool
10   during later part of this turn))

11 M: Well you've got to go and have your hands all <u>wash</u>ed if
12   you're going to have honey,

13   ((F then brings a cloth and wipes A's hands while she is still
14   by her mother, prior to which there is also discussion as to
15   where she will put down some chalks she is still holding; 45
16   seconds elapse in this omitted segment))

17 A: Now I'll have honey now (.) I'll sit (   )= ((moves to sit in
18   her chair))

19 M: =You're going to sit there=that's the honey chair is it?

20 A: Mm
21   (1.0)
22 M: Right

23 A: Here's the honey (   )?[B]((smiles as she says this, as F comes
24   into camera shot carrying the honey))

25 M: ((laughs)) Is this person ((pointing to A)) a bear really?=
26   ((by now F is also proffering the jar directly to A))

27 A: =No: No:[C] le:t mummy: ge:t i::t= ((with agonized voice
28   quality, sharp moves of head to face away to her right and

29   flailings of her arm in the direction of the honey; by the end
30   of her turn F, in reaction to this, has passed the honey to M))

31   M: =Oh I've ⌐D got it

32   A: ⌊NO:: NO::= ((with arm flailings and tearful
33   vocalization that continues after the end of the word))

34   M: =What d'you want me to do=

35   A: =Ge::t it fro:⌐m the ta-, ((all tearful))

36   M: ⌊I'll go and get it shall I,

37   A: Ge:t it fro:m the ta:⌐bl:e? ((still tearful))

38   M: ⌊O:kay I'll go'n get it from the table
39   ((then M gets up and goes to table))
40   (5.0)
41   M: Oh:: loo:k I've found some honey (.) fancy that, ((all done
42   with 'surprised' intonations))

Plate A

Plate B

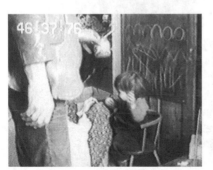

Plate C

Plate D

Father, mother and Amy are close to the dining table. There has already been discussion about playing shops, and Amy carries a bag that she has fetched for this purpose. F has just suggested to A that M be the shopkeeper:

1   A: C-c-come^{A}o:n? ((to M, as A moves across room))

2   M: ((laughs))=

3   A: =<u>You</u> sit o:n- o:n this: <u>chair</u> (mis ter) shopkeeper ((to M))

4   F: Ye:::s

5   F: ⌐Ye:s ((then chuckles))

6   M: └ I'm going to sit the:re am I, ((then M gets up to move
7   towards the chair))
8   (5.7)
9   ((during this pause M goes to the chair and F moves other
10   chairs about))

11   F: Ye::s the shopkeeper should sit (   )
12   (1.7)
13   A: No no: you ca::nt sit 'ere^B ((to F as she picks up a bag off
14   the floor; A infers that F was about to sit down
15   somewhere here))

16   F: We:ll I'm just putting this:-, ((as he moves a chair under the
17   table))
18   (4.2)
19   F: ((A passes a shopping bag to F)) Ye:s I know I've got to hold
20   tha:t
21   (2.1)
22   ((A turns for the first time to see where M is seated))

23   A: NO: NO: NO:::::::::::::::   NO:^{C}::::::::::::::::= ((to M;
24   intonations becoming more tearful in the course of the turn;
25   stamping and moving around room as words are said;
26   then, at end of turn, takes M's hand))

27   M: =^{D}Whe:re do I sit the:n ((smiley voice))

28 A: NO:::::::, ((pulling at M's arm to get her up, M laughing))
29   (.)
30 A: (GE::T U::P), ((though by now M is up))

31 M: Whe:re do I si:t? ((being pulled across the room, out of
32   camera shot from here on))

33 A: <u>GO: AWA:::::Y</u>,

34 M: Oh: dea::r I sat on the wrong seat I think

35   ((A has now taken M into an adjacent room, all out of
36   camera shot))

Plate A

Plate B

Plate C

Plate D

Mummy (gan get), and to her location problem in #4.2, when she said **(Oh) no no no 'pposed to do it .hh over .hh HE::RE**; these solutions attempt to rectify the deficient action or proposal by cueing an action that fits the child's expectations. Similarly in #4.3 such simple solutions are not used by the child. Here, although Amy says **No: No: le:t mummy: ge:t i::t** in the course of making it clear that she does not wish to take the honey being proffered towards her, it is also clear that the straightforward transfer of the honey jar from her father's hand to that of her mother is entirely unacceptable. Although the child may have been agreeable to my *initially* passing the honey to her mother, in that her face remains a picture of happiness as I approach them holding the honey jar (see Plate B), once I have attempted to pass the jar directly to the child matters take a different course. The action that I might have taken earlier, giving the honey jar to her mother for her to give it to Amy, now designed as a remedy to the trouble that has emerged, is not acceptable as a remedy. It is met by the tearful cry of **NO:: NO::** and then **Ge::t it fro:m the ta-**, together with attempts to push the honey jar further away from herself.

These reactions on the part of Amy in extracts 4.3 and 4.4 suggest that, for her, such simple solutions are inappropriate. What types of solution are appropriate then, or rather what are the characteristics of the solutions which prove acceptable to her? In #4.4 the solution is to remove her mother from the room, perhaps the most extreme form of sanction she felt entitled to exercise at this age, and, in effect, to abandon the projected course of action associated with the original request sequence (the game of playing shops). When Amy returns from putting her mother in the other room, after the transcript of #4.4 has ended, she seems undecided as to her next course of action when I ask her **So what are we going to do?** In abandoning the activity the child treats the mother's deficient action as having rendered the projected game non-viable. In #4.3 her reactions take a slightly different form. While, importantly, she rejects the solution of the honey simply being transferred from her father to her mother, she is prepared to accept a re-run by the mother of the overall activity that had been performed by the father, that of transporting the honey to her from the table on which it had been placed – she tells her mother to get it from the table (lines 35 and 37). It is interesting here that the mother does not then simply perform this activity as though she is repeating what the father has done, but she constructs this activity in the intonationally exaggerated way that makes it easily identifiable as an action being performed for the *first* time – **Oh:: loo:k I've found some honey (.) fancy that** (line 41).

Constructing a line of action in this way, in this type of sequential position, is, of course, rather unusual. Speaking and acting in such a way as to have what you say both replace and ignore that which has palpably taken place is not a common feature of adult/child interaction, nor indeed of any interaction. In acting as though this is the first time of finding the honey the mother, in effect, fictionalizes the past, but in a sequential position where such fictionalization is evident to the child. What makes it acceptable and apt for this occasion is its compatibility with the child's desire to have the act of fetching the honey from the table re-performed, and re-performed in a manner which avoids the blemishes which were associated with the first attempt.

At this point I want to put together two simple observations that have arisen in the course of the discussion so far. On the one hand, we have just seen that the child's solution to the parental deficiencies with which she is confronted in extracts 4.3 and 4.4 involves either the abandonment of the sequence or the redoing of a substantial portion of the activity prior to the deficiency's occurrence. In particular, simple solutions to the deficiency, like that proposed by the father's transfer of the honey to the mother in #4.3, are deemed inappropriate by the child. On the other hand, these same occasions are ones in which the child becomes upset, displaying a mixture of wrath, indignation and tearfulness. This neat symmetry suggests a connection between such displays by the child and the deficiency's lack of susceptibility to the kinds of simple solution that we saw being employed in extracts 4.1 and 4.2. It is because the parent's deficiency is linked with what is taking place in such fundamental ways as to render unfeasible the current trajectory of action that the child becomes upset.

Further evidence in favour of this linkage between emotional display and the lack of susceptibility of these occasions to simple remedy also occurs in cases like extracts 4.1 and 4.2, where I have shown how the child is capable of using simple solutions. It happens that in neither of these cases do we find the extreme forms of emotional expression that we have seen in extracts 4.3 and 4.4. Although the child can show signs of irritation (e.g. hand waving) when the parent attempts to give the child something she does not actually want, there is no suggestion of emotional reactions that 'flood through' other aspects of the child's behaviour on such occasions, nor of the other extreme reactions that have been identified in extracts 4.3 and 4.4. For example, I mentioned earlier how, in #4.1, the voice quality of **Mummy (gan get)** (line 12) was relatively neutral, not imbued with emotion of the kind that we find in Amy's **Ge::t it fro:m the** ta-, said to her mother at line 35 in #4.3. The evidence suggests, then, that wrath of the kind we find in extracts 4.3 and 4.4 is associated not with simple solutions of the kind employed in extracts 4.1 and 4.2 but specifically with flawed attempts to grant a request which are not susceptible to simple remedial solutions.

Sequential correlates of distressed reactions

We are still left, however, with the question of what, from the child's point of view, makes instances like extracts 4.3 and 4.4 not susceptible to simple solutions. What is it about #4.3 which leads the child to require her mother to get up and bring back the honey to her from the table, rather than just to accept it from her mother? What is it about #4.4 which leads the child to abandon the activity in question rather than simply to ask her mother to move to the correct position? I take it that one type of answer is not supported by the empirical detail within these sequences. This type of answer might focus on the presence of some internal psychological property such as frustration, the argument being that these more distraught reactions could be an outcome of high levels of frustration. Now the strength of that kind of argument hangs on what one takes to be indicators of frustration and the way that evidence pans out. A popular index might focus on the length of time, and difficulty, that it took the child to make her intentions understood in the situations in question. Paradoxically, using these features as indicators we would expect higher levels of frustration in extracts like 4.1 and 4.2, for it is in these sequences that the child's difficulties appear to be more prolonged in such respects. But, what precisely characterizes these extracts is an absence of the kinds of distraught reaction under discussion. A feature of extracts 4.3 and 4.4, and a feature to which I will return later in the chapter, is the suddenness of the child's distraught reaction when she is confronted by the predicament with which it is associated. Up to that moment everything seems to have been going relatively smoothly and there has been little or no sign of any 'build up' of frustration. In general, therefore, it appears that accounts framed in terms of an increase in levels of frustration are unlikely to capture or explain key features of the sequences in question.

In formulating my original question as 'what, from the child's point of view, makes instances like extracts 4.3 and 4.4 not susceptible to simple solutions?', I was trying to shift the focus away from the presence or absence of internal states on the part of the child towards considering the

potentiality of particular types of sequence to generate displays of particular kinds of emotional state.[2] So I shall approach this question by looking
at some earlier features of the relevant sequences. One aspect of this relates
to the original requests which led to these sequences getting off the ground
in the first place, together with the nature of the parents' responses to these
requests. The main point I want to make here is that the parents' later
attempts to grant these requests are, in fact, identifiable as deficient
attempts according to any strict interpretation of the original requests. In
#4.3 Amy's **Get me (a) honey** (line 1) and **You get it for me, (.) Put it on
the:re for me** (line 9) are directed at her mother. At no point in the subsequent sequence does she overtly ask her father to get her the honey, even
though it is her father who wipes her hands during the middle phase of the
sequence (lines 13–16). So there is an obvious basis for Amy to suppose her
mother to be the person who will actually give her the honey. In #4.4 Amy
specifically instructs her mother as to where she should sit in the pretence
activity about to get underway. She says **You sit o:n- o:n this: chair (mis ter)
shopkeeper** (line 3). Although her mother, in response, is displaying some
order of involvement in this projected play activity, she is, nevertheless, not
sitting in the chair that the child has asked her to. So, in both extracts Amy
has available to her a previously established basis, an accountable basis, for
treating the parents' later attempts to grant the requests as deficient. We
do not need to suppose, for example, that the child has some private notion
of what is involved in the granting of the request, and that the parent falls
foul of the child by virtue of not having had access to the internal notion
in question. If this were so we might expect to find such distraught reactions in circumstances where there appeared to be no prior basis for the
child to treat the parents' action as deficient – but this is never so within
these data. It is always possible, in such circumstances, for us to identify,
empirically, that what the parent does in response to the request is potentially discrepant to an understanding of the request that has been established earlier in a public, overt way. Although, therefore, such instances
may contain what appears to the parent, and others, as wilful and strange
behaviour, what is actually remarkable about them is the orderly attention
to an earlier understanding, which is always being displayed by the child.

A further feature of these two sequences is that, unlike those such as
#4.1, after making the request neither party has displayed any problem
with establishing exactly what it is that the child wants, and the child has

---

[2] For a useful formulation regarding the relationship of emotional displays among adults to
the sequences in which they are embedded see Heath (1988).

been led to believe that her request can be granted in the form in which it was originally made. Furthermore, in each case, the child has engaged in subsequent activities after making the request which seem predicated on the request being granted. In #4.4, after guiding her mother towards the chair, Amy continues her preparations for the pretend activity by picking up a carrier bag to give to me (in my capacity as co-shopper), and then forestalling what she took to be an intention on my part of sitting on another chair in the vicinity (lines 13–20). It is on turning around from these activities, at line 22, that she first sees her mother sitting in what, for Amy, is the wrong place. In #4.3 the only possible stated grounds for not granting the request for honey concerns the state of the child's hands. Hand washing is treated as a necessary condition for the granting of the request, so that when the child engages in the intervening activity of hand washing (lines 13–14) this is recognizable by her as both preparatory to, and fulfilling the conditions for, the granting of her request. Therefore, at the point at which the parents attempt to grant the child's request in extracts 4.3 and 4.4, the child has no grounds for supposing that the request will not be granted in the manner originally agreed upon.

These, then, appear to be the distinctive interactional circumstances which are associated with the extreme forms of reaction that occur later in these sequences. Prior to the parents' attempts to grant the request, the child has grounds for supposing that her requests have been adequately understood and has been led to believe that they will be granted; and the attempts to grant the request are themselves recognizably deficient in ways which I have described. Crucially, the child's subsequent behaviour displays these attempts to be deficient from the child's own point of view, and for the child to treat them as such requires the child, in part, to be matching the parents' attempt to grant the request with her own initial expectations concerning what the request entailed. This local, sequentially based understanding, which the child has grounds for treating as further confirmed by what the parent then does, appears to form a template which is used to judge the adequacy of the parents' eventual response to the request. Having been led to believe and hope that her request will be granted in a particular way these hopes are shattered. The kind of breach that has been created by the parents' response is not one that can be readily rectified through simple solutions; the order of breach that is involved undercuts and transgresses the child's sequential expectations in more radical ways, in ways that admit of only more extreme reactions.

Distressed reactions to offers of assistance

Over several recordings, from the age of 2;3 onwards, there are instances of a further puzzling kind of behaviour from Amy. On these occasions she says that she is going to obtain an object, but when the adult attempts to obtain the object for her, in the spirit of assisting her to do that which she is proposing to do, the child rejects the assistance on offer. For example, in one case the child is being dressed by her mother. She makes it clear during these proceedings that she wants to have a drink from her drinking cup, which is on a table close-by, but when I offer her the drinking cup she treats my offer as grossly inapt. This is suggested by both the distinctive ways in which the offer is rejected and the accompanying signs of emotional distress. This incident will be examined in more detail later, but first I want to discuss some of the other ways in which the child can deal with offers of assistance at these ages.

Offers of assistance to the child

Offers of assistance by the parent to the child can be made in, broadly, two types of situation. First, there are occasions on which the child overtly requests such assistance from the parent. Here the child usually has some problem in carrying through a course of action, and, in the light of this, solicits help. Bruner *et al.* (1982) note the existence from about 18 months onwards of ways of requesting which are designed to deal with this type of eventuality, and similar types of request can be found in our recordings of Amy at a parallel age. What is of more interest to us here is the second type of circumstance in which parental offers of assistance can be made, that in which they are not solicited by the child.

Unsolicited offers can again be broken down, very crudely, into two types. In the first, the parent either begins to engage in an act of assistance or proposes to engage in such an act when there is no overt suggestion from the child that she would wish to do the thing herself. In #4.5, for example, at 2;1, the child is in her high-chair by the table eating a boiled egg. After enquiring as to whether the egg is finished her mother makes her offer of assistance: she says **Shall I get that ou::t?** (line 7), meaning 'Shall I get out the remains of the egg for you?', tentatively taking hold of the spoon that the child is holding in the later part of this turn. The child replies **No::** and retracts the hand that is holding the spoon so as to indicate that she is not willing to let go of it. On first feeling this pressure her mother releases her hold on the spoon. In this kind of sequence, then, the child has means at her disposal for rejecting an offer, and, though there is a slight non-verbal *contretemps* over the holding of the spoon, there is no sense from the child that the parent's action is radically untoward. By this I mean that, although these are sequences that can generate child rejections of parental offers, they are not the ones that generate distressed forms of reaction by the child.

The second type of parental unsolicited offer is one that is either proposed or enacted in a position where the child has made it clear that she would wish to do the thing herself. An example of this also occurs in #4.5. After the child has stated that she does not want her mother to spoon out the egg her mother eventually goes on to make another offer to do this same thing; she says **well I can get it out with a spoon if you like** (line 14), to which Amy simply replies **No**. Here, however, the offer is simply made verbally; there is no attempt on the mother's part to enact it, by taking hold of the spoon, for example. The offer sequences in which more serious tensions potentially arise seem to be those in which, in the face of the child's stated concerns to do something for herself, the parent actually makes moves to do the act for her. One such sequence, which took place when Amy was 2;5, has already been discussed in chapter 3 (see #3.7, p. 75). On that occasion Amy was standing on a low chair, chalking, when she dropped her piece of chalk on the floor. As her mother, who was sitting by her, goes to reach for it Amy says **I'll pick it u:p**. Nevertheless, her mother picks up the chalk and actually proffers it to her. Another similar instance is presented as #4.6. Here a doll falls off the edge of the chair on which Amy is sitting. On seeing me reach down to pick it up for her she says **Oh (.) I'm going to pick it up** (line 6); nevertheless, I continue with my action of picking up the doll, and then I proffer it towards her.

In both #4.6 and the chalking incident, #3.7, what I have called unsolicited offers are being made by the parent. Both these occasions also illustrate the thinness of the further distinction that I have drawn between those offers produced when the child has made her opposition to them known and those in which such concerns have not been expressed. In each case the parent's initial act of reaching for the object is embarked on prior to a statement of opposition by the child, but the continuation of the action, after the child's statement of intent which is designed to preempt what it is that the parent is about to do, becomes one which is now in opposition to the child's preferred line of action. In general terms it is this latter circumstance, where the offer is in opposition to that which the child wants to do, which seems to have a special potential for creating distressed

4.5 2;1/6900

Amy is sitting in her high-chair eating a boiled egg. She is holding the
egg in her rh, mouthing it, and holding a teaspoon in her lh. Her mother
sits down by the table close by:

1	M:	Have you eaten your egg now?
2		(.)
3	M:	Is it finished? ((By now A has removed the egg from her
4		mouth, and is looking into it - she does this for the rest of
5		the sequence below. Her lh is resting on her tray))
6		(.)
7	M:	Shall I get that ou::t? ((towards the end of this turn M moves
8		her hand to hold A's teaspoon))
9	A:	No::,^{A} ((pulls the spoon from M's grasp as she says this))
10	M:	Can you do it?
11	A:	(mark) ((during this turn A puts her spoon down on
12		the tray and begins to take out some egg with her left
13		hand))
14	M:	Mm::: (.) well I can get it out with a <u>spoon</u> if you like
15	A:	No^B ((said as A puts egg in her mouth))

Plate A   Plate B

---

reactions on the part of the child. For this reason it is worth examining the
child's reaction to the parental proffer in each of these incidents.

In each case the child displays that she is unprepared to take the object
from the parent. In the chalking incident, #3.7, at line 4, she says **No leave**

Amy is sitting on her chair while her father, nearby, has just begun to read a newspaper. Lodged on the edge of her chair, behind her, is a large Russian doll. A's initial request below, which she aborts on knocking off the doll, concerns another matter entirely:

1   A: I wanta (.) have some^A (.) some photog- ((doll falls on
2   floor, A turns to look)) (.) oh (.) EH

3   F: Eh ((said in the course of his moving to pick up the doll: as
4   his hand nearly touches the doll A's next utterance
5   begins))

6   A: Oh (.) I'm going to pick it up ((during this F picks up the
7   doll and passes it towards A; well before it reaches
8   her, during the latter part of her turn, she puts out her left
9   arm as though to ward off the pass. F continues to move
10   the doll towards A, wanting to pass it to her; 1.0 pause
11   between A's turns))

12   A: I'm going to pick it up^B? ((pushing the doll away with her
13   hand as she says this: F lets it go and it falls back on the
14   floor))

15   F: (Oh) you're going to pick it up (.) ⌐allright ((during this he
16   resumes his original paper-reading| position:
17   simultaneously A begins to get| down from her
18   chair))

19   A: ⌊Yes ((A begins to get
20   off her chair. Then there is a discussion about the name of
21   the doll which prompts a delay in the child's moves to pick
22   it up. It is some 2 minutes before she eventually does so))

Plate A   Plate B

it on the floo:r, after which she climbs down from her chair and fetches the chalk herself. **Leave it on the floo:r** clearly means 'leave it on the floor for me to pick up'. In #4.6 her reaction to the proffer of the doll is to say **I'm going to pick it up** whilst pushing the object away in the direction whence it came (see Plate B). She then gets down from the chair, apparently in order to pick up the doll, but becomes diverted from this task by the conversation which ensues. It is not until two minutes later that the doll is eventually retrieved. One might think that in each of these extracts it may have been possible for the child to have had a special reason for wanting to retrieve the object herself, some special use that she was going to make of the object in its new location. When one examines the detail of these occasions, however, there is no such suggestion. On picking the object up the child does not put it to some different use from that which preceded its movement to the floor. The only motive she displays in choosing to pick it up appears to be the intrinsic one of doing it herself rather than having the adult do it for her. Indeed, this is one of the features which makes such behaviour all the more perplexing from an adult point of view.

One feature of note in these two incidents is the interest that the child displays in having the object put back into its original location. In #4.6 it is not that she just wants to pick the doll up from anywhere; the direction of the pushing makes it clear that it should be returned whence it came. These matters are made more overt in the chalking incident, #3.7, as the child actually says **No leave it on the floo:r**. The appropriate form of rectification being sought from the parent is the return to the preceding *status quo*. This return is clearly justified, for the child, by her original statement of intent, her stated intention to pick up the object herself. A further feature to note, however, is the absence of any special distressed reaction on the part of the child. This suggests that even though, from the child's point of view, the adult's reaction may be sufficiently out of order to merit being entirely played back, this is not an eventuality that presents special problems for her. Although the circumstances that present special problems, the ones that occasion distressed reactions, have parallels with occasions such as #4.6, in the last analysis they have further distinctive features that need to be uncovered.

Before turning to those incidents and those features I want to make a final point about the *potential* for distress contained in occasions such as extracts 4.6 and 3.7. Although there is no evidence of undue perturbance in the child's behaviour on these occasions, it is fairly easy, nevertheless, to see how such incidents contain the potential for this to occur. In #4.6, for example, this might have happened had the parent not put the doll back –

if, for example, he had continued to proffer it to the child. When dealing with young children we routinely identify such moments in interaction in which confrontation is only just round the corner, moments in which, if the interaction is not handled carefully, tears and tribulation are on the cards. One possibility in such circumstances is for the child's co-participant to tease or taunt her, knowingly to take advantage of such circumstances in order to wind the child up or in some way test her reactions. But much of the time carers are concerned to minimize the risk of upset occurring, so sequences are steered in directions where such outcomes are less likely. Although there are obvious analytic difficulties in making claims about phenomena in interaction that *nearly* occur it is, nevertheless, relevant to note that sequences like #4.6 are ones that appear to contain this potential for causing distress, but ones in which this is quickly defused.

Avoiding the potential for conflict contained in such sequences requires the parent to abandon the form of help which is being made available to the child, which in these cases consists of passing her an object. In this respect it is possible that such incidents have a special propensity for the generation of conflict. If we take it that a motivation to help the child is a common one among those who deal with children of this age, especially parents, then avoiding an outbreak of distress requires the abandonment of forms of behaviour – offers of assistance – which satisfy such pro-social parental concerns. So, instances like #4.6 come close to confrontation not just because the parent would have provoked this had he or she not permitted the child to engage in the action herself, but also because in these circumstances the parent has an available motivation for continuing the projected action, the powerful one of helping the child.

Distressed responses to offers

On each of the recordings between the ages of 2;3 and 2;9 there are at least two or three instances analogous to #4.6, ones in which the child, in similar circumstances, rejects an unsolicited parental offer of assistance. Most of them, like #4.6, run off quite smoothly in the sense that there is little sign of the child becoming in any way emotionally het up in the course of dealing with them. But on two occasions at 2;9 incidents in some ways parallel to those above do become the focus of emotional distress. One of these, the incident with the drinking cup that I briefly described earlier, is transcribed as #4.7.

Effectively, the sequence of interest begins at line 1 with Amy saying

Wanta dri::n:k (first), while she is being dressed by her mother. As she says this she attempts to push off the trousers that are being put on her, clearly with a view to moving towards the nearby table in order to obtain the drinking cup herself. The mother's response is to say **Yes you can have a drink well:** (.) **just let me do these up** (lines 2–3), that is she agrees to what the child is proposing but, through her final words, and her continued holding of the child, is making it plain that she wants first to complete the current activity: putting on her trousers. This impedance is met with **no:: no:::::** by Amy, words which already display a distressed voice quality; but the level of distress is radically escalated when I intervene, when I say **I'll get you a drink** (line 6). The child, in tearful and agonized intonation, says **No::: no::: no:::** (lines 8–9) and then **GO: AWA:::Y (please)** (line 13). Although I have had this evidence of her opposition to my offer I proceed to enact it in a fashion. I proffer the cup towards her, from a distance, as if to give her the opportunity to signal an interest in taking it, but not in such a way as to expect her to do so. Her response to this is to struggle forwards, whilst still being held by her mother, towards the cup, and to hit it with her hand (Plate C), whereupon I put it back on the table (lines 17–20).

There are several obvious parallels between the events so far in this sequence and the extracts which have been discussed in the prior section. The first is that in each case the child has made clear her own preference to engage in a course of action. More specifically, we can note certain common features as regards the ways in which she expresses this preference. At this age the child has available to her a variety of ways in which she can indicate that she wishes to do something. Some of these can treat her proposed course of action as in some way uncertain, as dependent on some order of concurrence on the part of her co-participant. What, then, can be noted about turns like **I'll pick it u:p**, in #3.7, **Oh** (.) **I'm going to pick it up** in #4.6 and **Wanta dri::n:k** (first) in #4.7 is that they are not ones which treat the child's proposed course of action as particularly problematic: in #4.7 the accompanying non-verbal behaviour, the child's attempted movement towards the table in order to pick up her cup at line 1, is especially important in this regard as it suggests that the action is not being viewed by the child, at that moment, as contingent on the nature of the parental response. From the child's point of view, then, these preference statements mark courses of action which are not contentious. The second parallel is that, in spite of having available this evidence of the child's preference, the parent, in each case, continues with his/her attempt to assist the child, by actually enacting a proffer of the object that the child

4.7 2;9/IV 12:00

Amy is having some trousers put on her by her mother. As the transcript begins she has just been moved from her mother's knee into a standing position on the floor. Her father is out of camera shot nearby:

1   A: Wanta dri::n:k^A (first) ((A pushes her trousers downwards))

2   M: └Yes you can have a drink ┌well: (.)┌just let
3   me do these up

4   A: └ ( )   └ (-)
5   no : : no : :┌: : :

6   F: └I'll get you a drink,=I'll get ┌you a drink,

7   M: └Have it ┌after

8   A: └No : : : no
9   : :^B: no : : :,= ((last two 'no's have sobs in them, and
10   child gesticulates with her left hand towards her cup, which
11   is on her tray by the table, as F moves towards it))

12 M: =Whats the matter,= ((M still putting on A's trousers))

13 A: GO: AWA:::Y (please) ((to F after he has picked up the
14   cup; all tearful))
15   (.)
16 M: Oh: dea:r ((still putting on trousers))

17   ((F proffers cup and A moves forward to hit it away^C; see
18   text; 1.0 pause))

19 M: Oh: dea:r

20   ((F puts cup on table))
21   (2.2)
22 A: Do:nt wa:nt i:t ((said in petulant tones as she looks down
23   at her trousers and as F moves into adjacent room))
24   (.)
25 A: hhhh No : : : := ((quiet, as if to herself))

26 M: =Silly sau┌sage

27 A: └((brief sob))

```
28                                          (.9)
29    A:      Put it on tha:t tra::::┌y ((to F, referring to cup; F in doorway
30            between rooms))        │
                                     │
31    F:                            └One thing I have to do this morning is
32            I have to give Deborah a driving lesson ┌sometime  ((to M))
                                                      │
33    M:                                             └Allright
34                                          (.)
35    M:      Okay
36                                        (1.9)
37            ((M, now finished putting A's trousers on, attempts to lift

38            her on to her knee; A resists this via her next 'no'))

39    A:      No::::::: putDit ba:::ck ((referring to the cup in later part of
40            the turn, that part of it being directed at F))
```

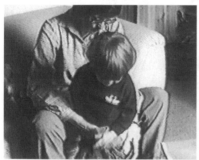

Plate A

Plate B

Plate C

Plate D

wishes to obtain for herself. Third, of course, the child rejects the proffer in an unequivocal manner.

Where #4.7 differs from the earlier sequences is in the level of distress displayed by the child at the initial suggestion of the parent engaging in the act of assisting the child: when I say **I'll get you a drink** (line 6). In earlier extracts the child either felt able to instruct the parent not to engage in the proposed act (#4.5) or simply brushed aside the parent's attempt to enact the offer, in ways which ran off with no overt suggestion of distress on the child's part (#4.6). In #4.7, however, what is different is that the child, when confronted with such a contingency, is not in a position now to engage in her preferred course of action. Whereas in #4.6, for example, she can immediately perform the action that she does not want her father to perform, namely picking her doll up off the floor, here she cannot do this. Specifically, she is prevented from doing so by virtue of being held by her mother.

In the other major incident of this kind, which also took place at 2;9, there are also circumstances which make it difficult for the child to enact her desired course of action. Here the child says that she wants me to go upstairs with her in order to fetch a toilet roll. From what she and I say it is clear that the need to replace a toilet roll must have been discussed earlier, though this discussion does not take place during the previous ten minutes of the recorded interaction. It may have been possible, for example, that parent and child had earlier agreed that a toilet roll needed to be fetched, even that the child should do the fetching. But leaving aside such uncertainties, uncertainties which render the analysis of this incident more difficult than that of #4.7, what is clear is that when I say **I've got it I've put it in the bathroom** (it referring to the toilet roll) Amy becomes very upset, running towards the bathroom, which is on the ground floor of the house, crying and saying initially **No no I want it**. The sequence is much more prolonged than #4.7 and the child's distress at what has taken place is more extensive. Without going into these details, however, what is generally clear is that the parent's pre-emption of the child's course of action – fetching the toilet roll – has rendered her proposed course of action not just difficult but also redundant, and that such an eventuality is intimately connected to the distressed reaction which she displays.

There are, then, similarities and differences between these instances like #4.7 and the offer sequences that I discussed in the prior section. The principal difference, the one I have just been dwelling on, relates to the child's capacity to engage in the line of action which she has stated as her preference. On the occasions when the child becomes distressed she is not in a position to do that which she wants to do, so it is this further interactional contingency which distinctively informs this kind of occasion. Before leaving #4.7, however, there are further points to be made concerning its trajectory after the point at which we left it – the child's knocking away of the cup being proffered by her father. It is to these that I now turn.

When discussing incidents like #4.6 in the prior section I noted that one feature of Amy's response to the proffer of the parent was to push the object away, in the direction from where it originally came. There seems to be a concern on her part, in such circumstances, to restore the positioning of the object to the preceding *status quo*. Something of this can also be found in the later part of #4.7, but further features are also present which in some ways make it distinct. What happens after the child knocks the cup away is this. She says **Do:nt wa:nt i:t** (line 22), a petulant **No::::** (line 25) and **Put it on tha:t tra::::y** (line 29). The **Do:nt wa:nt i:t** is somewhat ambiguous in that it could be a reaffirmation of the fact that she does not want her father to get the drink for her; but the details lend more support to an alternative interpretation. When she says this her father has already placed the drinking cup on the table, his back is towards her and he has just begun to move away towards an adjacent room. Therefore the child has no basis on which to presume that her father still thinks that she does want it. Nor is the utterance addressed towards her father – as she says this the child looks at the floor, and her father does not treat it as in any way addressed to him. What then seems more likely here is that she is now saying that she does not want a drink, that she has now changed her mind about wanting her drinking cup at all. If this is so then her father's action of offering her the cup has destroyed the very motivation that it was intended to satisfy – it has entirely spoiled the course of events anticipated by the child.

The other words I want to focus on are **Put it on tha:t tra::::y**. When her father first puts the cup back down he puts it on the dining table. In telling him to put it on the tray Amy is noticing that the place from which he has picked it up is not the same as that on which he has now put it down. She is insisting that it be put back on her feeding tray, the place from which it was first obtained, insisting that the situation be restored to the preceding *status quo*. Indeed, this insistence continues even after the subsequent discussion between her father and mother, when she says **put it ba:::ck** (line 39).

Amy's solutions to the circumstances in which she finds herself are, therefore, ones which minimally require the situation to be restored to its exact original state prior to the cup being lifted. Either she wants the line of action, in its totality, to be executed in the manner which she originally projected, or, if **Do:nt wa:nt i:t** means 'I no longer want the drink', the father's action is being treated as having even more radical implications: as having spoilt the nature of the whole enterprise.[3] So it is these kinds of solution which are linked with the distressed elements in Amy's behaviour in this sequence: distress, again, is associated with solutions which handle the contingency by either re-running it or abandoning it.

General themes

Reports of the distribution of conflict between mother and child in the age range that principally concerns us here, 24–36 months, suggest that it tends to occur in particular situations. Dunn, for example, finds that the two most common sources of conflict are destructive/wild behaviour by the child and breaches of family routines. In addition, she reports an upsurge at 24 months in conflict about caretaking matters (e.g. getting dressed, cleanliness), and there was also a fair amount of conflict over manners (e.g. saying 'thankyou') and rights (e.g. sharing, taking turns) (Dunn 1988:39–41). In this literature there tends to be a separation between examination of the workings of such conflict episodes and what is known as pro-social behaviour, especially with regard to the child's conduct. Pro-social behaviour refers to things like sharing and helping, behaviour which exhibits positive consideration for other people.

In the recordings of Amy certain of the types of conflict listed above are less prominent. Wild and destructive behaviour, for example, may occur rarely because, unlike most of the children studied by Dunn, she did not have a brother or sister at home; nor were recordings normally made when her friends were in the house.[4] Some of the incidents which have been discussed, however, could be construed as falling within some of Dunn's categories. Extract 4.7, for example, which involved the child having her

---

[3] The reader may be interested to know what eventually happens after the end of #4.7. After I have put the cup back on the table Amy picks up her cuddling blanket and vigorously sucks her thumb. Her mother then suggests that she, Amy, goes to get her drinking cup from the table. She then does this and drinks from it.

[4] In this respect it may be relevant to note the following from Dunn, about disputes at this age: 'Although the general pattern of the children's verbal protests and justifications was similar in conflict with the sibling and with the mother, it was noticeable that the most advanced arguments or claims were made to the mother rather than to the sibling' (1988:57). For further discussion of forms of child–child conflict characteristic of this age see Ross and Conant (1992).

trousers put on and her drink being passed to her, may fall under the rubric of 'caretaking matters'. A central paradox of these incidents that I stated at the beginning of this chapter is the intermingling within them of both conflict and pro-social behaviour. In them a parent is always trying to assist or help the child in some way but the sequential outcomes involve the rather extreme forms of distress which have been described. What seems to be possible then, as Shantz has also noted (1987:287), is that pro-social behaviour can play a significant part in generating conflict.

The question then arises as to how this comes about, why in such circumstances the child takes such a dim view of the parent's well-intentioned actions? Certain obvious kinds of answer do not appear to carry much weight. These incidents are not, for example, best viewed as the product of momentary childish whim because their occurrence does not display the random, inexplicable distribution that would be the corollary of such a claim. Nor is it helpful to characterize them simply as occasions on which the parent does something that the child does not like. While that is true, this does not discriminate them from the variety of other occasions on which this is obviously also true. Nor are they best viewed as arising out of the unavailability to the child of alternative, lower-key, methods of altering the course of events. In discussing both types of incident, those arising out of attempted grantings of requests and those out of attempted offers of assistance by the parent, I have demonstrated that the child has available to her alternative ways which could potentially have been employed in order to bring the parents' conduct into line.

What I shall do now is highlight certain themes that have emerged in the course of providing an answer to this paradox: first, the formative role played by sequential understandings; second, the nature of the distress contained within these incidents; third, their moral properties.

Sequential understandings

One of the systematic properties of the incidents which have been examined is that there is always a way in which the child is in the right. To say this is to say that in each case there are grounds for Amy to treat what the parent does as illicit, as misfitted to what she can feel entitled to expect on the occasions in question. The expectations to which the adults' responses are illicitly misfitted are ones which have their foundations in understandings that have been arrived at earlier on the occasions in question. When looking at this earlier interactional detail what has always been uncovered is an overt public basis for the child to expect subsequent events to unfold in a particular type of way. It is when events do not unfold in this way, in conjunction with other circumstances that will be mentioned in the next section, that distressed reactions take place. One necessary condition, therefore, for the emergence of these distressing incidents is a capacity on the part of the child to construct her conduct in the light of earlier forms of sequential understanding, a capacity that received documentation in the last chapter. The evidence I have discussed in the present chapter adds to that picture in important ways. It shows quite clearly that the child can use such expectations as a yardstick against which to evaluate subsequent action taken by other parties. In this way the relevance of such sequential expectations for the child is given further, independent, documentation.

In my discussion of sequential understandings contained in the last chapter I drew a distinction between understandings which were derived from within the same conversational sequence and those which had their bases in earlier sequences. Most of the sequences which have been discussed in the present chapter fall into the former category, they are same-sequence understandings. For example, in #4.3, even though other conversational topics occur between the child's stated desire for the honey and its eventually being passed to her, it is nevertheless the case that these other topics largely involve activities which are preparatory to the honey being made available to the child. The possibility of a relevant earlier sequential understanding was most explicitly touched on in connection with the toilet roll incident, anecdotally referred to on page 122, but there were also uncertainties here because the recorded interaction did not include key earlier events. In order both to bring out how earlier, non-same-sequence understandings can similarly inform occasions of distress, and to show how the significance of such understandings also extends into non-request domains of behaviour, I shall now briefly examine an incident which took place when the child was aged 2;5.

A highly abbreviated version of this sequence, which in real time spans some three minutes, is presented as #4.8. It begins with Amy sitting on her mother's knee, discussing whether or not she wishes to go out with me to the shop. Crucially, at line 8, Amy says **I'll leave this honey here and leave the top off**. In saying this she indicates that the honey jar she is eating from should be left where it is, with the lid off, so that on her return from the shop she can eat some more (line 15); her spoon is also laid on the table by the side of the jar. This arrangement meets with her mother's concurrence. It turns out that this is the key understanding that informs subsequent events.

Amy is sitting on her mother's knee by the dining table, father sitting in an adjacent chair. The mother's first question below follows on from earlier discussion about A going to the shop with F. During this first question and the subsequent three utterances A is moving the lid of the honey jar that is directly in front of her, and from which she has been eating honey.

```
1    M:    D'you want to go to the paper shop with daddy? (.) Or stay
2          here  with me
3                              (.8)
4    A:    ( )
5                              (1.3)
6    M:    (Mm) there's a problem ((ironic))
7                              (1.7)
8    A:    I'll leaveᴬ this honey here and leave the top off ((A
9          repositions the jar on the table during the first clause and
10         points to the top of the jar in the second clause))

11   M:    Mhm,
12                              (.)
13   A:    And I'll=

14   M:    =Why are you going to leave the top off

15   A:    And I will come back and eat it (then)  ((begins to get off
16         M's knee in later part of this turn))
```

((the trip to the shop is delayed because the talk turns to TV programmes that are on (see #5.5); in the course of this A takes her spoon and honey jar down from the table to the seat of a chair on which she is leaning; when the next segment begins F is wiping her hand with a cloth and is giving reasons why its not possible for her to put the TV on; the honey has not been talked about at all))

```
17   F:    No its not plugged in at the main: at  theeuh mai::n (.) plug
18         on the wa:ll   ((hand wiping ceases and A's hands go
19         to hold honey jar))
20                              (.9)
21   F:    Now let's put this back up here while we just go and get a
22         paper ((takes hold of the honey jar that A is holding, and by
23         end of this utterance has placed it at the back of the table))
24                              (.)
```

25   F: I think we're going to go ou:t-, ((during this utterance he
26   picks up A's spoon from chair and places it on plate
27   at front of table))

28   A: No- ᴮno:t goin:: ou((this word becomes an extended wail as
29   A begins to cry; during the initial words of the turn F takes
30   A's lh to wipe it))

31   M: Are you going to go to the paper shop now Amy? ((M comes
32   in from kitchen, A continues crying))

33   A: (No::t ye::t) ((said through sobs as she continues to cry))

34   M: Soo:n
35   ((crying continues and M picks A up and stands her on the
36   chair with her arm around her; 6 seconds between last
37   utterance and next))

38   M: Oo::::::::::h come on you're going to go to the paper shop
39   now, ((A still crying))

40   A: No::t ye::? ((said through tears as she continues to cry))

41   M: But daddy's going to go? ((M still holding A, kisses her at
42   end of turn))

43   A: No::: (I::: don::)= ((said through tears as A continues
44   crying))

45   F: =Well you don't have to go you can stay he:re then if you
46   want to,= ((F wipes A's mouth with a tissue as he says
47   this))

48   M: =Mm you can stay with me ((A still cries))
49   (1.0)
50   M: D'you want to do that?
51   (1.2)
52   A: I: do:nt wanna I: wa:nta go:: ((said through tears))

53   M: You're going to go with daddy are you?=

54   A: =Yeh I wanna lea::veᶜ(the top o::n),= ((during this she
55   points to the place on the table where the honey was, and
56   then, briefly, to where it now is, at the back of the table))

57   F: =Yes well ⌐ lea:ve it the:re ((F picks up honey jar and puts it
58   ⎢   in the position that A has indicated))

59   M: └ Tha:ts alright you can leave it there
60   (.)
61   M: ⌐That can sta:y the:re

62   F: └You can have it when you come ⌐ back

63   A: └ No: I wanta (   ),
64   ((as A says this, still in tearful voice, she picks up the
65   honey spoon from the plate and puts it back to its original
66   position by the jar))

67   M: You can leave it just like that and nobody will touch it
68   alright?

69   A: Ye:::s, ((voice still upset, but not tearful))

70   M: Fi:ne

Plate A

Plate B

Plate C

The child then gets off her mother's knee and says she is ready to go the shop; but then she changes her mind and suggests that before going out we might put a snooker programme on the TV. There is then a discussion of other programmes that she might have on, in the course of which she takes her spoon and jar of honey down from the table to the seat of the chair on which she is leaning. We then further discuss TV programmes while I wipe her hand. At lines 21–2 I lift the jar from her hands saying **Now let's put this back up here while we just go and get a paper**, meaning 'go out to the shop and buy a newspaper'. Amy does not attempt to restrain the movement of the jar, but she does gaze at where I am putting it, at the back of the table – that is, not in the position earlier agreed with her mother. It is these actions of mine which occasion the tears. Although her verbal reaction is initially framed in terms of not wanting to go out now, **No- no:t goin:: ou** (line 28), and although her parents initially (lines 31–53) treat the basis for her being upset as being a reluctance to go out, subsequent events (lines 54–70) strongly suggest that the basis of her distraught reaction is my positioning of the jar and the spoon, the infringement of the earlier understanding arrived at with her mother. Once she has these items relocated in their original position not only does her crying cease but it is also plain that she is quite happy to go out.

In earlier incidents discussed in this chapter the parental reaction that provokes the child's wrath is an attempt either to grant the child's request or to assist the child in obtaining her immediate goal. In #4.8 my 'illicit' act, moving the honey jar to the back of the table, is not designed in either of these ways. So this forms a further domain of interaction in which distressed reactions from the child can be found. A principal feature that this incident shares with those described earlier is that the child's distress again appears contingent upon her finding the parental action to be in breach of an earlier understanding, in this case one concerning the location of the spoon and honey jar. In #4.8, however, that understanding dates from an earlier sequence involving Amy and her mother. In these ways, as we found in the last chapter, earlier sequences can form, for the child, an on-going resource which informs the ways in which she both constructs her own conduct and evaluates the conduct of others.

The final point to make in this section concerns the nature of the earlier understandings which inform the child's subsequent conduct, both in the earlier distress incidents as well as #4.8. In none of these cases is it evident that the understanding reflects a broader, trans-contextual, script-like understanding about the event in question. For example, the child is perfectly happy on many occasions to receive food or a drinking cup from me. What, in part, gives extracts 4.3 and 4.7 the potential to become distressing incidents is not, therefore, some general precept about rejecting my offerings, it is the preceding *local* understanding on which the child draws. Although these incidents may look, superficially, as though they are about transgressions of normal routines they are nothing of the sort. They are about transgressions of local understandings which, by virtue of having been publicly established, now have a distinctive significance in the child's interactional world.

The nature of the child's distress

Other interactional features contribute to the occurrence of distress as well as the sequential understandings which I highlighted in the last section. These additional features are particular to the two kinds of sequence with which I have been principally concerned in this chapter: deficient attempts to grant the child's request and deficient attempts to offer her assistance. Distressed responses to deficient grantings occur where the child has been led to believe that her request is going to be granted, and where various subsequent events appear to be predicated on that presupposition. Distressed responses to offers of assistance occur where circumstances contrive to prevent the child carrying out an action herself. Nevertheless, the displays of distress that occur in each of these eventualities have certain properties in common, properties which distinguish them from displays of distress which one finds in other types of sequence. In order to bring this point out I will now examine a sequence that falls within this latter category – one in which the parent turns down a child request – and then I shall draw comparisons between the nature of the distress displayed in this incident and that displayed in the earlier incidents which have been analysed.

In non-granting sequences like #4.9 the distress is prompted by the parent's unwillingness to grant the request. Amy, near bedtime, wants to play farms, **Wanta play fa:rms** (line 1), but that is clearly not on my agenda nor to my liking at this time. In saying **Come on these things are going away now** (line 10) I am proposing to move the basket which contains the farm things into the storage cupboard, though only after a somewhat less than definite initial response where I make reference to an earlier occasion when the termination of the farm-making activity was initiated by Amy. It may be the case that the nature of that initial response, and the fact that I do not immediately proceed to pick up further toys or move towards the

4.9 2;5/V 39:40

Amy is being carried by her father into the room where the camera is when she makes the first request below:

```
1    A:    Wanta play fa:rms

2    F:    You wanta do what?
3                             (.)
4    A:    Play fa:::rms

5    F:    Pla:y fa:rms?

6    A:    Yea::hᴬ,   ((F puts A on floor as this is said))

7    F:    But we started playing farms and you stopped? ((then he
8          picks up toy basket))
9                             (.)
10   F:    Come on these things are going away  now ⌐=you help me
11         put them away,                             |
                                                      |
12   A:                                              └ (  )n:o::,

13   A:    No (hh hh)((i.e.vocalized, upset breathiness)) No: I- (.) I::,=
14         ((during this turn she sits on the floor and begins to handle
15         her toys))

16   F:    =We've had our game (.) we've played our- we've had ⌐ the
17         game of farms                                        |
                                                                |
18   A:                                                        └ No::
19         No : : : : : : : ᴮ : :, .hh No: : : : : : : :   ((intonation
20         becoming tearful towards the end of last 'no'; looking at F
21         for most of this time))

22   F:    We've got a lot of things to do yet ⌐ Amy we're- we're going
23         to be very very busy                   |
                                                   |
24   A:                                           └ No : : : : ooh ((upset
25         intonation; looking at F))
26                             (.)
27   A:   ⌐No:: ((not looking at F; plays with her toys))
         |
28   F:   └We- we've got lots of things to put away in the other room
```

```
29          as we:ll and we've got to go upstai::rs and we've got to,.hh
30                              (1.0)
31   A:     ehNo :⌐ : (hh hh) no: ((then full-blown crying))

32   F:            ⌊Do all sorts of things
```

Plate A   Plate B

storage cupboard after picking up the basket, implies, for the child, a possible basis for supposing the matter to be further negotiable.[5] But leaving aside this issue, the broad pattern which we find, both in this and in the few other non-granting sequences which take a distressed turn, is that the child's distress gradually escalates in the face of continuing intransigence on the part of the parent. This culminates in the full-blown crying which takes place after I say **and we've got to go upstai::rs and we've got to,.hh Do all sorts of things** (lines 29 and 32).

There are several contrasts to be drawn between the child's distress behaviour in this sequence and that which occurs in the incidents examined earlier in this chapter. First, whereas in sequences like #4.9 distress is associated with an escalation of the child's oppositional behaviour as the sequence progresses, in our earlier instances distress is built into, and a component part of, the child's *initial* reaction to the parent's deficient response to the request, or to the parent's deficient offer of assistance. In

---

[5] This matter of how the child monitors different kinds of parental response to her request, especially ones which do not express a willingness to grant the request, is something that is central to the workings of request sequences, and one which I do not address in this book. The term 'non-grantings' rather than 'rejections' is more apt in this context because parents appear to employ a variety of ways of turning down requests, which are not constructed as explicit rejections (e.g. lines 7–8 of #4.9). This makes all the more interesting the question of whether the child appears to make systematic inferences which are related to the design of the parental non-granting turn, its sequential positioning and so on. See Wootton (1981a) for an investigation of these themes in a large corpus of recordings of four-year-old children, and also McTear (1985:chapter 5).

#4.3, at line 27 (Plate C), the child's facial expression and words change instantly from happiness to distraughtness; in #4.4, at line 23, there is a similar sudden change when Amy sees her mother sitting in the 'wrong' position; in #4.7 the child is already somewhat upset by the time I make the offer of the cup, but after I do this, at line 8, matters take a serious turn for the worse; in #4.8, at line 28 (Plate B), distress is displayed as soon as I place the honey and the spoon in the 'wrong' position. In contrast with the gradual escalation of distress that sometimes occurs in the rejection of normal requests, as in #4.9, the timing and scale of the child's initial reactions in these other incidents is very sudden.

Second, in sequences like extracts 4.3, 4.4, 4.7 and 4.8 we find a range of behavioural options which are never taken up by the child in non-granting sequences such as #4.9. In non-granting sequences it is possible for the child to abandon her request, especially where she accepts that the parent is unwilling to grant it. But distressed abandonments such as that found in #4.4, where the parent is treated as having committed an offence, and as having been in the wrong in responding in some particular way, never occur in non-granting sequences; nor do we find the attempts by the child to restore the situation to the preceding *status quo* which are so common to the earlier incidents.

Third, the behavioural details of the emotional display itself also appear to be different. Specifically, forms of behaviour that seem endemic to many earlier sequences are not just the tears that we find in #4.9 but behaviour which seems associated with a sense of outrage and frustration. The stamping/canter-like movements found in #4.4 (Plate C) and the hitting of the cup in #4.7 (Plate C) are just the most obvious examples of this.

In general terms these observations suggest that the nature of the child's emotional display may be fitted, in a number of detailed ways, to the type of interactional contingency in which that display occurs. In this respect certain of these observations are clearly associated with the interactional matters which I discussed in the previous section. For example, the suddenness of the child's negative reaction is likely to be linked to the fact that at that moment it becomes evident to the child that the sequential expectation, which, for them, was underpinning what was going to take place, has now been breached. Some of the other observations above, notably those suggesting that these sequences contain distinctive forms of moral outrage, also connect with the moral theme which is the subject of the final section.

The moral nature of action

Within the literature on children there has been a tendency to demarcate the moral sphere of action from other aspects of their conduct. Piaget, and subsequent writers, for example, have given special attention to rules, to what kinds of knowledge the child has about rules and to whether moral rules are recognized by the child as having distinctive properties (Piaget 1932; Kohlberg 1976; Turiel 1983). The evidence pertaining to such discussions has principally been derived from situations – more often presented to the child as hypothetical rather than based on observations of actual child behaviour – which involve transgressions, conflict or disciplinary matters. This focus has received further legitimation from within the Freudian tradition, which also places special emphasis on matters to do with authority, transgression and punishment in its account of how children develop a moral sensibility (Emde *et al.* 1990).

More recent work, especially that of Dunn and her co-workers (for example Dunn 1988; Dunn and Slomkowski 1992), has shown that it is misleading to see the emergence of this moral sensibility as only being exhibited in, and shaped by, such disciplinary contexts. She shows clearly how moral matters can be touched on in the context of a wide range of activities in the homes which she studied; for example, teasing, humour, the handling of distress, co-operation and sharing, as well as transgressions and conflict, can be occasions on which matters relating to moral issues can find expression. In a way I want to go even further than Dunn and say that there are more fundamental ways in which, by the time the child is two years old, the design of her ordinary action attends to considerations which, for the child, have a moral force.

The considerations to which I am referring, of course, are the sequential ones which have been the focus of both the present and the previous chapter. Especially in the present chapter I have shown how sequential expectations can form, for the child, a yardstick against which to evaluate what takes place at a later time. In employing this yardstick the child is not dispassionately noting incongruities, she is treating these incongruities as consequential. In #4.6, for example, it seems plain enough that, when the child pushes the doll away, saying **I'm going to pick it up**, this move to rectify what is happening hinges on the occurrence of her earlier statement that she will pick it up herself. The earlier understanding, in this way, forms a basis or warrant for the child to stake a claim as to what *should* take place; and insofar as it can indicate what *should* take place the warrant is

being treated by the child as having moral force. Sequential understandings, then, have both cognitive and moral parameters.

What seems to be occurring in the distressing incidents which I have
examined is that in these particular interactional circumstances the child
acts as though she has no means open to her for rectifying the course of
action within its present trajectory. The moral force of the understanding,
however, is evidenced by the very fact that the child reacts so negatively to
the activity of the parent (rather than just going along with events as they
have turned out) and by the *nature* of the child's reaction. The distinctive
features of the latter have been addressed in the previous section. In this
regard it is most important that on most of these occasions the child
requires that the situation should be returned to the preceding *status quo*.
Such a requirement in part expresses a judgement as to the inappropriate-
ness of what has taken place, but it also claims an entitlement to have the
action re-run in a particular way, and again speaks to the child's recognition of the moral force of the expectations to which she is orienting.

Perhaps the most extraordinary feature in all this is the *public* basis of
the sequential understanding that is available to the child, and the way in
which there is, because of this understanding, a sense in which the child is
always in the right. On the face of it, child behaviour like that which occurs
in many of these transcripts approaches what is often referred to as 'spoilt'
behaviour in English society, behaviour which we think of as only being
understood, if understood at all, as intrinsically childlike in some way, as
beyond reason or as regressive to some anterior state.[6] Such a folk designa-
tion is deeply misleading. Parallel 'spoilt' behaviour is not evident in the
recordings prior to 2;5, and, according to my arguments, its occurrence is

---

[6] Discussions about the 'terrible twos' in child guidance literature for parents usually present
the child's untoward behaviour as an outcome of general developmental processes. Leach,
for example, treats it as a consequence of the twin, but contradictory, desires of wanting
to remain a baby and wanting to be independent. She suggests to parents that, with more
experience of language after the age of two, the child 'will at last be able to see both the
unreality of most of his worst fears and the reasonableness of most of the demands and
restrictions which you place on him. He will turn into a reasonable and communicative
human being' (1980:327). My argument is that at least some of the emotional turbulence
associated with the 'terrible twos' is an outcome of the child developing more sophisti
cated communicative skills of the kind which I have described, of her becoming a reasoning, communicative human being. Nevertheless, Leach is surely correct in stating that
further developments in 'reasonableness', after the age of two, are the order of the day. For
example, in many of the incidents which I have been discussing what is noticeably absent
from the child's behaviour is any expression of gratitude to the parent for the kindly assistance which the parent is attempting to make available. The emergence of 'gratitude' is a
matter that has received rather little attention in the research literature, though see Harris
(1989: chapter 6) for a related discussion.

predicated on the child's use of interactional and sequential skills which are themselves a significant developmental achievement. Specifically, it is restricted to circumstances in which the parent's action is discrepant with an overt, public understanding that has earlier been established. By virtue of this restriction the child displays a selective attentiveness to the public, accountable world of shared understandings. It is the parent who is in a way breaching these understandings and making the distress possible. So, in order to account for the 'spoilt' behaviour of the child, behaviour which in fact turns out to have quite orderly properties, the first things we should look for are ways in which the sequence has been 'spoiled' by the parent.

In this chapter I have been mainly examining sequences in which the child has exhibited unusual and distinctive forms of distress. It has been shown that orderly, local sequential understandings lie at the heart of the events in which this takes place. These understandings, together with other circumstances, make it possible for the child to expect sequences to unfold in a particular manner. Where this does not happen the child's reactions suggest that she recognizes that this is the case, and in reacting as she does she documents what for her is the binding nature of the understanding in question. Therefore, the emergence of a capacity to operate with such understandings brings with it new forms of moral sensibility regarding what ought to take place. I now go on to explore further ramifications of these understandings, ways in which they enter into the child's deployment of new linguistic designs for making requests during the course of her third year of life.

5

The emergence of two request forms

A central proposal of the two prior chapters has been that, at around the age of 2, the child's capacity to make use of sequential knowledge informs her behaviour in request sequences in important ways. Amy's actions are often bound up with understandings which normally have their basis in the sequences of interaction which precede these acts. In chapter 3 I showed how these understandings have a bearing on the child's use of imperatives, while in chapter 4 it became apparent that certain forms of distraught behaviour on the part of the child come to be intelligible once the nature of relevant understandings within earlier interaction has been traced. In these ways the child treats such understandings as a relevant context for the actions in which she engages; indeed one might say that in orienting to such understandings the child's capacity to respect aspects of the context in which she acts undergoes a major transformation when contrasted with her behaviour at, say, 16 months. She is now in a position to take account of, and adjust her behaviour in the light of, local, sequence specific knowledge. The sequence in which she is involved is thus permitted to inform and shape what she does, and what she does can display a sensitivity to these local circumstances.

These same observations and arguments also have a bearing on an important general question that has not as yet been overtly raised. This question concerns why the child should develop such a variety of ways of making requests so early in her life; why, for example, could her purposes not be satisfied by just employing a single format for making requests? Clearly, a single format would not suffice because it would not permit the child to differentiate, along the lines I have identified, the types of interactional circumstance in which she finds herself. This question becomes even more pointed, however, during her third year of life because at this time important further developments within her request system take place.

During this year although the child continues to use most of the request forms that I have been examining, such as imperatives, she also comes to use a number of further request forms, notably interrogatives such as 'Can I have x?'[1] In fact, by three years of age children have an almost bewildering repertoire of request formats to draw on, and what I shall be trying to do in this chapter is to trace the interactional laminations of some of these developments. These laminations turn out to have a relevance to the question of why such a variety of request forms come to have a use for the child of this age.

The developmental relationship between the newly emerging request forms and the ones which have been in prior use is a complex one to analyse. Broadly, it is possible that the new forms take over certain interactional duties previously handled by request formats in earlier use. Alternatively, it is possible that the new forms are used so as both to recognize and deal with interactional contingencies which were not previously addressed. Exploring these possibilities involves, therefore, detailed comparisons with the use of earlier request forms, and because of the scale of this enterprise the analysis to be presented here will be quite restricted in scope. It will be confined to two of the newly emerging interrogative formats, 'Can you do x?' and 'Shall we do x?', though, in the course of this, reference will also be made to the use of certain other new request forms.

The discussion is organized into two main sections. In the first I will examine alterations in the circumstances in which the child uses certain imperatives, and I shall argue that between the ages of two and three there is evidence to suggest that the child adopts an alternative request form, 'Can you do x?', for dealing with some of these circumstances. In effect, the child can adopt this device where she wants the parent to do something but has no sequential warrant of the kind that has, in previous chapters, been identified as having a distinctive association with her use of imperatives. In the second section I will principally examine the newly emergent interrogative form 'Shall we do x?' I will show that it has a particular affinity with certain interactional circumstances, and I will discuss the shifts in interactional sensibility which the use of this form entails.

In the course of these sections, therefore, I will also be showing some of the ways in which the child's sequential and interactional awareness is undergoing change between the ages of two and three, as well as demonstrating ways in which this awareness serves to differentiate some of the

---

[1] For an overview of psycholinguistic research on the emergence of interrogatives in English see Ingram (1989:454–65).

standard linguistic designs which the child comes to adopt. At the core of my argument is the claim that the motivation for the adoption of these designs is an interactional one, that these designs serve to encode and further differentiate forms of understanding which are either present or imminent within the child's interactional system. Essentially, it is an argument which is epigenetic in character in that it identifies ways in which the structure of considerations drawn on by the child at an earlier stage of development lays the basis and motivation for the emergence of new linguistic designs at a later stage.

Imperatives, interrogatives and non-warranted action

The requests with which I shall be concerned here occur in what have been called, in chapter 3, non-offence contexts. That is, they are mainly not employed for dealing with some sort of offence that the parent has committed, is committing or is about to commit. In chapter 3 I argued that a substantial proportion of non-offence imperatives were used in circumstances in which a certain type of sequentially based understanding was available to the child. More specifically this understanding provides the child with a basis for expecting the act required of the parent to be concordant with what the child knows of the parent's own preferences in that situation. The first point to be made about non-offence imperatives on the recordings in the second half of the child's third year is that they continue to be associated with this same kind of interactional circumstance. In fact, where imperatives are used in the months subsequent to 2;5 the existence of such sequentially based understandings can be marked in more overt ways within the construction of the imperative. At 3;1, for example, we find several instances of the word 'then' being incorporated into non-offence imperatives, as in #5.1. This word turns the action required by the imperative into one which is in some way expectable in the circumstances, the basis for this expectation lying in earlier events. In #5.1 there is obvious evidence, in lines 1 and 2, that both parents now expect someone to shuffle the cards, in order to play the game. Amy's imperative at line 5, **Give y'all yer ca::rds te daddy the:n**, draws on this warrant, and the inclusion of the word 'then' appears to mark the sequential connection between that warrant and the course of action that the child is now proposing. The word 'then' first accompanies requests constructed as imperatives at 2;9, and both at that age and 3;1 it *only* accompanies requests formatted in this way. In chapter 6 some possible implications of this will be addressed further.

    In chapter 2 I noted that at age 2;5, and earlier, Amy could also, on a

5.1 3;1/II 26:27

Amy, her mother and father have just finished playing a card game. The next game requires some boards on which to put the cards. Amy has just finished giving out one of these boards to each player:

1 M: Who's gonna shuffle 'em

2 F: Yea:h who's gonna shuffle them
3   (1.2)
4 F: ┌( )

5 A: └Give y'all yer ca^A::rds te daddy the:n ((in early part of this
6   turn A gestures with her rh towards the cards that M is
7   holding; chuckles from M and F after the turn))
8   (1.5)
9 A: Here y'are da:d   ((A passes F her own cards))

Plate A

---

small number of occasions, employ imperatives in circumstances where no sequentially based warrant was available to her. These imperatives can be loosely described as ones in which the child is asking the parent to do something which is directly in the child's, rather than the parent's, immediate interest. They include, for example, instances in which the child asks a parent to fetch her milk or move an object for her. Whereas imperatives like **Give y'all yer ca::rds te daddy the:n**, in #5.1, deal with forms of action which are not exclusively of benefit to the child, these others display a more single-minded self-interest. Fortunately, this rather nebulous characterization occasionally receives formal marking within the design of the child's imperative. This takes the form of the phrase 'for me', and is illustrated by the following instances, all of which occur at 2;5. None of them are said in the circumstances most often associated with the use of imperatives: ones in which the child has a sequential basis for supposing that what she is asking for is compatible with the parent's preference:

Get some chalks out of there for me
Get some more chalks for me
Put it on there for me
Get some more ma drink for me mummy
Get that for me

These instances, then, make up a clearly marked subset of the wider and fuzzier set of non-offence imperatives in which the child, without any sequential warrant, asks the parent to do something which is in the child's rather than the parent's interest. The phrase 'for me' can also be found appended to imperatives when Amy is 2;9, the next recording session; and at both 2;5 and 2;9 this phrase can also accompany the 'You do x' form of request, as in:

You hold that for me
You get it for me

Between 2;9 and 3;1 there is a decline in the frequency with which the child uses non-offence imperatives. This is documented in Table 5.1 where it is clear that by 3;1 this decline is evident both with regard to the raw frequency with which imperatives occur and with respect to their proportionate use in comparison to the other major non-offence request forms. A major component in this decline is the reduction in the fuzzy set of imperatives which the child is using to further her own immediate and exclusive interests. As this set is fuzzy no attempt will be made to quantify this decline in these terms. Instead, as I have done previously, I will focus on the subset marked with the phrase 'for me', taking these as the most clearly marked cases of such imperatives. The major finding here is that at 3;1 and 3;5 this phrase, with one exception, is no longer to be found in any imperative request; in addition, it is not appended to any 'You do x' request design at these ages.

The exception, which occurs at 3;5, is presented here as #5.2. Here Amy is down from the table, where at this age she normally now sits on a chair or bench, unconfined by the high-chair, apparently taking little interest in the food put out for her. Her mother mentions the jelly babies in lines 1–2, and, when responding to the child's **I want my jelly babies** in line 5, clearly implies that they will be made available to Amy. In saying **Get fi:ve for me**

Table 5.1

Distribution of certain child request forms* between the ages of 2;1 and 3;5

Age	2;1		2;3		2;5		2;9		3;1		3;5	
Request type	N	%	N	%	N	%	N	%	N	%	N	%
Imperatives	19	25	35	40	35	47	50	53	18	32	21	23
I want x	27	35	34	39	26	35	33	35	7	13	39	43
I like x	29	38	5	6	0	0	0	0	0	0	0	0
You do x	2	3	12	14	10	13	10	11	3	5	15	17
Can I/you	0	0	1	1	1	1	1	1	15	27	8	9
Shall I/we	0	0	0	0	3	4	1	1	13	23	7	8
Total	77		87		75		95		56		90	

Note: * Negative versions of these request forms are excluded, as are imperatives accompanied by the word *NO* and imperatives using the verb 'Look'. Only requests to either parent are included.

(.)no::w, therefore, Amy has an obvious basis for treating her request as being potentially in accord with her mother's understanding. To this extent, then, this imperative with 'for me', unlike those occurring at ages 2;5 and earlier, *is* informed by the kind of sequential warrant more broadly associated with non-offence imperatives.

At 3;1 and 3;5, therefore, there is a marked decline in those imperatives which I have described as self-interested, this decline being indexed by the virtual disappearance of the phrase 'for me' from the imperative constructions which do occur at these ages. In the only instance at these ages in which this phrase is retained, in #5.2, the imperative *is* informed by a local sequential understanding, which renders it analogous to the other non-offence imperatives in use by the child at this time. One implication of all this is that by 3;1 and 3;5 there is a closer connection between non-offence imperatives and the kinds of interactional circumstances with which they were only associated at earlier ages. By 3;1 it is difficult to find a non-offence imperative in which the child is not drawing on some locally available sequential warrant of the kind that has been amply illustrated in chapter 3 and #5.1.

With regard to Table 5.1, one reason for the decline in imperative use at 3;1 and 3;5 is likely to be, therefore, the decline in the use of imperatives by the child to ask her parents to do things for her 'out of the blue'. The question then arises as to how the child, at 3;1 and 3;5, handles the interactional exigency in which, at earlier times, she used self-interested imperatives. Where she is asking the parent to do something for her 'out of the blue', how does she go about this? My argument will be that these are the circumstances which appear to attract the use of one of the child's new interrogative request designs, 'Can you do x?'

In order to produce a 'Can I/you?' request the child has to master the necessary syntactic rules for producing this type of yes/no answer question. Amy's mastery of these rules seems to be well advanced by 2;5. By then she can produce forms like **Do you want some of these, Is this breakfast** and **Have we got any jam**, sentences which suggest that she has some control of the basic capacities for constructing formal yes/no answer questions. This competence is by no means even across all yes/no questions. For example, instead of saying 'Do you want x?' Amy sometimes produces forms like **Want to do some chalking mummy?**, forms that she relied on heavily during the recordings immediately previous to the age of 2;5. Sometimes necessary words are omitted, as in **Are going now?** ('Are you going now?'), and there are even occasional failures to invert the auxiliary

5.2 3;5/VII 3:15

Amy is down from the table, where she has left some food, fiddling with
some folders on a nearby shelf. Her mother is out of camera in the
doorway to the next room:

```
 1   M:    Now we'll have to uh: have your jelly babies soon and have a
 2         bath so⌐ you'd better eat-

 3   A:           └ AI want my jelly babies=   ((now thumb in mouth,
 4         holding cuddling blanket, looking at M))

 5   M:    =Well eat your mackerel paté up as we:ll,
 6                         (2.6)
 7         ((in this pause A moves back towards her seating position at
 8         the table, trying to suck her thumb and hold her blanket at
 9         the same time; does not look  at M again for the rest of this
10         sequence))

11   A:    Get fiB:ve for me, (.) no::w
12                         (1.1)
13   A:    Plea:se ((then A moves to pick up some of her food))

14   M:    Good (.) carry on with your mackerel paté and I'll get your
15         sweeties as well
```

Plate A   Plate B

---

verb, as in **He has hands?** ('Has he got hands?'). Table 5.1 shows that
instances of 'Can I/you?' requests can be found from 2;3 onwards, though
their early identification is made more difficult by this child's tendency to
contract the initial word 'can' to something like 'cn', where the 'c' sound

is little more than a glottal stop. However, these requests do not occur with any frequency until 3;1, and the issue of why this might be so is a matter that will be taken up later.

For the moment I shall focus on the instances of 'Can you do x?' that this child produces up to and at 3;1. These are listed below, together with summary versions of the interactional circumstances in which each occurs:[2]

a. 2;5 **Can you get it** (said whilst sitting on her mother's knee, and asking her mother if she will fetch Amy's drink for her from a table in the same room).

b. 2;9 **Can you put that piece in the dustbin for me** (Amy is peeling a banana, and, after taking off the first strip of skin, proffers it towards her mother as she makes this request).

c. 3;1 **Can you hold that for me a minute** (said as she proffers a chalk towards her father, when he is drinking tea from a cup, holding the saucer in his other hand).

d. 3;1 **Can you be my little baby** (said as she sits on her father's knee, thumb in mouth and holding her cuddling blanket, as a first attempt to initiate a bout of fantasy play when, in fact, her father is just trying to start getting her dressed. The real meaning of these words can be taken as 'Can I be your little baby?').

e. 3;1 **Can you shuffle them up please** (said as she has finished getting some cards out of a box in preparation for playing with them. Said to her father as he is sitting on the floor nearby).

f. 3;1 **Can you put the light on for me** (said to her mother after Amy has said that she is taking some toys into the other room to play; she wants the light put on in the other room).

g. 3;1 **Can you move it near my seat for me** (sitting on her mother's knee she turns to resume sitting in her chair at the table; as she turns she makes this request to her mother to move a bowl on the table closer to where she is going to sit, so that she will be able to eat from it).

Within four of these 'Can you do x?' constructions we find the phrase 'for me'; in fact by 3;1 this phrase seems to have entirely migrated from the imperative and 'You do x' constructions with which it was earlier associated to this 'Can you?' form. In these four cases the child wants the parent to engage in an action on her own, the child's, behalf – to effect an action

---

[2] Two of the child's 'Can you do x?' productions are omitted from this list. One occurs in the type of offence context which is not being considered in the present discussion, and the other is not a request – it appears to mean 'Are you able to do x?'.

that is helpful to, and in some cases necessary for, the child's own projected course of action. They are self-interested forms of request in that the beneficiary of the requested act is clearly going to be the child: there is no sense in these cases that the act required of the parent forwards some line of action which is to the benefit of the parent.

This 'self-interest' feature is not characteristic of all these 'Can you?' requests. For example, in (e) it is plain that the child intends that the card game should be a joint one involving both her father and herself. Shuffling the cards is a prelude to this line of action – playing cards – in which both she and her father will be active participants. However, this instance does share one feature with all the rest of these 'Can you?' forms. They all occur in sequential positions in which the child does not have a basis for supposing that the action which she is proposing is in line with current parental preferences. Compare, for instance, (e) with #5.1, both of which concern the shuffling of cards prior to a card game. Whereas in #5.1 the child has ample basis upon which to suppose that her parents are willing to engage in another game, this is not so in (e). Here, prior to the request being made, Amy's father has expressed several reservations about playing cards again at that particular time (though without categorically rejecting it), and, although there has been a lapse of time between that discussion and the child's request, the child has no basis, at the time of making it, for supposing the parent to be willing to play the game.

The general points I want to take from this discussion of imperatives and 'Can you do x?' forms in the period between the ages of 2;5 and 3;1 are as follows. During this time imperatives in non-offence sequences become increasingly associated with circumstances in which the child has a basis for supposing that what she is telling the parent to do is in line with understandings that have been arrived at earlier in the interaction. In particular, the child comes not to select imperatives where, out of the blue, she wants the parent to do something to assist her own lines of projected action. By 3;1, there is every suggestion that *one* method the child uses to make requests in these interactional circumstances that are no longer handled through the use of imperatives is to employ 'Can you?' constructions. In particular, they can be used where the child wants the parent to do something which is in the exclusive interest of the child, and where there is no local understanding that suggests to the child that what she is asking for is in line with what the parent expects to occur. In effect, by 3;1 the child displays that imperatives are no longer suited to handling certain interactional circumstances, and that the 'Can you?' form is now one appropriate device that is to be used instead. Where the child wants the parent to do something which is in the child's own interest, without a sequential warrant, then she can elect to employ a form which overtly gives her recipient *choice* in the matter.

In the final part of this section I want to consider the more difficult question of why there should be this decline in self-interested imperatives between 2;5 and 3;1, and the related question of why 'Can you do x?' constructions should be chosen to take on their interactional role.

One way of approaching this transition might be to view it as an outcome of changes in the child's cognitive processing capacities during this time period. For example, various research has suggested that early in the child's third year of life she becomes increasingly able to take into account the desires and wishes of other people with whom she is dealing. Wellman and Woolley (1990), for example, have shown that children aged 2½, in experimental situations, are capable of making appropriate inferences about people's actions on the basis of knowing their desires. So one might argue that the concern to frame requests as yes/no questions, questions which formally recognize that the other party may have contrary desires, is sensitive to the emergence of those underlying cognitive skills.

There are a number of reasons which suggest that this line of argument would be weak with regard to the issues that we are dealing with here. The most important is the fact that at a much earlier age, 2;1, this child has demonstrated, in a variety of ways, that she is capable of taking the views of other people into account in the design of her actions in request sequences. This is most overtly marked in cases where the child asks the parent if he or she would like to engage in some action, instances like **Daddy ye like do it again?** and **Like another one daddy?** (see especially extracts 3.2, 3.3, 3.10 and 3.11 in chapter 3). Furthermore, other forms of data were also presented in chapter 3 which suggest that by 2;1 the child can systematically take account of understandings which have emerged concerning what the other party views as preferable or acceptable. I have shown there that, where such understandings exist, then this forms a sequential environment which has certain affinities with requests constructed as imperatives. If the child's request selection can take account of the existence of such understandings then this suggests that a cognitive processing capacity necessary for taking account of the views and understandings of other people is already in place at 2;1, several months before the child is making the transition from imperatives to 'Can you do x?' constructions that is our concern here. So, a cognitivist account, framed in the terms I have described, is weak in two ways. First, the emergence of the interrogative in question, 'Can you do x?' does not coincide with the emergence of an interest in the mental states of other people; the latter predates the former by many months. Second, it is difficult to see how a cognitivist account could explain the decline in the particular type of imperative, which I have called self-interested imperatives, that seems to be in some way connected with the emergence of these interrogatives.

A second line of approach to the transitions in question might be to see them as shaped by the reactions of the parent to the request behaviour of the child. Clearly, parents can require the child to repair the form in which she makes requests at this age. Through a variety of repair initiators, such as 'Pardon?' and 'What do you say?', and prompts, such as 'Please', the child can be required to re-do or repair the original version of her request. If such repairs are systematically initiated on requests constructed as imperatives, and if the parent makes it clear that forms such as 'Please can you do x?' have a preferred status, then over time one might expect the child who heeded such cues to use fewer imperatives and more request forms such as 'Can you do x?'

The strongest evidence in favour of such an argument is the fact that where the parents do initiate repair on imperative requests, then the subset of non-offence imperatives that is especially vulnerable to this is those which are not embedded in sequences where local understandings warrant that which the child is telling the parent to do. In short, it is those requests which I have called self-interested imperatives that tend to be queried in this way, the most overt of these being those which, prior to 3;1, are constructed with the phrase 'for me'. For example, at 2;5, 2 of the 6 child imperatives which include this phrase are subjected to repair initiation in which the adult seeks some form of politeness repair; none of the other 33 non-offence imperatives which occur at this age is similarly dealt with by either parent. There is some suggestion then that it is specifically in the context of self-interest imperatives that the parents are drawing attention to inadequacies of this kind in the use of the bald imperative. Having said this, there are a number of further reasons why too much weight cannot be attached to such parental behaviour in accounting for the transitions that are my concern here.

First, the sheer incidence of parental repair initiation of this kind is very low within parent–child interaction in the home. For example, in an analysis of the responses of Scottish parents to the imperative and 'I want x' requests of 4 children aged nearly 4 years old, I found that, of 517 such requests, only 8 attracted politeness repair by a parent (Wootton 1986). Their incidence is somewhat higher on the recordings of Amy, but it is still a relatively infrequent phenomenon in the home setting. Second, in both the Scottish data and the present recordings, where the parent does initiate such repair, a next turn by the child which simply states 'Please' is taken as an adequate response by the parent to his or her request for repair. This implies that from the parental viewpoint it is not the use of the imperative *per se* which is faultable but such uses which exclude the word 'please'. So, if the child were to include 'please' in the construction of her imperatives, which she begins to do from 3;1 onwards, then the concerns of the parent will be met. In short, the system of politeness repair adopted by the parent does not require a decline in the use of imperatives by the child. Third, there is no evidence, either before or at 3;1, that the child, when responding to such repair initiations, spontaneously substitutes an interrogative request design for the imperative that she used in her initial request. Up to 3;1 there is, for example, no evidence of the child, after using an initial imperative, replying to subsequent repair initiators such as 'Pardon' or 'What do you say?' by resorting to a 'Can you do x?'[3] So this constitutes further evidence for the claim that, for the child, these initiations of politeness repair are not addressing the adequacy of the imperative as an initial request format. Although these are environments in which the child is being encouraged to reconsider the design of imperatives, they are not ones in which the child is being encouraged to switch from imperative to 'Can you do x?' formats.

The tentative argument that I wish to make about this transition is as follows. First, it is important to emphasize that the decline in non-offence imperative use and the upswing in the use of 'Can you do x?' forms from about 2;9 are linked. It is those instances in which the child does not have a sequential warrant when using her imperative which decline in occur-

---

[3] Extract 5.2, line 13, contains an instance of the child producing the word 'please'. Here it occurs after a pause occurring subsequent to her use of an imperative. It is possible here that the child treats the non-reply of the parent, as signified by that pause, as a basis for identifying the parent as finding some problem with her use of the imperative, the word 'please' being employed as a remedy to the problem. But we also find children of this age appending a 'please' after briefer pauses at the end of their request turns, and it may be the case that in doing this they are producing late self-monitorings as to the inadequacy of their request designs, which are not specifically touched off by the absence of a parental response. My arguments in the text, however, do not hang on such details. What is interesting about cases like the one in #5.2 is that, in comparable sequential positions, the child never changes the initial format in which she chooses to make her request. After using, say, an imperative, she never then spontaneously re-designs her request into a 'Can you do x?'; at most she adds a 'please', as she does here.

rence, and it is these circumstances which seem to have an affinity with
'Can you do x?' designs. How does the child become aware that the absence
of a sequential warrant matters for the construction of such imperatives?
To some extent such an awareness may be induced by occasional parental
repair initiation on such imperatives, of the kind I have alluded to above.
Perhaps more fundamental, however, is the fact that in her wider non-
offence imperative usage the child has routinely been taking account of her
parents' views and preferences in deciding on whether or not to use an
imperative since 2;1. Within that sector of her request system that is
employing these imperatives, therefore, there is an in-built tension between
acting in a way that respects the views of the other in some domains and
not in others. For a while, between about 2;1 and 2;9, the child operates a
system which perpetuates this tension, but what is happening at 3;1 is that
the child extends her concerns with the views of the other into situations
in which she wants the parent to do something but where she has no
sequential warrant for treating the parent as being prepared to go along
with this. Her way of doing this is to employ a question, one which asks if
the parent could do this for her. 'Can you do x?' questions, therefore, orient
to the absence of bases in mundane reason for the child to make presump-
tions about the nature of the parents' involvement in situations where she
requires their assistance. In general, this is a type of constructivist view of
request development which places more weight on the internal tensions
involved in using the system available to the child than on the shaping of
these matters by those involved with her. It suggests that there are pressures
encouraging the emergence of such interrogatives which are largely
endogenous to the request system itself and independent of the specific
nature of the parental input.

This type of account raises a number of further questions which also
need to be addressed. For example, where the child does not have a sequential warrant why does she not simply switch to using an alternative request
design that is already available within her repertoire, one like 'I want x';
why does she need to employ an interrogative? I shall come back to such
matters in the concluding section of this chapter, but at this stage I shall
consider a fourth type of account which, on the face of it, has an obvious
potential relevance to any consideration of the emergence of interrogatives.

One possible argument is that the emergence of interrogatives such as
'Can you do x?' is a simple function of the child acquiring the capacity to
form these questions in a syntactic sense. There are a number of matters

that complicate this argument and make it less compelling as an explanation of the transition that I have been concerned with than the one I have
proposed above. First, there is some evidence, already alluded to, of the
child being able to form both yes/no-answer questions, and specifically
'Can you do x?' questions, well before their upswing in occurrence at 3;1.
While it is, therefore, the case that the linguistic capacity to use such questions is a necessary condition for their wider adoption it may not be a suf-
ficient condition. So this creates a need for further accounts, like the one I
have offered, of the processes which are conducive to their adoption.
Second, simply to appeal to the emergence of the competence to construct
such questions as an explanation of their occurrence in no way accounts
for why they appear to be chosen to do the particular job that they do, or
why they have the affinity that they do with certain kinds of interactional
scenario. From the evidence I have offered, for example, there seems little
doubt that their emergence is specifically linked with situations which have
earlier been handled through certain imperatives. That order of connection
and complexity remains unaddressed within any account that exclusively
focuses on the emergence of a competence to construct such questions.

'Shall we?' interrogatives

The other type of interrogative design that we shall be concerned with in
this chapter is that prefixed by the words 'Shall we?' In various ways it is
misleading to refer to many of the relevant instances as requests, one overt
indicator of this being the absence of the word 'please' from both 'Shall
we?' and 'Shall I?' questions at this age. Whereas this word can accompany
a number of other request designs this is not the case here.[4] Often, 'Shall
we?' questions intuitively seem to be more like suggestions than requests,
but, rather than approach their analysis in stipulative, definitional fashion,
I shall, instead, be describing the characteristic interactional positions in
which they are used and the roles which they appear to play there. In
general, what the analysis will reveal is that the use of this interrogative
brings into play a recognition by the child of the *joint* nature of some line
of action in which she is engaged with her recipient. Although there are
ways in which, prior to her use of 'Shall we?', the child can involve other

---

[4] The absence of 'please' in the construction of 'Shall I/we?' questions is not just a feature
of Amy's data. In my study of twenty children aged just four years, based in Aberdeen, no
such co-occurrence is ever found with the equivalent type of question found in that Scottish
dialect, namely 'Will I/we?' questions.

people in joint lines of action, the use of 'Shall we?' designs brings something distinctive to these occasions. It turns out to be a way in which the child can display the continuation of such an understanding through a stretch of interaction. In adopting and using 'Shall we?' forms, therefore, the child is at the same time displaying a sensitivity regarding to whom a line of action belongs, and who has entitlements to be considered in relation to it.

Table 5.1 shows that 'Shall I/we?' constructions occurred within Amy's recorded speech from 2;5 onwards. In fact, all the instances at 2;5 are formatted as 'Shall we?', and I shall begin by examining one of them.

Although **Shall we make a farm**, at line 13 in #5.3, begins in a sequential position where it has been agreed that some form of game will be played, there is, as yet, no warrant for selecting the particular game in question: farms. For example, there has been no related prior discussion concerning farms. So, to suggest playing farms, in the form of a 'Shall we?' question, is to make the matter of which game is to be played into a matter of choice, one about which the child's recipient is to have a say. By this age Amy already has other techniques available to her for treating her recipient as having a say concerning some line of action in which she clearly wishes the recipient to engage. In the earlier recordings at 2;3, for example, the matter of playing with farms was again initiated on several occasions by Amy. One technique that she uses both there and on other types of occasion (see, for example, #5.4, line 1) is to create a question out of a want statement, as in **Want make a little farmyard daddy?** On these occasions the child's accompanying gaze and waiting behaviour, in addition to the questioning intonation, make it patently clear that these are genuine questions rather than 'want'-statement requests. So, while Amy's **Shall we make a farm**, in #5.3, treats her recipient as having a say in what is to happen next, the earlier availability to the child of such alternative questioning techniques suggests that, while this is an important property of 'Shall we?' designs, it is not in itself developmentally novel.

The interactional position in which **Shall we make a farm** occurs is of a rather particular kind. The main point I want to make here concerns what, for the child, is the nature of the parent's involvement when asking this question. **Shall we make a farm** occurs in a sequential position in which the participation of the parent is relatively assured. Although the parent has, at lines 4–5, expressed reservations about playing another game at this time in the evening, most recently he has acceded to the child's demand with **Well we'll have one game**, at line 10 – a form of words which makes

5.3 2;5/V 36:58

Near bedtime Amy tries to persuade her father to play with the toy farm animals; A is holding a toy pipe, fiddling with it:

```
1    A:    Pla:y with 'em
2                        (.8)
3    A:    No:┌::w
4    F:        └Its- no its too late to start playing ┌now its-  its ┐time
5              to be thinking of bed now?=             │               │
6    A:                                                └Pla:y with em ─┘
7    A:    =Pla:y with them  ((at the end of this turn A bends down to
8          start taking a toy from the bowl of toys))
9                        (.9)
10   F:    Well we'll have one game
11   A:    Yeah
12   F:    One quick game with them (.) right?
13   A:    Shall we make a^A farm
```

Plate A

---

clear his agreement to his being involved in the ensuing game. It is in this interactional position, then, that the child says **Shall we make a farm**, one in which she has an obvious basis for supposing her recipient to be favourably disposed towards both permitting and participating in a joint line of activity.

The 'Shall we?' occurring in #5.4 has parallel interactional features. Here, in what will by now be familiar to readers as the 'chalking situation', Amy, at line 21, says **Shall we do some cha:lk(hh)in .hh Bo:th do so:me**, the word 'both' being emphasized and prolonged. Again, this occurs in a situation in which Amy has explicit grounds for expecting her mother to be involved in the chalking activity: for example, earlier in the sequence, in response to Amy's **Want do some chalkin: mummy::?**, at line 1, her mother replies **Ye:s**, and after moving over to the blackboard her mother continues to stand by it throughout the sequence, as though expecting to be further involved.

Two main lines of argument about these cases now need to be put together. On the one hand, these 'Shall we?' turns are occurring in sequential positions in which the child has a basis for expecting parental joint involvement in some activity, but on the other these turns exhibit that choices remain to be made by her recipient. The latter is clear enough in #5.3, where the matter of which game to play has yet to be decided. #5.4, however, merits a further word as it may appear that the child already knows the answer to her question **Shall we do some cha:lk(hh)in .hh Bo:th do so:me** prior to asking it. After all, the mother said **Ye:s** earlier to Amy's **Want do some chalkin: mummy::?**, and it is clear enough even then that Amy herself wants to do chalking, so in what sense do choices remain to be made when the child says **Shall we do some cha:lk(hh)in .hh Bo:th do so:me**. Potentially important here is the mother's question **What are you going to draw**, at line 17. Whereas 'What are *we* going to draw?' would have displayed a continuing expectation by the mother that they were *both* going to be involved in some way in drawing, **What are you going to draw** can be treated as representing a possible shift away from such a position, as now supposing that only Amy will be drawing, or, possibly, that Amy will be doing her drawing first, before her mother. Either way, the child's special emphasis on 'both' in **Shall we do some cha:lk(hh)in .hh Bo:th do so:me** suggests that she is not treating any understanding arrived at earlier as having decided the matter of what exactly is going to take place, even though it is clear enough that there is to be some form of joint involvement in the chalking activity.

By this stage the special basis for the occurrence of 'we' in these questions will be becoming apparent. As they spring out of situations in which there is an expectation of joint action between the child and her recipient then the inclusion of the 'we' displays an orientation to this contingency by the child. In such a situation the child, through her use of 'Shall we?' designs, presents her recipient with a possible line of action for recipient

5.4 2;5/III 2:34

Mother has just suggested to Amy that she might like to do some
chalking, upon which M offers to put on the light for her in the corner of
the room by the board. As M does this A says:

1   A: Want do some chalkin: mummy::[A]?

2   M: Ye:s
3   (1.6)
4   M: Shall I: (.) shall I: rub this off now? ((picking up cloth and
5   pointing to board))
6   (.)
7   A: L̲o̲o̲k̲ (.) daddy's made a ship for ye ((pointing to picture on
8   board))

9   M: Oh:⌐ that's nice isn't it
             ⌊
10   A: ⌊ No: lea: :-,

11   M: I'll leave it on ⌐shall I
                            ⌊
12   A: ⌊( )

13   A: ( )

14   M: Oka:y where's the chalks=here are the chalks ((M picks up
15   box and puts it on stool for A))
16   (1.5)
17   M: What are you going to draw

18   A: And I:'ll get a chai:r, ((runs to other side of room to get
19   chair))
20   (.)
21   A: Shall we do some cha:lk(hh)in .hh Bo:th [B]do so:me,

22   M: Both do some okay

Plate A   Plate B

either to agree to or to reject. For although it is clear in these cases that the child would like to do the thing being proposed in the 'Shall we?' question there is still a clear sense that the child is not presuming that her recipient will wish to do this also. In this respect these question designs have features which make them more like suggestions rather than requests, a point which other evidence, to be presented later, will further substantiate. At this stage, however, I want to pause and look back into the recordings prior to age 2;5, in order to consider how the child handled in the past those interactional circumstances that now, at 2;5, seem to be associated with 'Shall we?' designs.

My reasons for being interested in this bear on fairly central issues concerning the relationship between forms of language and the interactional circumstances to which they relate. Developmentally it might be the case that a new linguistic form, such as 'Shall we do x?', represents a way of handling an interactional exigency which supplants some other way of handling parallel exigencies that occurred in the past. Really, to speak of 'supplanting' is always too crude, as the adoption of an alternative device for handling an interactional contingency always in some sense gives a different character to the interactional contingency itself. Speaking crudely, however, what I found to be the case with the 'Can you do x?' requests, discussed in the previous section, was that by 3;1 at least some of them have come to replace a sub-set of imperatives, to be used in a parallel interactional environment. In contrast, a further possibility is that new linguistic forms may orient to an interactional exigency which has not been previously addressed within talk. In the case of 'Shall we do x?' designs, the evidence from earlier recordings suggests that it is this second possibility which is more pertinent in this case. I will now explain this more fully.

Prior to 2;5 Amy had linguistic resources available to her which she could have used to perform actions akin to her use of 'Shall we?' designs at 2;5. Most notably, as described earlier, she could use questions like 'Wanta do x?' Having obtained her recipient's agreement to engage in some form of joint action, she could then have followed that up with a further question to establish which specific kind of joint action was to be the focus of attention. For example, at 2;3, as at 2;5, there are, as I have already noted, several sequences which involve me in playing farms with Amy. These are usually initiated by Amy, by her saying things like 'Wanta make a little farmyard?' After my (occasional) agreement to this line of action what she could then have gone on to say would have been things like 'Wanta get the cows?' or 'Wanta do this first?', things that would have recognized an entitlement on my part to have a further say regarding what was to happen next. However, in such circumstances, subsequent to some line of joint action being agreed on, Amy does not enact such turns or other sentence designs which operate in similar ways. She does not treat her partner as having any entitlement to have a say in how the line of action is to proceed subsequently. In other words she does not, on earlier recordings, use forms of words which appear to function in analogous ways to 'Shall we?' designs at 2;5. Where she does use questions such as 'Wanta do x?', both at 2;3 and 2;5, these questions are only used to broach the possibility of some line of action in an initial way. Her use of **Want do some chalkin: mummy::?** in #5.4, line 1, is but one example of this. Such questions, therefore, do not occupy interactional positions parallel to those in which 'Shall we?' designs occur.

What seems distinctive about 'Shall we?' designs, therefore, is as follows. First, they occur at this age, 2;5, in sequential positions which are immediately subsequent to the other party displaying some measure of agreement to engage in a course of action with the child. Second, in occurring after such a preliminary agreement they imply that that agreement – or that understanding in our normal terminology – does not necessarily entail a willingness to go along with that which the child is now proposing. Third, and specifically through their adoption of the term 'we', they claim that the joint character of the understanding is a matter of continuing concern, that it is not a matter of the child's preference or the parent's preference, but that this can be a matter susceptible to resolution in the interests of both parties. These designs are distinctive with regard to the accomplishment of this work in that I cannot find obvious precursors which operate in parallel ways in parallel interactional positions in earlier recordings.

What their use brings into being, therefore, is a new type of orientation by the child to a type of sequential understanding, one which acknowledges the continuing jointness of the child's involvement with her recipient. In this sense these question designs are interactional as well as linguistic inventions.

This analysis of 'Shall we?' designs holds for the majority of those which appear between 2;5 and 3;1, the age range with which I shall be concerned. But there are two further kinds of use that appear within this period which also merit attention, and in the remainder of this section I shall try to delineate them. In the first we find a capacity to detach the concerns of the 'Shall we?' question from the immediately preceding sequence; in the second, this question design is employed on occasions in which misdemeanours, or potential misdemeanours, are being handled by the child.

Detachable 'Shall we?' questions

In extracts 5.3 and 5.4 we have seen that the child uses the 'Shall we?' question to specify further a general line of action to which the parent has agreed. After the parent has agreed to play with her, in #5.3, the child uses **Shall we make a farm** in order to establish what the nature of the play is to consist of. There is, then, a connectedness between the nature of the initial agreement and the line of action being proposed by the child through her use of **Shall we make a farm**. In the third instance of the use of this design at 2;5, #5.5, this connectedness is less apparent.

When Amy says **Shall we put snooker o::n**, at line 14, the circumstances are that there has been agreement about the feasibility of her going to the paper shop with me (see #4.8, p. 127, for the transcribed detail). Although she then delayed the onset of this shop activity, with **No: jus:- in a minute**, at line 8, the position remains that I have indicated a current preparedness to engage in joint activity with her – going to the shop. The activity which she then goes on to propose, watching television snooker, was one in which, at that time, she and I often engaged together. It is not, however, one that is directly connected to the prior agreement to go to the shop, in fact it is topically disconnected from that agreement. In effect, Amy is using the sequential position in which the parent has committed himself to one form of joint action as a favourable one in which to broach a new line of joint action.

At 2;5 and 3;1, although 'Shall we?' questions can be detached in the sense I have just outlined, they remain for the most part embedded in

Amy has agreed with her mother that she would like to go to the paper
shop with her father (see the early part of #4.8 for this discussion). She
gets down off her M's knee, and moves to stand close to F:

1	A:	I want to go: no::w

2	F:	You want to go: to the paper shop,

3	A:	Mm:,
4		(2.0)
5	A:	Are going now? ((looks at F))
6		(.6)
7	F:	Well we could go now

8	A:	No: jus:- in a minute ((moves around chair to face F))
9		(3.5)
10	A:	In a minute, ((quietly, smiling broadly both here and
11		subsequently))

12	F:	In a minute?
13		(.8)
14	A:	Shall we put ^{A}snooker o::n?

15	M:	((laughs))

16	F:	What'd she say? ((to M))

17	M:	Shall we put the snooker on,

18	F:	((laughs))

19	A:	Shall we do: i::t

Plate A

sequences in which the parent has initially agreed to engage in some form of joint action with the child. At 3;1, however, there is one case in which this no longer happens. Here, in #5.6, there appears to be no prior commitment to any form of joint action with the child either in the immediately preceding talk, which has been about Amy's imaginary friend, or at any earlier point on the recording. Indeed, it may be the absence of any such understanding that informs the laughter, at line 9, which accompanies the parental rejections of the child's **Shall we go upstairs**.

Because of the topic-initial nature of **Shall we go upstairs** the basis upon which the child might suppose this to be a line of action that may be compatible with what is currently happening is not available to us as analysts. It could be connected to the observable fact that both parents appear to have finished their meal, and that they are not engaged in any recognizable activity which could be construed as making them unavailable for the venture of going upstairs. In this regard it may be relevant that when Amy turns to get down from her chair, at lines 5–6, she is looking away from her mother. So she does not see her mother's subsequent act of picking up her teacup in order to drink from it; but to suppose that the absence of parental activity could inform Amy's suggestion about going upstairs is rank speculation. The chief point to note is that by 3;1 the use of 'Shall we?' designs by the child is no longer confined to those occasions on which there is some immediate sequential warrant available to her for supposing the parent to be willing to engage in some joint activity. As in #5.6, they are probably by then being used in ways which implicitly claim some other basis for expecting parental compliance.

'Shall we?' questions used to handle offences

For the most part in this chapter I have not had cause to look at the use of requests in offence sequences, sequences in which the child acts as though some offence is being, has been, or may about to be, committed, or may be about to be committed. At the age of 3;1, however, there are two instances in which 'Shall we?' questions are used by Amy in such circumstances, and as they contain particular features of interest they will now be examined. Two aspects are of special note. First, although the child says 'Shall we?' do something, it is the child herself who in fact does the something in question. Second, and unlike in any other cases that have been discussed so far, the child actually begins to do the action before completing her 'Shall we?' question. So, although these are constructed as questions the child does

5.6 3;1/VI 6:13

Amy, her mother and father (out of camera) are sitting at the table
towards the end of a meal. M and A are discussing A's imaginary friend:

1   A: She'll come to our house ^Aanother da::y

2   M: And what will she do when she comes

3   A: She'll pla:y with our toys? ((smiles and looks at M))

4   M: Mm::=

5   A: =Shall we go ^Bupstairs ((as she speaks she turns to get down
6   from her chair))

7   F: No=

8   M: =Not at the moment no ((M here raising her teacup for
9   drinking)) ((then M and F both laugh))

10   A: Well I'm goin upstairs anywa:y

11   F: Look well what about these vegetables here, ((pointing to
12   unfinished food in A's dish))

Plate A   Plate B

---

not wait for an answer, and although she gives the impression that both
parties are to be involved in the action, through her use of the inclusive
pronoun, only *she*, in fact, is initially involved.

   The first of these two occasions is presented in #5.7. Here the **it** in **shall**

5.7 3;1/III 14:13

Amy and her father are by the kitchen sink, having just completed some washing up. As the sequence begins A has her rh on a tap; water is coming out of one of the taps, washing away the remaining suds in the sink:

```
1   F:   Oka:y you watch it while the soap goes^A  ((then F picks up a
2        towel to dry his hands))
3                           (3.3)
4   F:   And I'll put thee: uh: ((A then leans forward and turns on a
5        tap with her lh; it jets loudly))

6   F:   Ooh not too ha:r┐d

7   A:                   └ Jus- jus- shall we^B (turn) it down┐a bit
8        ((during this turn A turns the tap jet down))

9   F:                                                       └ Ye::s
10       ((smiley voice, then laughs))

11  A:   That's too (     ) isn't it, ((smiling and brief turn to F and
12       away again in middle of the turn))

13  F:   Its too ha::rd, ((probably a correction of the untranscribed
14       word in A's prior turn))
```

Plate A

Plate B

---

we (turn) it down a bit, at line 7, refers to the water flowing out of the tap that the child is standing in front of. She has just turned the tap on further so as to speed up the process of washing away the soap-suds in the sink, so much so that the force of the water jet from the tap is noticeably increased.

When this occurs I immediately say **Ooh not too ha:rd**, at line 6, so that, irrespective of whether Amy finds the water pressure a problem, it is made clear to her that I find it a problem. In saying **Shall we (turn) it down a bit,** Amy is proposing a solution to this problem, and proposing it in such a way as to recognize that the matter is one of concern to the parent as well as herself. This is conveyed through her use of the interrogative form and the pronoun **we**; but these words are stated as she is actually moving to turn down the water. In this way they offer an account, an explanation, for the action she is undertaking. So, she is simultaneously recognizing that the problem is also one for the parent as well as for her, and drawing on this as a basis for putting a solution immediately into place.

In #5.8 the bare bones of what takes place are clear enough though the interactional details are more complex. The topic of the bear crops up in Amy's talk with her mother. In the course of this, at lines 2–4, Amy gets up and walks to where the bear is lying in a carry-cot on the floor, briefly addressing the bear as she does so, at line 6. On arriving at the carry-cot she takes hold of an official-looking document, which is leaning against the carry-cot, in her right hand. Clearly, if she is going to pick up the carry-cot, which she subsequently does, the document will need to be disturbed. After turning to look at me, quite close to her but currently operating the camera, she then lifts up the document, saying to me as she does so, at line 13, **Shall we pick 'i:s up**.

Whereas in #5.7 the existence of a problem was made explicit by the parent prior to the child's 'Shall we?' question, in #5.8 there is no suggestion of this. Nevertheless, the child acts as if a problem may exist, and that problem is clearly connected with the document leaning against the carry-cot. As soon as she first touches this document she looks towards me (lines 8–12), behind the camera, thus creating a first opportunity for me to comment on the question of what is to happen to it. So, in not just moving it herself, and in turning to me, Amy treats the moving of the document as not a matter that she can unilaterally decide, but as one which may require the involvement of another party. Just over a second elapses after she first looks towards me. In effect, I have been given an opportunity to offer guidance but, for whatever reason, have failed to do so. It is then that the child says **Shall we pick 'i:s up**.

In these ways Amy makes it clear that her co-interactant has an entitlement to be considered when it comes to relocating the document. She also continues to signal such an entitlement in a number of ways from this point onwards. The choice of **we** in **Shall we pick 'i:s up**, and the fact that she chooses an interrogative form at all are of obvious relevance here. In addition, the sustained gaze at her father, which accompanies these words, invites a reaction from him, a reaction that could either confirm the

5.8 3;1/VIII 35:01

Amy and her mother are talking in a quasi-pretend way about doing
things that are 'naughty'. M's first utterance below is related to this;
father is operating the camera:

1	M:	I think that that teddy down there's a bit naughty
2	A:	She isn't she:'s my little ba:bee::= ((A gets off her chair in
3		the later part of this turn and walks towards the bear, which
4		is in a carry-cot near the camera))
5	M:	=Oh:::
6	A:	Hello? (.) Wha:t's the matter: ((to the bear, in distinctive
7		intonations; by the end of this turn she is holding a
8		document which is leaning against the side of the carry-cot;
9		then she looks up at F))
10		(1.0)
11		((during this pause A looks^A at F while her hand holds the
12		document in its original position by the carry-cot))
13	A:	Shall we pick 'i:s up^B ((lifts the document as she says this,
14		but looks at F continuously))
15	F:	Ye:s just leave that on the chai:r ┌ because we'll need to- ((A
16		puts document down on chair │ during F's turn))
17	M:	└ Mm that's daddy's isn't it

((Amy then lifts up the carry-cot by its handles and carries it
and the bear to the other side of the room))

Plate A   Plate B

appropriateness of the action that she is taking, or otherwise; but the line of action proposed in the question is also in itself interesting, in at least two ways, for its bearing on the involvement of the parent. First, to say **Shall we pick 'i:s up** is to turn the current position of the document into an undesirable state of affairs. The only way it is undesirable from the child's point of view is that it is leaning against her carry-cot, so any shift in its positioning (e.g. to elsewhere on the floor) would act as a solution to her problem. The child, therefore, in selecting **up**, meaning 'up off the floor', is selecting a new position which is more than just compatible with her own interests; it is a position which, as is evident from her scrutiny of the parent's reaction, is specifically designed to be endorsable by the other party. The second feature of interest in **Shall we pick 'i:s up** is that the destination of the object is not specified (compare 'Shall we put this on the table?'), nor is it initially prefigured in the movement of the child's hand when she first moves the object. These, then, constitute yet further ways in which the other party is being permitted by the child to have an involvement in the movement of the object.

An important common feature of extracts 5.7 and 5.8 is the fact that the problem that the child's 'Shall we?' turn addresses is a problem for *both* parties to the interaction. Even though the parent does not say as much in #5.8 we have seen that there are many ways in which the child tells us, and her father, that, for her, this is the case. Her **Shall we pick 'i:s up** is anticipating the problematic nature of engaging in some next line of action, and in displaying this anticipation she indicates her awareness that that which might be a problem for someone else is, by virtue of this, also a problem for her. In each case the 'Shall we?' turn proposes a solution to the problem that both parties share, and it is, presumably, this fact, the fact that the child is trying to assist the other party as well as herself, which makes her feel entitled to enact the solution as well as to present it verbally, in an interrogative fashion. It is in these specific kinds of circumstance, then, that we find interrogative forms which have the unusual features that I initially identified – use of the inclusive 'we' when the child is in fact the agent, and the performance of the proposed act prior to recipient being given a chance to give a response.[5]

---

[5] I have already noted in connection with #5.8 that a case can be made that the child, at lines 10–12, is giving me an opportunity to react prior to embarking on her 'Shall we?' question. That is an important feature of this extract, though, as I say here in the text, it remains the case that, when she is enacting the 'Shall we?' question, she is moving the document prior to giving me the opportunity to provide an answer. In these various ways which I am describing here Amy is, of course, documenting her analysis that the document belongs to me in a way that it does not belong to her. For an interesting discussion of ways in which these considerations can enter into how people move objects, and suchlike, see Goffman (1971: chapter 4).

To complete this discussion of 'Shall we?' questions which deal with actual or potential problems I want to compare them with a further question design that is certainly available to the child by 2;9, namely 'Shall I?' questions. In the main, the latter work in quite different ways to the 'Shall we?' questions that have occupied us in the latter half of this chapter. Rather than furthering some joint course of action, they are largely constructed as offers of assistance to the other party. In an instance at age 2;9, for example, Amy's mother returns to the living room, carrying with her a dryer that she has been using to dry her own hair. On seeing this Amy says, in topic initial position, **Shall I put it away or no:t**. Here there seems to be no basis for the child to suppose that her mother has a problem in putting the hair dryer away; but some offers do appear to orient to the existence of such problems. Their usage, therefore, takes place in sequences which have certain parallels to those I have just been discussing – instances in which 'Shall we?' constructions were employed to solve problems. What is interesting, however, is that the problem configuration in which such 'Shall I?' questions are used is different in important ways to that in which 'Shall we?' questions occurred. Take #5.9 as an example. Here Amy is engaged with me in doing some washing up. The specific local events which lead her to say **Shall I get it**, at line 13, appear to hinge on my having difficulty in cleaning a spoon. Note especially how I continue to rub the spoon immediately after saying, at line 9, **I think its off now**, so that Amy has a continuing basis for identifying me as having a problem here. The action that she clearly, though not explicitly, is proposing to do – scrubbing it with her pad – is designed to achieve the object of my endeavours: cleaning the spoon. The point to note here, in contrast with extracts 5.7 and 5.8, is that the problem she is proposing to assist with is principally *my* problem, not her problem. There is no sense with any of these 'Shall I?' questions, where they do in some way overtly concern themselves with a problem, that the problem is a problem for the child. It is because of this that they come across as offers of assistance rather than proposals for solving a problem that has arisen for both the child and her recipient. When employing 'Shall I?' and 'Shall we?' questions, therefore, there is every sense that, for the child, a key interactional axis for their differentiation is the matter of *whose* problem the problem is. This, in turn, suggests that such interactional parameters both inform, and are articulated through, the emergence of these new 'request' forms.

5.9 3;1/III 6:24

Amy and her father are both doing the washing up, each cleaning
separate objects. A looks towards the object that F has been scrubbing at
for some time; she does not look at F at all in this sequence:

1   A: What you do:ing[A]

2   F: Trying to scrape that (.) dirt off the:re ((F continues scraping
3   the object))
4   (.9)
5   A: Where,
6   (1.0)
7   F: Just the:re,
8   (.9)
9   F: I think its off now ((continues scraping at the object after the
10   end of this turn))

11 A: ((moves her rh, holding her brush, towards F's object, then
12   speaks))
13   [B]Shall I get it,=

14 F: =Ye:::s that's a good idea give it a hard rub with that
15 A: ((A starts rubbing the object))

Plate A   Plate B

The overall pattern of request development

In the final section of this chapter I want to contextualize the principal
findings that I have been presenting in the chapter as a whole by discussing
them in the light of trends which have been identified in previous chapters.

We have seen that in the first half of her third year of life (2;1 – 2;5), this child has the capacity to take into account, through her request selection, the presence or absence of relevant understandings. In general, where an understanding exists which leads the child to expect that a proposed course of action is compatible with that envisaged by her recipient, then she selects the (non-offence) imperative form to encode such a request. At this age, then, the expectability of action is a major interactional pre-occupation of the child. Also consistent with this is the fact that such a concern is also made manifest in other ways at this time, ways which I have not as yet directly touched on. If we look at the less standardized sentence designs that the child uses to enact her request-related business at these ages, what we find is a flowering of verb forms and other devices which place a special emphasis on social obligation. Here is a sample:

2;1
Mummy have to get the medicine now
Mummy supposed eat it
I'll have to get it
I supposed t'have it
2;3
Get- better eat your tea-cake now
Blue bear you musn't do that
Don't lick that knife daddy (.) 'pposed to cut it up
I had'te hold it (i.e. 'I have to hold it')

The bindingness of social and sequential obligations appears to be a major motif for this child during the first half of her third year of life, and in attending to it she, and other children of this age (Gerhardt 1991; Stephany 1986), have cause to develop a variety of constructions such as those illustrated above.

At this same time, 2;1 – 2;5, we have seen that the child can also employ questions in organizing the involvement of the other party in lines of action which she is about to undertake. Prior to 2;5 these questions are almost exclusively concerned with the preferences and desires of her co-interactant. The child can make use of this knowledge in a number of ways. For example, if the parent is not interested in becoming involved then the child may decide not to engage in the activity. If the parent *is* interested then we have seen that the child can draw on this knowledge to instruct the parent as regards what should be done next, especially through her use of non-offence imperatives (as in, for example, extracts 3.2 and 3.3).

There are, however, important differences between these early questions and the new question forms such as 'Shall we'? and 'Can you?' that emerge from about the middle of this year. The child is using these new question forms so as to seek parental agreement to some line of action upon which she wishes to embark, or one which is directly in her own interests. The parent's preference is now officially taken as being of relevance not just to the parent's conduct but also to that of the child. The question types that the child comes to use with regard to requesting have one generic property: they are all yes/no interrogatives; which is to say that they all explicitly seek the alignment of the recipient towards the course of action being proposed. In seeking such an alignment the absence of such information is treated as a relevant absence in the circumstances. The child does not change over willy-nilly from non-interrogative forms to interrogative forms at this time. She continues to use non-interrogative forms such as the imperative when there is an appropriate sequential warrant. In using yes/no interrogatives she is pro-actively seeking a recipient warrant for engaging in some course of action where no such warrant exists. The important questions, then, concern how, when and why these alterations in the nature of interactional understandings take place.

In this chapter I have been exploring this process for a limited number of the interrogative request forms that the child comes to adopt. One important general conclusion is that the interactional circumstances are not all of a piece in this respect: that the different interrogative forms are likely to have an affinity with, and thus a capacity to differentiate, distinctive types of circumstance. This has two implications. First, any account of the considerations which enter into the child's orientation to the absence of warrants will need to be couched in terms of her grasp of specific interactional configurations. Second, the child's adoption of such interrogatives is likely to display certain forms of developmental unevenness. If the adoption of any one form is designed to handle a particular type of interactional configuration, then this does not necessarily imply that the child will find a use for other interrogative types in other types of sequence at the same time. Indeed, there is a suggestion of this sort of developmental unevenness within these data. 'Shall we?' constructions, for example, appear to be in wider use at an earlier time – 2;5 – than 'Can you?' constructions. The adoption of all forms of interrogative request does not appear to take place at the same developmental time, a fact which also argues against any explanation of their use pattern in terms of general syntactic rules which may be common to the construction of such yes/no questions.

The interactional configuration most often associated with the earliest 'Shall we?' questions is one in which the child's recipient has just committed him/herself to some form of joint activity with the child. In then employing a 'Shall we?' question the child acknowledges both the *joint* nature of the undertaking and the entitlement of her recipient to further consultation with regard to the subsequent activity. Prior to the age at which such questions first appear – 2;5 – the child has been able to broach with her parents the possibility of their engaging with her in joint action. What is new at 2;5 is the capacity to encode within the subsequent sequence the continuation of this type of understanding about the joint nature of the undertaking. This emerging sensitivity as to who any line of action belongs to, who has entitlements to be considered in relation to it, was also brought out in other ways within the discussion of 'Shall we?' questions. For example, it turned out to be a key parameter differentiating the child's use of 'Shall we?' and 'Shall I?' Whereas 'Shall I?' questions are offers of assistance with problems which are not characteristically problems for the child, in those 'Shall we?' forms that were constructed as solutions to problems there were strong empirical grounds for supposing that the child was treating the problem as being one for both herself *and* her recipient. In this connection it is also worth noting that from 2;5 onwards we also find other utterance designs which incorporate inclusive pronouns. The most obvious request form which falls in this category is 'Let's do x.' Whereas 'Let me do x' is in use from 2;3 onwards, 'Let's do x' is first used at 2;9. This also suggests, therefore, that at around the middle of her third year the child is developing some sensitivity regarding to whom a line of action belongs.

There are good grounds, then, for supposing that at, or shortly after, 2;5 there is a shift in the child's capacity to encode understandings which differentiate the nature of the involvement of the child's recipient in any course of on-going action. Specifically, through 'Shall we?' questions, and possibly through other linguistic designs such as 'Let's do x', the child can now encode new forms of sequential understanding, ones in which both parties to the interaction are taken to have a joint stake in any particular course of action.

The interactional concerns that the child has when producing 'Can you?' questions are ones which she has also had in the months preceding the adoption of this question form. She wants the parent to do something for her, to assist her in some way. In previous months this type of concern is usually made evident through her use of either imperative forms or 'You do x' designs, and in particular through ones which incorporate the words 'for me'. And in these cases there is also no suggestion that the child has available to her a sequential warrant, an understanding, which offers some assurance of parental compliance. This contrasts with the circumstances in which the child often uses other imperatives at these earlier ages, circumstances in which such a warrant normally exists. I have tried to show that the decline in self-interested imperatives is specifically linked to the emergence of 'Can you?' request forms, that 'Can you?' forms come to be one way in which the child handles the circumstances in which she previously deployed certain imperative request formats. If this is so then it seems to me that what prompts the child's use of 'Can you?' forms is a recognition that in the circumstances no warrant is available to her. The seeds of this new request form, therefore, lie partly in the child's earlier experience in taking account of understandings which orient to the preferences of the other party, and partly in the child's earlier proven capacity to enquire into the preferences of her recipient. The 'Can you?' request co-ordinates such skills and considerations with respect to lines of action that are directly in the domain of the child's interest. In doing this it marks a sensitivity as to *who* the beneficiary of the request is to be, whereas in 'Shall we?' questions what is being interactionally marked is *who* any line of action belongs to.

At this stage it is necessary to make certain points about the relation between these request forms and the circumstances with which I have frequently described them as having an affinity. By using rather fuzzy terms like affinity I am trying to avoid giving the impression that the relationship between these request forms and the circumstances in which they occur is a deterministic one. Where, for example, the child finds herself in a contingency in which she wants the parent to do something for her, but one in which she has no warrant for expecting parental compliance, I am not wanting to argue that the 'Can you?' request, by the age of say 3;1, is the only technique available to the child. Similarly, where the child has a commitment from the parent to engage in some form of next action I am not wanting to say that the only way, at the same age, that the child will then proceed with a subsequent request will be to employ a 'Shall we?' request. Empirically, such propositions would simply not be true. One reason for this is that the child always has choice of action within any given interactional contingency: so, for example, when a parent agrees to some form of joint action the child may then, at 3;1, tell the parent what to do through an imperative rather than employ a 'Shall we?' request. More fundamentally, however, this way of thinking about the relationship between the request form and the circumstances in which it occurs is misleading. Instead of thinking about these two facets as separate it is important to recognize that in key ways they are interconnected, that they have a reflexive relationship with each other. So there is also a sense in which the type of request form used instructs us to identify the circumstances as being of a particular kind whilst these same circumstances inform the nature of the request form itself. It is for this reason, as I have said earlier in the chapter, that the employment of particular request forms has the capacity to transform their contexts of occurrence in particular ways. Indeed this point is especially pertinent to the analysis of requests which, when functioning as sequence initial types of interactional object, eventually come to have the capacity to entail particular versions of the nature of the unstated context to which they relate.[6]

All this gives a particular kind of status to the findings I have reported. Instead of dealing with request forms and the circumstances in which they occur I am really dealing with nexuses containing both aspects. I have been trying to identify systematic properties of these nexuses, ways in which they both contrast and connect with each other and with those which occur at earlier or later dates. It is important, however, that these nexuses have distinctive types of utterance design at their core, new standardized types of questions such as 'Can you do x?' and 'Shall we do x?' As far as I can tell all children develop such variable and standardized questions at around this time. Where such systematic linguistic differentiation takes place there is clearly a need to inspect the practical interests that these serve within the child's life-world. In this respect the interactional parameters of these nexuses provide a specification as to the nature of these practical interests. These parameters appear to revolve around forms of sequential understanding which become elaborated during the course of the child's third year. My analysis of these nexuses has by no means been exhaustive. Several new request forms, notably 'Can I do x?', have not yet been subjected to analysis along these lines. But I hope to have provided a basis for taking seriously the possibility that the child's new request forms

---

[6] By 'context' here I am especially referring to states of knowledge and belief that can be drawn into play through the construction of requests. So, when, for example, a four-year-old makes a sequence initial request by saying 'Some day please could I just go over to Martin's house for just one night?', there are obvious features of the request's design which suggest that, for the child making it, a favour is being asked, and that her recipient is not being viewed as potentially well disposed towards what is being asked for.

have systematic and distinctive connections with forms of sequential understanding. They have, to misuse Goffman's term, the capacity to put interaction on different 'footings', and it seems likely that it is this capacity to encode new forms of human sensibility which make them, or their equivalents in other languages, both necessary and ubiquitous.

6

General skills involved in early requesting

This chapter is divided into three sections. In the first two I shall be considering research from social linguistics and developmental psychology respectively, research which has been influential in shaping the picture that has been formed of the skills of the two-year-old. The aim here is to set the main findings which I have reported into the context of these two traditions, so as to bring out relevant consistencies and tensions. In the third section of the chapter a summary is presented of the overall argument emerging from this book, focusing especially on its implications for connecting the study of cognitive and interactional processes.

Social linguistics and politeness

Over the last 20 years there has been a steady accumulation of information about the ways in which young children make requests. In chapter 2 I described the main developmental changes in this regard between the ages of 12 and 24 months. Here the focus will mainly be on the period immediately after 24 months, and in particular on research which has brought out ways in which the child's choice of some particular way of requesting is sensitive to social considerations. By 24 months all normal children are capable of producing requests in a variety of linguistic guises. We have seen within my own data, for example, that by then Amy standardly made use of imperative constructions, ones framed with the verb 'want' and ones framed with 'like'. In addition, she was also capable of using a variety of less standardized constructions with request-like intent. During the course of her third year she also acquires further types of request construction, notably formal interrogatives such as 'Can I/you?'. In approaching the matter of how the child makes a request selection from the alternatives available to her at these ages the focus within the social linguistic tradition has been on the ways in which such selections are influenced by forms of social knowledge that the child either has acquired or is in the process of acquiring.

Research which has explored these themes has principally been concerned with measuring the frequencies with which the child draws on the various request designs in her repertoire in different types of 'context'. The parameter of context that has been most frequently explored is variation in the person to whom the child is making her request. For example, several studies have shown that the child is more likely to use imperatives when speaking to her mother than to her father (Becker 1982) and that she is even more likely to use imperatives when speaking to a younger brother or sister (Dunn and Kendrick 1982), while less likely to use them to an adult who is not a member of her immediate family. There are a number of recognized difficulties in interpreting the significance of these statistical variations. Becker, for example, notes that the differences in request usage to mothers and fathers may be a function of the child being involved with different activities with each parent (1982:11). Ervin-Tripp and Gordon (1986:70–1) make a similar point when attempting to explain the differential use of imperatives to mothers and fathers. For them imperatives are associated with routine activities, their more frequent use to mothers being a function of the higher incidence of co-operative activity in mother–child pairs. So for them this pattern is a product not so much of the fact that the child is using different ways of speaking to her mother or father as it is of the typical circumstances surrounding the nature of this talk. The question then arises as to what makes circumstances more or less conducive to becoming co-operative and non-contentious. Research in this tradition postulates that a variety of considerations may bear on this: for example, matters of ownership and intrusiveness (e.g. which objects belong to whom), local rights and entitlements (e.g. whether the child is normally allowed to do this thing), politeness, the child's estimation of the difficulty for her recipient of granting the request, and so on (Becker 1982; Ervin-Tripp and Gordon 1986). Request selection is, therefore, principally viewed as a site to which the child brings different kinds of social knowledge. Quite how this knowledge is drawn on by the child in specific instances is usually not addressed within this approach, but showing that the child may be capable of taking such knowledge into account, as well as suggesting developmental patterns in this regard, is one of the principal achievements of this body of work.

The research that I have reported in this book has focused in more detail than is normal on the circumstances in which requests are actually made. The main potential tension between my arguments and the social linguistic tradition concerns the role and status of general trans-contextual knowledge that the child may bring with her to any social encounter. Within social linguistic research, special prominence is given to this kind of knowledge, but in earlier chapters I have presented various arguments which suggest that, for the child of this age, it is of weaker significance than the distinctive local configurations of knowledge which bear on any request sequence. This kind of point is most readily documented in my earlier discussions of the notion of *scripts* (e.g. pp. 37–8, 90). This notion is generally used to describe those forms of knowledge which the child has derived from her past experience, an awareness of which can be conveyed by her in a variety of ways on specific occasions. Repeatedly, however, I have identified difficulties in accounting for what takes place on such occasions in these terms. It can be shown, for example, that where the child is making requests for exactly the same thing (e.g. to get down from the table) to exactly the same person then the request can, nevertheless, be made in radically different linguistic guises on different occasions. To appeal to scripts, or other forms of trans-contextual stored knowledge, therefore, leaves undiscriminated the bases on which the child selects one way of making her request rather than another. Similar points have been made on a number of other occasions in this book. When discussing the distressing incidents in chapter 4, for example, I noted that they often appeared to be about matters which might be construed as 'routines': everyday caretaking issues like getting the child dressed. These are events to which the child might be expected to bring general trans-contextual knowledge, and the forms of deviance identified by the child within them might be expected to hinge around the infraction of expectations formed on the basis of this knowledge. When these incidents were examined, however, it was not this kind of knowledge which proved to be integral to their workings. Instead, what turn out to be of key importance, both in these and many other types of sequence, are locally operative understandings. It has been a relatively straightforward task to identify these understandings. Fortunately, they are not mysterious kinds of internal events which require the analyst to engage in complex inferential gymnastics. They are publicly oriented to within the explicit details of prior interaction, and it is the infraction of these local and public expectations, not the infraction of general caretaking patterns, which forms a critical basis for the occurrence of the child's distressed reactions. Such local understandings are also entangled in many other aspects of the child's request behaviour. It has been shown in chapter 3, for example, that the use of imperatives to the parent by the child, even when as young as two years of age, is sensitive to their existence. Baldly, the child's selection of imperatives has a particular affinity with sequences in which she has a basis, a warrant, for telling the parent what to do, a warrant that arises out of events in the recent past.

The kind of account I have offered is, nevertheless, not incompatible with many of the empirical findings within the social linguistic tradition of work. Take, for example, observations which have been made about one four-year-old child's use of imperatives by Gordon and Ervin-Tripp (1984). They note that the use of imperatives by this child was canonically associated with 'shared or routine activities' and occasions on which the child was not concerned necessarily to obtain something for himself. They also note that reasons and justifications rarely accompanied such imperatives. If, as I have argued, the child's use of imperatives is associated with interactional circumstances in which the child often has a basis for supposing his or her recipient to be willing to engage in the action proposed in the request, and indeed is to become even more closely associated with such circumstances between the ages of two and three (see chapter 5), then these kinds of finding seem perfectly commensurate with my arguments. For example, in the early part of chapter 3 we found that, where the child knows the preferences of the parent, she uses imperatives to instruct the parent as to how to implement his/her line of action. If the child's orientation to local understandings yields behaviour of this kind then one might expect imperatives to be more frequently used in circumstances where the child does not necessarily have a direct self-interest in the course of action in question. In fact, Gordon and Ervin-Tripp come close to foreshadowing my argument in their more general suggestion that when the child employs imperatives he expects his recipient to be compliant. In a sense, what I have been examining in this book is the variety of bases which can inform the nature of the expectation which the child holds. What my analysis reveals is the significance of the local sequential context in which the imperative is embedded. It is because the child becomes capable of identifying and drawing on local understandings – skills that seem to be in place by two years of age – that she can recognize the uncontentiousness of that which, through her use of imperatives, she is requiring of the other party.

What seems to be clear from my account is that there is a kind of symmetry for the young child, aged about 2, between the procedures available to her for accessing social knowledge and the kind of knowledge she thereby makes use of. From the age of about 18 months she is capable of articulating, and operating with, joint local understandings, most notably through the negative constructions discussed in chapter 2 (see p. 42). By the age of 2, she is capable of drawing on, acting in the light of, prior local sequential understandings. The capacity to make use of these understandings is the mechanism through which it is possible for the child to gain some order of access to the particular shape of the culture to which she is exposed, a culture which may, of course, vary along a number of parameters such as type of family and type of society. Participating in such processes permits the child to develop, at some level, a script-like knowledge of the ways in which her world works, as is evidenced from studies of children's memory at this age (Bauer and Thal 1990; Nelson 1993). But I would argue that it is misleading to see the child's request behaviour as in any way a simple reflex of this knowledge, of what she knows about the social routines and typical happenings in her world. Her on-line behaviour continues to be sensitive to the nature of the local understandings that pertain to any given occasion. It is the specifics of these to which the child appears to accord principal significance because it is these which continue to have a direct bearing on her request selection and other facets of her behaviour.

There are, then, both potential continuities between the results which I have reported and those of the social linguists, and ways in which my own analyses place greater emphasis on the detailed workings of interactional processes. Grounding an analysis in these details is also important in other ways. I take it that social linguistic research, like research in the tradition of conversation analysis, is, at some level, concerned to identify not just contextual correlations with conduct but aspects of the context to which the people we are studying, children in this case, can be shown to be attending in some way. Paradoxically, when we claim that children can recognize the salience, through their request selection, of a variety of contextual features such as age, status, familiarity and the like, then, when we approach the analysis of any particular instance, we have too much in the way of potential explanation rather than too little. We face the task of demonstrating which, if any, of these possible 'influences' is operative, in what way and how such a recognition is displayed by the child. These issues and ways of dealing with them are central and foundational matters for conversation analysis in a way in which they are not for the social linguists, for whom they remain largely unaddressed (Schegloff 1991a). The conversation analytic solution is to focus, *in the first place*, on identifying the kinds of procedure and knowledge which are being displayed by the people being studied as having some significance for them, on locating how the particular sense of any given scene is brought into being by the participants. Getting to grips with interactional detail and trying to discover, and show, the order of event that has significance for the child, therefore, has been a central aim of the approach that I have adopted.

The picture of social linguistics that I have painted so far has, if only implicitly, pushed into prominence those of its representatives with a social cognition and correlational inclination rather than the growing body of work which has examined the discourse of request sequences in more direct ways. A number of theoretical approaches, such as speech act analysis and discourse analysis as well as conversation analysis have shaped this latter work. I do not intend here to compare or adjudicate on the merits of these approaches.[1] Importantly, the work, as a whole, has drawn attention to parameters of interaction within request sequences which my own analysis has left largely unaddressed – for example, how the child attends to the involvements of her recipient and gains their attention, ways in which the child manages breakdowns of understanding within such sequences and the various techniques which the child can use to deal with actual or anticipated opposition to what she wants (see Garvey 1984: chapters 4 and 5; McTear 1985: chapter 5). In the remainder of this section I do, however, want to touch on one facet that this and other writing on requests has addressed, namely 'politeness', as it connects with some of the arguments which I have been putting forward, especially those in chapter 5.

Requests between the ages of two and three have a special interest in that they are one of a small number of sites within talk where, across cultures, the child is sometimes explicitly coached in how to say something (Gleason, Perlmann and Greif 1984; Snow, Perlmann, Gleason and Hooshyer 1990). Parents in most cultures appear to target requests in particular when it comes to indicating that the way in which the child has said something is inadequate. In English-speaking countries there is every suggestion that the word 'please' has a special significance in this regard. Through the addition of this single word, for example, a request can be converted from one that is deemed deficient by the parent into one that is considered adequate. Requests are, then, one domain in which the child is encouraged to exercise a self-monitoring of her talk for the adequacy of the lexical format chosen to do the business in hand.

---

[1] For overviews of the merits of these various approaches see Coulthard (1977), Levinson (1983: chapter 6) and Drew and Heritage (1992).

There are a number of possible investigative angles that one can take with regard to the tuitional processes engaged in by parents. For example, for such tuition to work the child must have mastered the repair procedures which are drawn on by the parent subsequent to the child producing a request deemed deficient. In English, at this age, these procedures revolve around the production of turns like 'Pardon?', 'What do you say?' and 'Get me a drink what?' – turns designed to have the child then produce an improvement on the original way in which the request was expressed. The success of these parental interventions is therefore – like much of the child's language learning – predicated on the child's more general grasp of the workings of a repair apparatus.[2] Another angle is to examine the sequences in which such tuition occurs in order to identify further orderly properties which they possess. For example, one such property is that within request sequences this kind of tuition takes place in circumstances in which the parent is going on to grant the request, not to reject it (Wootton 1984). In this respect there are similarities between this and other tuitional activity in which parents engage, in that parents appear to choose positive environments in which to engage in such work. For example, when they make offers to children at about 2 years of age they may ask the child to say 'thankyou' where the child accepts that which is offered, but not 'no thankyou' where the child rejects the offered item. In another type of sequence, one in which the parent is trying to teach her child how to stand up for herself in disputes, Miller has made similar observations about children aged 1;7 – 2;4 and their parents (P. Miller 1986). Miller describes how parents attempt to give this coaching via what she calls 'teasing', by developing exaggerated and mock confrontational lines of dispute with their children. An important feature of this is that the parent does not graft this teasing onto an already established state of genuine mutual acrimony, onto a sequence in which some actual dispute has already emerged between the parent and the child. Instead, the parent adopts a teasing mode (through things like sing-song intonation and emphatic stress) as her *initial* mode of involvement in such sequences. Here again, even where the object of instruction is conflict management skills, the child is being taught about such things in an environment which minimizes any dissension between the parent and child. This is the kind of interactional site which appears to have special attractions for instructional work at this age.

While these angles seem to me important, in that they point to ways in

---

[2] For an overview of research relating to repair, clarification and the like see McTear (1985:164–200). Tarplee (1993) develops this line of investigation in highly original ways.

which the young child's behaviour is lodged within sequences which may have analysably generic properties, they remain ones which are less stressed within the literature on 'please' and politeness. In one sense there are good reasons for this. To describe the properties of sequences in which, say, 'please' is solicited, and their resemblances to other types of sequence, as I have done above, still leaves unanalysed the nature of what it is that the parent is trying to get the child to recognize through being required to say 'please'. Rather than trying, however, to adduce evidence which might have a bearing on this question, research in the social linguistic tradition has tended to treat 'please' as one of a number of markers of 'politeness'. As children, in experimental or quasi-experimental settings, appear to show some level of agreement on which request forms are more polite than others, and as they tend to switch request forms in similar ways when asked in such circumstances to make requests more nicely, it is taken, therefore, that the dimension of politeness is germane to understanding their on-going conduct. It is often claimed on these grounds, for example, that interrogative requests are markers of politeness, and what often seems to be implied is that politeness is a type of mental yardstick that is available to the child when making her request selection.

An appeal to politeness as, say, being linked with the use of interrogatives has obvious explanatory weaknesses. If the child has grasped the notion of politeness then why is it not the case that she is always polite? Why do we continue to find variation in request selection once she is capable of using interrogative constructions? There is clearly a danger of answering this type of question in a circular way: interrogative requests, which are markers of politeness, are selected because the child wants to be more polite, and not selected when she does not. The solution to this type of problem in general theories of politeness, such as the one proposed by Brown and Levinson (1978, 1987), is to make specific predictions and connections between types of interactional circumstance and the selection of utterance designs which are more, or less, polite. These theories, however, drawn up with regard to patterns of talk among adults, cannot be simply extrapolated backwards into childhood as some of their crucial parameters are susceptible to developmental change (Ervin-Tripp and Gordon 1986:71). For example, in Brown and Levinson's theory it is posited that request selection is connected to the speaker's estimation of the kind of imposition which the request places on the request recipient, what they call 'negative face': expressed crudely, the greater the imposition the more indirect the request. In developmental terms, therefore, it is only when the child develops the capacity to make inferences about the imposition being placed on another that the kinds of consideration addressed by Brown and Levinson can come to shape request selection. However, it is generally agreed, within psychological research on young children, that children under the age of three have rather little capacity to make such inferences (see next section of this chapter). Indeed, even among four-year-olds there is little, if any, overt sign of children displaying attention to the burden which their request may be placing on their recipient (Wootton 1981a). So it is not at all clear what bearing a theory of politeness formulated along Brown and Levinson's lines can have on the emergence or use of different forms of request, some of which are interrogatives, by the child under the age of three. Such problems with the notion of 'politeness' could be approached through the construction of a developmental theory of politeness, though to my knowledge no such theory has been proposed.

An alternative tack, in line with some other recent work (Gerhardt 1990, 1991),[3] is to examine in detail the ways in which different types of utterance design are embedded in local interactional configurations, in order to identify what, for the child, are the salient features being taken into account through her use of, say, interrogatives. This is the tack that I took in chapter 4 where I examined Amy's use of the interrogatives 'Can you do x?' and 'Shall we do x?' There I offered various empirical grounds for believing that 'Can you?' requests were used, after about the age of 2;5, to broach matters which had earlier been broached through a sub-class of imperative constructions. In effect, the adoption of this interrogative is a solution to the child's recognition that, when making a certain type of request, there is no sequential basis available to her for expecting parental compliance. The capacity to make such a recognition seems to me an outcome of the child's prior experience, from about 2 years of age onwards, in taking these types of understanding into account when making selections between her available request forms. 'Shall we do x?'

---

[3] Gerhardt's important papers contain good overviews of work in both linguistics and psycholinguistics which relates to the modal-catenative forms 'hafta', 'needta' and 'wanna'. In addition, her 1990 paper explores the various discourse functions which 'hafta' constructions can perform in different sequential positions within the talk of two three-year-olds; and her 1991 paper, using the same corpus, attempts to plot the distinctive semantic meanings of all three of these modals. Her procedures of analysis are similar to those within conversation analysis in that they pivot around detailed inspection of the evidence contained within the sequences in which these forms occur. In particular, especially with regard to 'hafta' constructions, she develops sophisticated ways of showing how their use is sensitive to what has taken place within a sequence whilst also having the potential for being context-creating.

questions seemed to be quite different in character. They hinge around understandings regarding to whom some line of action belongs, who has a stake in what is to take place. Their adoption seems to be bound up with their capacity to encode such considerations. In general, therefore, it seems likely that it will be possible to identify particular interactional configurations which have distinctive associations with different types of interrogative request. I have argued that it is the capacity of these interrogatives to display a sensitivity to these considerations which is germane to their adoption by the child.

The aegis of 'politeness' potentially draws our attention to a wide range of matters within parent–child interaction, matters which can be investigated in a variety of ways. There seems little doubt that the child is being encouraged to pay special attention to the words she uses when making a request. The manner in which this is done and the skills required of the child in accommodating such a concern on the part of the parent seem appropriate subjects for interactional study. Social linguists seem keen to infer from the existence of such processes that a broader range of child actions, and for that matter actions of adults, can be accounted for by shared social knowledge about politeness, thought of in a more general sense. A focus on the nature of this shared knowledge, both in work on children and adults, has underplayed the variation in request use *within* our interactions with particular people in particular settings. Careful examination of such variation suggests that the linguistic selections used to make requests attend to, and have systematic connections with, interactional considerations. It is these considerations which are likely to form the core axes around which young children's request differentiation takes place, and it seems to me that a specification of these considerations and the procedures involved in taking them into account offers a more likely route towards identifying the ways in which the request behaviour of children is socially organized.

The cognitivist tradition

By the 'cognitivist tradition' I mean to refer to research, mainly carried out by psychologists, which has viewed developmental alteration in the child's behaviour principally as a function of changes in underlying thought processes. The focus within this perspective is on the description of these processes and on the mechanisms which bring about changes in their nature. The foundational work here is, of course, that reported in the writings of

Piaget and his co-workers. Even though there is increasing doubt as to whether there are *general* stages of development of the kind postulated by Piaget – stages which cut across the child's grasp of different types of knowledge – nevertheless within particular domains there remains a good deal of evidence for stage-like accomplishments (see Karmiloff-Smith 1992 for a recent overview). What remains especially influential regarding Piaget's legacy is his constructivist approach to the child's development of knowledge: action at any one time is always a function of the cognitive procedures which the child brings to that action, though it is in the course of engaging in action that the potential is created for those procedures to be altered. Although there is some division within the tradition over what is hard-wired from the start within the child, there is agreement, I think, that the object for study is the unfolding of cognitive procedures; in practice, this involves paying special attention to the continuities and discontinuities which pertain between the cognitive procedures which are to be found at different ages in the child's life.

For my purposes here, what is of special interest is what this cognitivist tradition has made of developments within the period that has been my concern within this book, about 18 months to 36 months of age. By comparison with the rest of his work Piaget has rather little to say about this period, but what he does say has been of some significance. In particular, he suggests that the onset of pretence and deferred forms of imitation, at around 18 months, marks the emergence of a capacity to work with true mental representations of objects and actions. When, for example, the child acts as though a banana were a telephone, which she may do at any time from about 18 months onwards, she knows that it is not really a telephone, but at the same time she can act as though it were. In Leslie's terms (1987) she has learned to 'decouple' the real status of objects and events from other, symbolically based, ways in which those events and objects can be construed. Therefore, within the cognitivist tradition, as articulated by both Piaget and later researchers, the emergence of skills in processing symbolic information, at or around 18 months, is taken as a major benchmark in children's development.

Within more recent cognitivist research attention has focused rather heavily on certain transitions which take place shortly after the child is about three years old. This research into what is often called the child's 'theory of mind' has, as this phrase suggests, investigated when the child recognizes that other people have minds and what she makes of how other people's minds work. One well-known discovery that researchers in this tradition have made about four-year-olds is that they can understand that someone's behaviour can be based on a false belief. Suppose a child leaves a sweet in a basket and then leaves the room. Another child moves the sweet to a drawer in the first child's absence. The first child returns. Most four-year-olds who have witnessed such a train of events acted out in doll play, when asked where the first child will look for her sweet, will say that she will look in the basket. That is to say they will recognize that the child can be operating with a belief that they know not to be true. Three-year-olds, especially younger three-year-olds, are likely to say that the child will look in the drawer. Such findings as these suggest to many that after the age of three there are major alterations in the child's information-processing capacities (see for example, Astington, Harris and Olson 1988).

Explanations of the emergence of these skills tend to focus on their cognitive prerequisites. In the case of false beliefs, for example, while there is no unanimity among psychologists as to the nature of the postulated cognitive procedures which differentiate the behaviour of three- and four-year-olds on the kind of task that I have just described, nevertheless the *type* of answer being put forward is clear enough. Either it is held that the four-year-old is now co-ordinating her capacity to take account of other people's beliefs with other schemata that she holds concerning how beliefs can arise, or it is thought that it is only at four years of age that the child can represent to herself the representing relationship that may exist between a belief and circumstances relevant to that belief (see Olson and Campbell 1993:21). Either view, in one way or another, seeks to explain the four-year-old's behaviour in terms of a transformation of the child's internal cognitive processing procedures. What usually remains weakly specified in such accounts are the processes which propel the child from one stage of development to the next. Here, if only implicitly, most writers rely on processes akin to those of accommodation and assimilation which figured in Piaget's thinking about such matters. The child's thinking develops new forms of accommodation in the context of her practical action because these are necessary for her to grasp the realities of the ways in which the world actually works. In this connection, Piaget himself laid conceptual emphasis on disagreement processes, ways in which, in social interaction, it becomes clear to the child that the understandings which she forms are not necessarily the only, or the correct, interpretations of events; but within this tradition these processes remain largely unexplored empirically.

In chapter 3 I touched on ways in which the kind of account I have been offering relates to one branch of cognitivist research, namely that on autism (pp. 91–3). This is a disorder on which this type of research has shed much light in recent years. For example, autistic children appear to have syndrome specific difficulties in making inferences about other people's beliefs as indexed by their performance on the kind of false belief task to which I have already made reference. Influential attempts to explain this fact, as is usual within cognitivism, have sought to identify the seeds of such a limitation in features of the autistic child's cognitive processing capacities at earlier stages in the child's development. In this vein, Baron-Cohen (1991), for example, has identified the relative absence among younger autistic children of forms of pointing which are simply designed to draw something to the attention of another. The absence of these stands as an early indicator of these children's limited interest in, and concern with, the perspectives of other people. While not wishing to deny that there could be cognitive, or other, precursors specific to autism, my argument stressed ways in which, following from my observations about a normal child, the practical activities of autistic children are not such as to provide them with experience in taking other people's views into account. Because they initiate so little contact with other people, and because such initiations appear to form such an important site for the child in making use of what I have called understandings, autistic children do not place themselves in a position where their conduct has the potential to be informed by public shared knowledge as to either their own preferences or those of other people. It was argued, therefore, that the relative absence of such experiences may contribute significantly to the lack of skill shown by autistic children in taking into account the perspectives of other people in social interaction.

Within the account that I have offered there is clearly a distinct set of emphases regarding the key parameters involved in the child coming to have knowledge of other people. For me the fulcrum of this process is the way in which the child makes use of what has previously been said on any occasion – local knowledge – in constructing her subsequent lines of conduct. Children who do not actively involve themselves in interaction in an initiatory capacity, such as children with autism, avoid gaining and practising such skills. Here, however, rather than developing this theme in the context of research on autism, I shall take it further by examining its relationship to some research on normal children. The research in question is the mainly experimental work of Wellman and his colleagues, work which I take to be within the tradition of what I have called 'cognitivism', and my first step will be to sketch in some of its main features.

The research of Wellman (Wellman 1990: chapter 8; Wellman and Woolley 1990) is of special interest because it addresses developments between the ages of two and three, the age range that has also been my focus. His concerns are principally with the ways in which the child can make use of information about other people's mental states in her reasoning, and his inclination is to see the much older (four-year-old) child's eventual success with false belief tasks as emerging out of an earlier facility for making inferences about mental states. What interests him in particular is a developmental change that occurs between the ages of two and three. He argues that at two the child can make appropriate inferences on the basis of knowing other people's *desires*, but that at three the child can also take into account people's *beliefs*. Take an example. The child is told about a character called Sam who 'wants to find his puppy' but 'the puppy is lost, and it might be hiding under the garage *or* the porch'. The child is also told that 'Sam thinks his puppy is under the porch', i.e. Sam's belief. Whereas three-year-olds will predict that Sam will look under the porch, two-year-olds, in Wellman's tasks, are much more prone to make inappropriate predictions. In similar experimental set-ups they are, however, capable of using knowledge of people's desires in appropriate ways. For these reasons Wellman sees two-year-olds as desire psychologists – as being capable of taking the desires of others into account – but not as belief psychologists.

The range of experimental work which Wellman brings to bear on these arguments is wide, and this present discussion does no justice to it. In part this is because what interests me as much as these empirical claims is the explanatory context in which they are set. Where does the two-year-old's interest in and facility with other people's desires come from? For Wellman it is based on the child's long-standing differentiation – traceable into her first year of life – between persons and objects, on her recognition that distinctive forms of causality apply to human beings (Golinkoff 1975; Leslie 1984). How does it come about that the child develops the capacity to make inferences from beliefs, between the ages of two and three? Here there are at least two important facets to Wellman's position. First, it is because the child who can only operate with a desire psychology will find aspects of the world puzzling or inexplicable – in his words, 'A revision of desire psychology is necessitated by the predictive and explanatory failures of that reasoning scheme' (1990:230): shades here of the Piagetian position mentioned earlier. Second, it is because a range of information is available to the child which encourages her in the direction of belief-type reasoning. Not all of this information is gleaned from the communicative context in which the child finds herself, but, among that which is, Wellman identifies as of possible significance such things as explicit teaching about mental phenomena (e.g. talk about the nature of dreams), the use of mental metaphors and the use of everyday mental terms such as verbs like 'think' and 'know'.

There are several compatibilities between Wellman's arguments and those developed during this book. In particular we agree that the two-year-old has a facility for taking into account the preferences and desires of other people. One way in which this has been apparent within my data is through the child's request selection. For example, the child's use of imperatives in what I have called 'non-offence' sequences has, from an early age, a special affinity with interactional circumstances in which the child has a basis for expecting the action she is instructing the parent to do to be in line with what she knows of parental preferences. In displaying this grasp of knowledge regarding what another person wants she is displaying a grasp of what Whiten and Perner call 'second-order mental states', a form of mind reading (1991:14). What differentiates Wellman and myself is our account of what makes this possible. For Wellman, as already noted, it is made possible because, from early in her life, the child recognizes that distinctive forms of causality apply to persons as opposed to objects. Whilst not wishing to dispute the empirical observations on which this is based, my own emphasis is a more Wittgensteinian one (1953). A key step in identifying the kind of grasp of other people's minds that the child has is that of identifying the ways and procedures through which the child displays attention to such matters in publicly observable action. Instead of asking the question 'What are the cognitive precursors to the capacity to take account of the desires of other people?', the more pressing question from my perspective is 'What are the publicly available forms of action through which such knowledge is expressed, and how have those forms of action evolved?' In fact, within this latter approach the major 'findings' of an analysis will consist of a specification of the forms of action in question, together with their systematic properties. It is this kind of specification that I have been attempting when examining, for example, the distinctive forms of interactional organization associated with the different request techniques which are available to the child.

The picture that emerges from my research has, to my mind, at least one major advantage over that of Wellman, though this point applies more generally to forms of explanation which are drawn on in the cognitivist tradition. It concerns the matter of making inferences about what is in the mind of someone else. Let us accept that the 24-month-old child has the capacity to treat other people as having desires. Now on any given occasion these desires may be of different kinds – desires to eat something, to read, to go out and so on. This gives rise to two related questions. The first is: how does the child select a desire attribution that is relevant for the particular occasion in question? The second is: how is the desire attribution timed so as to co-ordinate with the local interaction *at that moment*? For the child to make a desire attribution so as to co-ordinate with the actions of her co-participant in systematic and mutually intelligible ways the child must have available to her procedures for resolving these matters. The cognitive tradition is weak with regard to these issues. At the most we usually find statements to the effect that the application of the cognitive capacity will improve with practice, once the child figures out ways of making inferences that work in the local circumstances – the counter-intuitive implication being that for some time the child's desire attributions will be poorly co-ordinated. What a cognitivist *could* argue is that in order to answer such questions as the ones I have posed consideration needs to be given to pragmatic skills of the child as well as cognitive ones. Presumably, the kinds of pragmatic skill they might identify might be ones like those which I have identified in earlier chapters, ones to do with the child's capacity to manage local sequences of action and to act on the basis of understandings contained therein. The question that then arises, however, is what explanatory purchase is gained by suggesting that underlying cognitive skills play a key role in accounting for such desire attribution behaviour on the part of the child? If it is the case that we can identify sequential patterns and practices which contain both procedures which allow the child to access and make use of knowledge about other people's desires, and procedures for selecting *particular* desires at *particular* times, then one might argue that the key apparatus for managing such inferential behaviour is the sequential practice in question. Broadly, the analyses presented in earlier chapters demonstrate that this is the case. In these circumstances the key psychological substrata are either those which are brought into being by these practices or those which are already in position so as to undergird them.

In summary, the cognitivist tradition has problems in handling the question of other minds when this is formulated as 'How does the child make inferences about the internal states of other people in a coherent intelligible way in interaction?' For this tradition there must be an on-going 'problem' of other minds because the social procedures and social knowledge which create bases for mutual alignment are marginalized. If these procedures routinely involve the child in taking account of the desires of other people and if these procedures routinely resolve the 'problems' which I have described above, then it seems likely that it is these procedures and their mastery which are centrally involved in the emergence of a capacity to take account of other people's internal states. The mastery of such procedures involves the child in attending to *local* understandings which have emerged. It is these local understandings, rather than the 'representations' which the child brings with her to any occasion, which appear to be her central concern.

Many of these points also apply to Wellman's account of the emergence, between two and three years of age, of a capacity to make systematic inferences from knowledge of other people's beliefs. Again there are resemblances between his arguments and those in previous chapters, especially chapter 5. There, I have argued that, in the course of her third year, the child displays new and more complex forms of awareness as to assumptions she can make regarding her recipient. With respect to the child's use of 'Shall we?' request constructions, for example, there is a strong suggestion that where the child uses this device she is exhibiting a particular kind of analysis of the situation in which she finds herself. It is one in which the other person to whom she is speaking is also being treated as having a stake in, a potential view about, the course of action that the child is proposing. Here it does not seem to be the case that the other party is treated as having a specific desire; but their special connection with the line of action being envisaged is being recognized by the child through the selection of this form of question. Through adopting a wider variety of request constructions of this kind during her third year, therefore, the child reveals an implicit capacity to discriminate different kinds of consideration which bear on the matter of how her request recipient should be treated.

All this is perfectly commensurate with Wellman's claim that the child develops a surer grasp of inference processes regarding other people's beliefs during this period. Again, however, the two forms of explanation differ significantly. Wellman focuses, as is usual within cognitivism, on the inadequacies for the child in operating with a desire psychology, and, less usually, on the child's exposure to talk about beliefs. The latter is less usual because it could make the acquisition of the skill in question contingent on a particular type of environmental input, a leaning towards empiricism which is generally rejected by psychological cognitivism, and one that I, also, have not favoured. The account of change that emerges from my chapter 5 resembles mainstream cognitivism in that it is heavily constructivist and epigenetic; but the parameters in my account which undergo differentiation during the third year hinge around forms of sequential understanding. Once the child, early in her third year of life, begins to orient to such understandings then, in subsequent months, they come to inform the ways in which she uses both the old and new request devices which are available to her. My argument has been that it is these understandings which serve to differentiate, and which come to inform, the ways in which the child makes her request selections, and it seems to me that it is they which are likely to motivate the flowering of new request forms which takes place among all children of this age.

Although an interactionist approach of the kind I have been developing throws up findings which are not inconsistent with those of cognitivism, certain important tensions are evident. At their heart, I think, is the focus within cognitivism on the child's store of representations and cognitive procedures which she brings with her to any given occasion. It is the transformations in this kind of enduring knowledge which the cognitivist seeks to describe and account for. While I have not wished to deny the existence of such knowledge, the findings which I have reported suggest, nevertheless, that this viewpoint overlooks certain systematic and important interactional processes which are evident by the time the child is two years old.[4] Around that time the child develops the skill to identify and draw on local knowledge which has been made apparent within prior interaction. Because this knowledge is contingent and local I have chosen to use the term 'understanding' to describe it rather than a term like 'representation', the latter indexing forms of knowledge which have a more enduring status within the mind. Understandings are important for the child because, as we have seen, they come to inform her behaviour in a whole variety of ways, ways which cut across such distinctions as that between emotional

---

[4] To some extent such an overlooking is fostered by the very design of the experiments which figure so prominently in cognitivist research. In this regard, Varela, Thompson and Rosch's remarks about cognitive science are also apt for cognitivism. They write that in cognitive science 'the usual tendency is to continue to treat cognition as problem solving in some pregiven task domain. The greatest ability of living cognition, however, consists in being able to pose, within broad constraints, the relevant issues that need to be addressed at each moment. Those issues and concerns are not pregiven but are *enacted* from a background of action, where what counts as relevant is contextually determined by our common sense' (1993:145). The present book, in a sense, is seeking to explicate the mechanisms involved for the child in first drawing on contextual knowledge, seeking to unpack what could be meant by 'common sense' in this quotation. Unfortunately, Varela *et al.*'s discussions of the latter seem uninformed by the now extensive research within micro-sociology, from Garfinkel (1967) onwards, which has taken the explication of common sense as its objective.

and cognitive behaviour. In attending to such understandings the child treats that which has just publicly transpired, earlier agreements and so on, as material to her line of conduct. It is this local interactional world that now patently has a privileged status for the child. Although it is an inter-actional world which is not as yet subject to the same forms of interpersonal discipline as are found among adults – the kinds of discipline identified by Goffman (1959, 1983) and subsequent researchers of the interactional order – it is one with quite distinct properties. Because under-standings can inform the shape of subsequent actions, new forms of accountability are created: the child can, for example, recognize inconsis-tencies between an understanding and what subsequently takes place, this in turn forming the basis for forms of protest and complaint. In short, this new local world to which the child attends has highly orderly properties, an orderliness that centres around people being held accountable to the stances which they have adopted; it is this kind of orderliness, together with its potential correlates, that goes unrecognized within cognitivism. At the least, the workings of this local order suggest themselves as a candi-date mechanism through which the changes within the child's mind, iden-tified within cognitivism, are brought about. Viewed more radically, this local order entails, and brings into being, cognitive skills of a kind quite different from those emphasized within cognitivism.

The correlates of this new accountable local order are important because, for it to work for the child in the ways in which it does, certain psychological skills are routinely required, and thereby fostered. Various remarks to this effect have been made in the course of this book. In the final section these arguments will be collected together in the course of summarizing the book's general proposals.

Overall statement

Within the cognitivist tradition there has been a continuing individualist emphasis, as pointed out by a number of writers (for example, Ingleby 1986; Sinha 1988). Although the child's encounters with other people play a significant part in the accounts of development which emerge from this tradition, the significance of these encounters is thought of in quite particular and limited ways. They can be viewed as a source of informa-tion which introduces tensions within the child's existing stock of knowl-edge, thus touching off revisions of that knowledge; they can take the form of occasions on which the child is presented with adult exemplars, or corrective feedback, which guide the trajectory of the child's development; they can form environments which, to a greater or lesser extent, influence the child's speed of movement through the stages of development which are on the cognitive agenda in question. Principally, however, the child's cognitive development is seen as an internal, epigenetic process, the shape of which has its own logic, one which, though contingent on interactional engagements, is not essentially structured by them. This vision of development generates a series of characteristic alignments and problematics. Within such a framework it becomes obvious both to treat the study of language and thought as separable, and to accord primacy to thought when it comes to adjudicating on the relative significance of these two parameters. What this tradition has to resolve, what comes to be a central problem by virtue of its individualist emphases, is how the child can come to know the world in the same way that other people do; how, for example, the child gains access to the workings of other people's minds and her local culture.[5]

From Vygotsky onwards a variety of alternative traditions have proposed less individualistic accounts of human development (for an overview see Ingleby 1986). In general they emphasize the difficulty of excising the stuff of cognition from the pre-existing, socially shared and cultural elements which imbue both the artefacts which surround the child and her dealings with other people. These alternative traditions have spawned various types of enquiry, ranging from more Foucaultian attempts to identify the properties of the cultural regimes to which the child is exposed to those closer to the concerns of the cognitivists, such as that of Vygotsky himself.

These alternative traditions carry with them their own internal tensions and difficulties. Take that of Vygotsky as an example. His general genetic law of cultural development appears to stand as a manifesto for research which seeks to connect the study of the individual psyche with the social formation in which it is nurtured – 'Any function in the child's cultural development appears twice...First it appears on the social plane, and then on the psychological plane. First it appears between people as an inter-psychological category, and then within the child as an intrapsychological category' (1981:163). As Sinha has noted, however, such a position is susceptible to various orders of logical problem:

If the individual cognitive subject is seen as being an internalised product of social life and organization, and not a product of biology, then what is the nature of the

---

[5] For useful discussions of these matters which look at them in detail see Coulter (1983), Sinha (1988) and Forrester (1992). See my discussion of Wellman on p. 190 for my version of some of the problems faced by cognitivism.

subject (or proto-subject) which is initially responsible for the act(s) of internalization? To say that this is itself biological is simply to push the problem down a level, for the capacity to become 'fully human' is also a uniquely human characteristic...despite its interactionist and dialectical impulses, the Vygotskyan theory of internalization reproduces in its internal logic the very divisions between the natural and the cultural, and the individual and the social, which it strives to overcome. (1988:102–3)

Such problems might have been overcome, or at least respecified, had Vygotsky attempted the thoroughgoing exploration of the dynamics of inter-individual conduct suggested by the terms of his manifesto. In practice, however, as various writers have noted (Wertsch 1985: chapter 7), this was not to be. Later research has attempted to redress this kind of limitation. That of Bruner (1983), in particular, amounts to a sustained attempt to demonstrate the interconnections between the language games in which the child is involved with her carers and her mastery of natural language. For him there are important ways in which cultural and linguistic mastery go hand-in-hand. He argues that carers, in effect, provide lessons for the child in the kinds of consideration which are relevant to engaging in different speech acts. For Bruner this kind of parental shaping takes place, in the context of requesting, through the information provided by the parent when a request is turned down.

The issue of how the child's behaviour is socially shaped is one which all those working within less individualist traditions have to face. In part that involves showing *that* development is socially shaped, and in part showing *how* this shaping takes place. At the beginning of this book, in chapter 1, I identified a particular way of thinking about the latter aspect which seems to be prevalent among those, such as Bruner, with less individualist leanings. The key aspects of this view, to put it crudely, are that the child extracts social knowledge from encounters, stores it in long-term memory and then draws on this knowledge base in later encounters. In this way the socially shaped knowledge base has the potential to inform and constrain the child's actions on a variety of different occasions. This kind of imagery informs a variety of such research, from the theoretical writings of G. H. Mead to the speech act analyses of Bruner and the script approach of Nelson.

My own line of analysis, which also has less individualist leanings, has focused on tracing the ways in which the young child first recognizes the existence and relevance of knowledge which is external to herself in her immediate social world. In particular, I have been concerned to identify the procedures through which the child gains access to such knowledge and makes use of it. One thing I hope to have demonstrated is that the imagery drawn on by writers such as Mead, Bruner and Nelson to account for these matters is misleading with regard to how the child *first* organizes her activities so as to display attention to important elements of contextual knowledge.[6] Instead of becoming social by picking up standard patterns and expectations which have a trans-situational relevance, the young child becomes social through having the flexibility to attend to local, sequence specific considerations. Being burdened by habits, scripts and so on would be a hindrance in such a process. The opportunity offered by discourse is the availability of orderly ways which permit interpersonal alignment to be negotiated on each and every occasion, and of ways which permit much more fine-grained co-ordination than is possible without discourse. It is out of these understandings and these modes of interpersonal alignment that the child's cultural awareness is fashioned.

By examining Amy's request selections and other properties of her request sequences it has proved possible to demonstrate that from the age of two onwards her conduct displays a special sensitivity to a particular order of knowledge – sequential knowledge. It is through coming to take account of that which has gone before, through this order of sequential attentiveness, that the child's actions come to be systematically aligned with, and to display recognition of, the interactional context in which she is operating. I have, somewhat loosely, described such sequential knowledge as 'understandings', but more important than the name which it is given are the properties which these understandings have been shown to possess. Three of these are of particular significance: their local nature, their public nature and their moral nature.

6 Although the lines of analysis developed in my book have in no way emerged as a result of trying to 'apply' Sinha's general approach to the study of mind, they are, nevertheless, broadly consistent with many of his conclusions. For example, I obviously agree that 'discourse introduces new levels of signification thereby rupturing, displacing and re-constructing the fabric of the social and the impersonal world alike. Such displacements and re-organizations are also constitutive of the subject and his or her psychological capacities' (1988:72). One thing I hope to have done is to have identified some of the precise ways in which the child's mastery of discourse permits her a particular kind of access to the semiotic systems of the culture to which she is being exposed. However, whereas Sinha deploys conceptual arguments of this kind in order to develop, and thus preserve, the centrality of 'representations' as conceived within the overall framework of cognitive psychology, my own arguments do not lead in this direction. There *are* important links between discursively based understandings and psychological processes, as I have tried to suggest, but there are various analytic reasons for being wary of re-instating an up-dated version of 'representations' as lying at the heart of these processes. For an overview of these reasons see Coulter (1983, 1989) and Varela, Thompson and Rosch (1993:chapter 7).

Local nature

The understandings which inform the child's actions are local in two respects. First, they are of recent origin. The earlier events with which a later request can have a reflexive connection, thus creating an understanding, are usually ones occurring either in the same sequence of talk or in a sequence within the recent past. Instances of the latter are of special interest because here the child is already displaying the capacity to make back-connections to more remote sequences. During subsequent development this facility is one which will become extended much further. By the age of four, for example, it seems fairly clear that the child can often build her initial requests in ways which seem to be sensitive to how this, or similar types of, request have been dealt with in the past (cf. chapter 5 fn. 6). Already, at two years of age, the child is displaying some skill in making such back-connections, though here these connections only seem to revolve around events in the recent past.

Second, the understandings are particular to the events in question. Specifically, they do not usually 'reflect' trans-situational knowledge, and they have the capacity to override generally expectable conversational patterns. The fact that these understandings do not usually reflect trans-situational knowledge has been documented many times. For example, in the distressing incidents discussed in chapter 4 there was every suggestion that a key element concerning the way in which they worked was the fact that the parent was infringing an understanding being held by the child. In every case there was no suggestion that the understanding in question represented something like a normal standard expectation concerning this kind of event. Amy's mother was not normally expected to sit on Amy's tiny chair (#4.4, p. 106), and it was not normal for me to pass food to Amy's mother for her, then, to give it to Amy (#4.3, p. 104)! The understandings were, in this sense, specific to those particular occasions. These same incidents also demonstrate how these understandings have the capacity to override conventionally expectable sequential patterns. Often, for example, the child will accept adult offers of assistance; what seems to touch off the child's rejection of such offers in extracts 4.3 and 4.7 (p. 120) is the fact that they are out of line with her locally operative understanding.

Public nature

The 'public' nature of these understandings refers to the fact that the child's conduct seems systematically sensitive to agreements and preferences which have been *overtly* established within earlier talk. In the non-offence sequences which I examined in the early part of chapter 2, for example, the child systematically employed imperatives where there was evidence available to her that what she was telling the parent to do was compatible with what the parent wanted to do, a pattern which became even more robust over the course of her third year, as was mentioned in chapter 5. In this way the child's request selection displays an orderly relationship, and thus a sensitivity, to the existence of such overt agreements. But paying attention to that which has been agreed or stated as a preference does not always guarantee harmony. Where the child has earlier identified, publicly, her own preferred line of action then the contravention of this line can have distressing consequences, as we have seen in chapter 4. In this regard it is most important that it *only* seems to be on occasions on which such publicly established understandings are infringed that the child exhibits the forms of distress described in chapter 4. Presumably, many other events take place which are not to her liking. What matters now, with regard to how she conducts herself, does not seem to be the sheer nature of some parental act but whether or not that act is in line with understandings which have been overtly arrived at. The significance that an act has now comes to be a function of its position in the web of interactional dealings in which it plays a part. An implication of this is that the child now has an incentive for paying privileged regard to jointly available public understandings. These now form an integral part of the main story-line of interaction.

Moral nature

Sequential understandings also create bases for the child to entertain expectations about how interaction *should* unfold. By drawing on them the child, in effect, uses them as a basis for deciding what ought, or ought not, to happen. Most notably this is demonstrated through the ways in which the child can identify parental actions as faulted. In chapters 3 and 4 it has been shown that this process can take a number of forms. The child can, for example, treat her own earlier statement about a preferred line of action as a basis for then rejecting a parental attempt to further that line of action in a different way (for example #3.7, p. 75); or she can reject parental assistance which infringes an earlier agreement that has been made with the parent as to how events will proceed (for example #4.3, p. 104). Detailed examination of the forms of outrage associated with the latter circumstances, as reported in chapter 4, suggests that they represent the most extreme expression of the child's moral sensibility at this time, and that they have features which distinguish them from the child's behaviour on other occasions in which her desires are thwarted. There seems little doubt that it is the infringement of sequential expectations which occasions this distinctive outrage. If this is so then this suggests that, for the child of this age, her moral sensibility is not so much an outcome of absorbing a parentally superimposed set of moral concerns as it is of operating with expectations which take their warrant from recent events within the interaction.[7] It indicates that early moral sensibilities are an epigenetic outcome of the kind of communication system that the child is operating with, and that sequential skills play a pivotal role in this process.

In demonstrating that the child, from about two years old, organizes her conduct with respect to understandings which have the properties described above we are also beginning to specify what, for her, routinely constitutes the relevant context that is taken into account in assembling her lines of conduct. In comparison with the child's world at, say, sixteen months, the parameters of what matters for the pursuit of a given line of action, what is relevant to it, have shifted in quite radical ways. Action now takes its significance from the system of understandings with which it interconnects, a system which operates on local forms of knowledge and which permits rather exact forms of interpersonal co-ordination.

The fact that previous agreements and statements can now be drawn on by the child means that these parameters must be ongoingly monitored by her for their potential relevance to what is taking place.[8] It has been argued,

---

[7] I would like to thank Dr Maureen Cox for bringing this point home to me.

[8] The fact that the procedures which I have identified offer a systematic basis upon which the child can derive access to the phenomena of agreement and cooperation is most important. This permits distinctive forms of involvement with other members of the human species, forms of involvement which are radically different from the forms of tactical exploitation which have been emphasized in recent, more ethological writing, about the development of apes and early hominids. Levinson, in the language of game theory, expresses the key point as follows: 'Humphrey's (1976:19) seminal paper on the social function of the intellect uses the zero-sum game as a model of the computational demands of social life...My point is that zero-sum games *merely* require decision trees for different contingencies; coordination games require deep reflexive thinking about other minds, and constitute a much more demanding intellectual task' (1995:256).

especially at the end of chapter 3, that this has a number of implications
for the cognitive equipment which the child brings to interaction. First,
particular requirements are placed on memory. If any request selection is
made in the light of the presence or absence of local understandings then
a memory is required which can store such understandings. The analysis
suggests, therefore, that there is a premium on, and an incentive for the
development of, short-term memory in the management of these interactional processes. Second, because action can now be contingent on earlier
claims made by the parties involved, the unit of time which the child is
required to attend to is shifted backwards. Specifically, the relevant units
which govern the distribution of her attention are discourse units like
topics. Because it is necessary to monitor such units and the alignments
taken within them, these units must come to shape the child's temporal
consciousness. A third facet relates to the matter of how generic, trans-
situational knowledge can arise. Note that even at the age of two this kind
of knowledge is not entirely absent. Work on scripts and pretence, for
example, suggests that by then the child does have some order of access to
trans-situational knowledge (e.g. Bauer and Thal 1990). If the lines of my
analysis are correct then particular requirements are placed on the child's
mind if this latter type of knowledge is to expand and become more
robust. If it is the case that the two-year-old assembles a sense of the social
world in which she lives from local understandings, then more generic
knowledge, of various kinds, in turn has to be extracted from this myriad
of local events. What is required of the child is a cognitive apparatus which
enables this type of extraction to take place. Fortunately, one of the
achievements of connectionist research has been to demonstrate that it is
possible for the mind to 'find' generic patterns of orderliness on the basis
of just such bits and pieces. In particular, it seems likely that the child's discovery of such generic knowledge does not require her to be given direct
instruction regarding the generic parameters. For a useful overview of
recent work on children which bears on this point, see Plunkett and Sinha
(1992).[9] In these ways the picture of the workings of the mind to emerge
from within connectionism seems compatible and consistent with the
emphasis on local forms of understanding that has emerged from within

---

[9] Having said this, the demonstrations of such matters within connectionist research largely
employ computer simulations which contain procedures (e.g. corrective feedback mechanisms) whose bearing on actual interaction processes is less than clearcut; and they display
no attention to, or interest in, the orderly nature of interaction processes. For further difficulties with the connectionist approach see Valera, Thompson and Rosch (1993:148).

my own analysis: at least, some such apparatus as that identified from within connectionism seems logically to be required by my findings if the child is eventually to acquire more sophisticated, generic, trans-situational knowledge.

In chapter 1 reference was made to a further domain of cognition to which the analysis that I have offered may be connected, namely reasoning skills. Certain findings which I have reported are relevant to this, and as these have not yet been brought together or systematically addressed I will now take the opportunity of doing this.

Practical reasoning

In Wellman's (1990) research with children aged 2½, referred to in an earlier section of this chapter, one thing that was of interest to him was the child's ability to take into account people's desires when making predictions as to how these same people would behave. That research demonstrates that children of this age can make systematic and appropriate use of knowledge about people's desires. For them to do this, however, they have to be in possession of reasoning skills: the capacity to make inferences of the form 'If we know x (a type of desire) then expect y (a type of action)'. One question one can ask, therefore, is from where such skills come. Research which has focused on linguistic aspects of the emergence of such reasoning skills has dwelt rather heavily on the child's capacity to display logical connections *within a turn of talk*, especially on the child's mastery of connective words like 'and', 'if' and 'but' (Braine and Rumain 1983). The sequential processes on which I have been focusing in this book, and various further specific findings, suggest, however, that what takes place *between turns at talk* may also be germane to the emergence of such reasoning skills.

It follows from the analysis that has been presented that, when making a request at around the age of two, the child can adopt various alignments in relation to what has been said in earlier turns at talk. For the sake of argument let me just deal with three. The first, and least interesting for our purposes here, is that prior talk may be treated as not having a bearing on the child's current request-like concern. In the second, the child's request can be consistent with an agreed understanding. In #3.3 (p. 64), for example, Amy's imperative **And put that paper down in the (room)**, at line 4, occurs after the parent has indicated a willingness to engage in chalking. The child's imperative identifies an action that is clearly connected to that earlier understanding, its connection being of the form 'If action x is to be done (mother is to do chalking), then condition y must be satisfied (she needs to put down the paper).' In making this connection, therefore, the child is enacting a reasoning procedure. Crucially, the operation of this procedure needs to presuppose rather little about the child's prior mastery of reasoning processes, it needs little 'bootstrapping'. All that is required of the child is a certain amount of real world knowledge, a capacity to think in terms of means–ends relations (which she has had for some time) and the possibility of connecting her talk with a prior understanding. What is also interesting, of course, about line 4 of #3.3 is that the child may be marking this type of connectedness through her use of the initial word **and**. In requests at this age, this word, as was noted in chapter 3, only occurred in sentence-initial position with imperatives which were constructed so as to have this consistent relation to prior understandings; and, as was noted in chapter 5, it is this same type of imperative which, later in the year, appears to attract use of the word 'then', usually in sentence-final position (see #5.1, line 5, p. 141). In general, therefore, these various forms of evidence suggest that, in taking account of earlier understandings in such cases, the child is involved in using reasoning procedures which serve to establish relationships of consistency which obtain between turns.

The third type of alignment that the child can take with regard to a prior understanding is to treat a subsequent action, by the parent, as inconsistent and incompatible with that understanding. This can take a number of different forms within the data which I have analysed, but for the purposes of my argument here I will just mention one. Extract 4.3 (p. 104) involved Amy in requesting some honey. An initial understanding was formed that she could have some after her hands were washed, but when I make as if to pass the honey direct to her (line 26) this is treated by the child as grossly inapt (line 27). What seems to be happening here is that the child's initial understanding about how events would proceed took the form of 'the granting of this request will involve a number of features, A, B, C etc.' where, minimally, 'A' stands for the honey transferrer being her mother. When 'not A' occurs then an incompatibility is created in relation to that earlier understanding. So, reacting as she does involves the child in making a judgement about the incompatibility of a parental action with the understanding which preceded it.[10]

---

[10] It is possible, here, that there are resemblances between the inference procedure being drawn on by Amy and certain of the inference schemas of natural propositional logic identified by Braine, notably his schema 4 in Braine (1990). In heading this section 'Practical

Our original question, posed in the context of Wellman's findings, though of general relevance to developmental research, concerned from where the child's capacity to make inferential reasoning arises. What sorts of practical activity, including linguistic activity, require and foster the exercise of such skills on the part of the child? In part, no doubt, we can accept the Piagetian claims that they are embedded in an earlier sensori-motor period, in the child's grasp of features like the means–ends relations – a grasp which may in certain ways be independent of, and anterior to, the kinds of communication skill which I have been discussing. There may also be other ways in which the experience of using language feeds into the emergence of logical skills (Falmagne 1990). It follows from my analysis and argument, however, that they are also entailed by the child's capacity to draw on earlier sequential knowledge. This makes it possible for her, at later points within those sequences, to develop alignments in relation to that earlier knowledge. These alignments involve the child in accomplishing embryonic forms of logical inference, along the lines which have been illustrated above. And because there are obvious interactional incentives for the child to take account of sequential understandings, so there are also inbuilt incentives for the cultivation of such logical inference procedures. In short, an orientation to sequential knowledge on the part of the child is likely to implicate, and encourage, the emergence of new forms of practical reasoning.

This line of argument carries with it implications which seem to be supported by other lines of research on children. If reasoning skills are fostered in the ways I have described above then, from the age of about two onwards, these skills are likely to be more developed in some domains than in others. In making sequential connections what the child is generally taking into account is some earlier statement which has conveyed a desire or a preference on the part of one of those involved in the interaction. It is on knowledge about features like these, which bear on lines of human action, that the child is routinely drawing, and it is this type of reasoning about humans which is likely to become the site in which her reasoning skills develop most rapidly. So, in general, we might expect the

reasoning', following Braine and Rumain (1983:270), I indicate a preference for steering away from the analytic commitments involved in such formal logics. See Coulter (1991) for a useful overview of some of the considerations bearing on this. In general, it seems to me that Coulter's recommendations, both here and elsewhere (for example, 1983), that reasoning be investigated *in situ*, as praxiology, are well founded, though it remains important that the reasoning procedures being identified in the more formal logics have, as Braine and Rumain recognize, close resemblances to those found in practical reasoning.

child's mastery of reasoning skills to develop more rapidly with regard to reasoning about human action than it does with regard to, say, the relationship between objects. Within the research literature on children between the ages of about two and five there seems to be a good deal of evidence that this is likely to be so. For example, in experimental tasks involving the kinds of logical and quasi-logical skills of concern to the Piagetian tradition there is ample evidence that children can display more advanced levels of proficiency when tasks are presented in human-like scenarios (Donaldson 1978; Light 1986; Cox 1991). In these ways, children appear to be at their best in contexts where they can deploy forms of reasoning which are suited to the understanding of human action.

To write in the above vein is to give the impression that the child's reasoning about human action is just temporarily more advanced than the child's reasoning about the world of objects; that eventually, as Piaget imagined, all humans come to share an access to a cognitive logical apparatus which is specifically fitted to discerning forms of orderliness to be found in the natural world. There are grounds, however, for being sceptical of this vision.[11] While it remains the case, as I have argued above, that human forms of communication carry with them the capacity to engage in forms of logical thinking, it also seems to be the case that this thinking insists on bearing a social imprimatur. The most sophisticated thinking to be found within the pre-literate societies is profoundly saturated with animism, as the earliest of anthropologists recognized (e.g. Frazer 1890), and animistic modes of thought continue to inform the thinking of adults in a variety of ways within the advanced industrial societies, even in domains which we view as free from such superstition (see Levinson 1995 for a good overview). So, the fact that the child's reasoning procedures are specifically geared to reasoning in animistic, human terms, from about two years of age onwards,[12] appears to be consistent with a bias which exists, and has existed, in all human thought. Tracing the ontogeny of such a bias, the matter that I have been touching on in this section, remains one of the more important tasks for developmental research.

---

[11] For an overview of the conventional cross-cultural evidence relating to Piaget's universalistic claims see Dasen and Heron (1981). In general, it suggests to me that the evidence in favour of the theory becomes weaker as one moves through the child's developmental cycle.

[12] In addition, it should be noted that there is a range of evidence suggesting that children much younger than the age of two treat objects and persons in distinctive ways (e.g. Trevarthen 1979; Leslie 1984).

Final remarks

To recap, it has been shown that the sequential understandings which inform the child's request conduct from the age of two onwards have certain general properties: they are local, public and moral. An orientation towards them also seems to entail and foster certain types of cognitive skill. This aspect has not been thoroughly explored, but some indication has been given of the nature of this entailment with regard to such aspects as memory, practical reasoning, knowledge of other minds and the child's awareness of time. More importantly, for my purposes, it appears that these understandings play a significant part in making sense of the child's behaviour within a variety of domains which are normally given separate treatment in studies carried out on children. Not only do they have systematic connections with request selection, and with the emergence of new request forms, they are also tied up with various phenomena associated with social conflict and emotional expression, and with the emergence of particular forms of moral sensibility. To this extent my arguments suggest important links between these various domains, ways in which a mastery of sequential skills has a generic and core significance for much of the child's behaviour at this age.

My central concern in this book has been with request selection and request differentiation. Request differentiation is especially intriguing as the repertoire of requests available to the child at the age of two is really quite large. Why then should the child, equipped with such a repertoire, bother to refine it even further in the course of her third year? Or, putting the question in an evolutionary context, why should early humans, equipped with such skills, with no 'models' as to other usages, come to find it necessary to evolve yet further ways of making requests? General theories of politeness, especially that of Brown and Levinson (1978), offer one kind of answer to this latter question. Further request forms, or elaborations of existing forms, become necessary because they are a means through which respect for 'negative face' can be displayed, a means through which a speaker can exhibit their recognition that in asking someone to do something they are placing a burden on that person. These considerations clearly come to have great import for human societies in that they are not just oriented to through request techniques, they are also officially encoded through the ways in which societies have both formal and informal rules which distribute the entitlements of people to make demands of various kinds upon each other. This kind of answer does not work well, however, when considering children's request differentiation during their third year of life. At that stage there is little or no evidence that children, in their request activity, orient to the potential burden they are placing on the other party. Even at four years of age, for example, there is no evidence of children withdrawing their requests, on finding evidence of the parent being unwilling to grant them, on the grounds that what they are asking for poses difficulties for the parent (Wootton 1981a). Such withdrawals seem to be prompted simply on the basis of the firmness of the parental rejection, on the basis of the child forming a judgement as to whether or not the parent is likely to accede to the request. Although parents may be training children to recognize, from an early age, that their co-operation should not be taken for granted, by occasionally encouraging the child to say 'please' for example, there is little suggestion that the two-year-old understands this as indexing specifically that a burden is being placed on the parent.

There must, therefore, be other bases upon which children differentiate their request behaviour in the course of their third year, and, for the same reasons, these bases may also have a relevance to the bases for such differentiation employed by early humans. In chapter 4 I have explored this matter with regard to two request forms which emerged during Amy's third year, 'Can you do x?' and 'Shall we do x?' Each of them has an affinity with a distinctive set of interactional circumstances. There is more than a suggestion that 'Can you?' requests are used in certain of the circumstances in which, at an earlier age, the child was prepared to use imperatives, and that in these same circumstances imperative use declines. A crucial feature of these circumstances is that in them the child does not have available to her a sequential basis which warrants her request. In drawing on a new, interrogative, form in such circumstances I have argued that the child is recognizing the *absence* of a warrant and remedying this by seeking the assent of her recipient. 'Shall we?' questions are first employed in a particular kind of circumstance, one in which there is a pre-existing understanding that the child and her recipient will engage in a line of joint action. The employment of this type of question at a later point in such sequences encodes in a new way the child's continuing understanding regarding to whom the line of action 'belongs', whose problem the proposal in the question seeks to resolve. 'Shall we?' questions, therefore, have a distinctive connection with understandings of this kind.

What, therefore, does the request differentiation which takes place in the child's third year differentiate? The potential answer seems to be that it differentiates interactional understandings. Because adults contribute to the substance of these understandings, by virtue of their shared, public character, the potential is created for these understandings to be shaped by the local culture to which the child is exposed, for the child's competences to be culturally as well as linguistically specific. Within such systems of understanding, however, there are also internal bases which create a potential for change within the system, and it is these which have been given greater emphasis within my arguments in chapter 4. With regard to 'Shall we?' questions, for example, it was noted that prior to their use the child had the capacity to organize and orient to a specifically *joint* activity with someone else. What 'Shall we?' questions do, therefore, is to extend that kind of understanding into a subsequent sequence. They represent a novel way of orienting to such an understanding, novel with respect to the sentence format selected and with respect to the sequential position in which such an orientation is displayed. But the seeds of such an orientation were clearly laid at an earlier time; there is, therefore, an inbuilt incentive for the intellect to find ways of extending such an understanding into further talk, and 'Shall we?' questions represent one means of accomplishing this.

From the arguments which have been put forward it seems clear that many of the understandings which I have been examining are likely to be of common concern to all children, in all cultures, between the ages of two and three. At around the age of two, for example, one might minimally expect all children to adopt alternative request techniques (linguistic designs) which permit the discrimination of two types of occasion: first, ones in which what they are asking for is compatible with what they know of the other person's preferences; and second, ones in which this is not the case. The extent of these cross-cultural parallels, however, is an empirical question which cannot be taken further here, mainly because of insufficiently fine-grained analyses of young children's request behaviour in other cultures. What, however, will certainly be common to all children will be an orientation to, and grasp of, *some* forms of sequential understanding of the kind that I have been describing. Therefore, what will be common to all will be those cognitive procedures necessary for the implementation of such a grasp. To this extent the arguments which I have offered are consistent with the possibility of there being universal psychological substrata which underpin those forms of mundane reasoning that lie at the heart of everyday affairs. But the properties of these substrata together with the potentiality for their emergence are likely to be critically conditioned by those forms of sequential and interactional organization with which the child begins to get to grips at about the age of two.

References

Apte, M. L. 1974. 'Thank you' and South Asian languages: a comparative sociolinguistic study. *International Journal of the Sociology of Language*, 3:67–89.

Astington, J. W., P. L. Harris and D. R. Olson (eds.) 1988. *Developing Theories of Mind*. Cambridge University Press.

Baron-Cohen, S. 1991. Precursors to a theory of mind: understanding attention in others. In A. Whiten (ed.) *Natural Theories of Mind*. Oxford: Blackwell, pp. 233–52.

Barthes, R. 1957. *Mythologies*. Paris: Editions du Seuil.

Bartlett, F. C. 1932. *Remembering: A Study in Experimental and Social Psychology*. Cambridge University Press.

Bates, E. 1976. *Language and Context*. New York: Academic Press.

Bates, E. and L. Silvern 1977. *Sociolinguistic development in children: how much of it is social?* Program on Cognitive and Perceptual Factors in Human Development, report no. 10. University of Colorado: Institute for the Study of Intellectual Behaviour.

Bauer, P. J. and D. J. Thal 1990. Scripts or scraps: reconsidering the development of sequential understanding. *Journal of Experimental Child Psychology*, 50:287–304.

Becker, J. A. 1982. Children's strategic use of requests to mark and manipulate social status. In S. A. Kuczaj (ed.) *Language Development*, vol. II. New Jersey: Erlbaum, pp. 1–35.

Bloom, L. 1973. *One Word at a Time: The Use of Single Word Utterances Before Syntax*. Cambridge, Mass.: MIT Press.

Bloom, L., K. Lifter and J. Broughton 1985. The convergence of early cognition and language in the second year of life: problems in conceptualization and measurement. In M. Barrett (ed.) *Children's Single-Word Speech*. London: Wiley, pp. 149–80.

Braine, M. D. S. 1990. The 'natural logic' approach to reasoning. In W. F. Overton (ed.) *Reasoning, Necessity and Logic*. New Jersey: Erlbaum, pp. 135–58.

Braine, M. D. S. and B. Rumain 1983. Logical reasoning. In J. H. Flavell and E. M. Markman (eds.) *Handbook of Child Psychology*, vol. III. New York: Wiley, pp. 263–340.

Brown, P. and S. C. Levinson 1978. Universals in language usage. In E. Goody (ed.) *Questions and Politeness*. Cambridge University Press, pp. 56–290.
  1987. *Politeness: Some Universals in Language Usage*. Cambridge University Press.
Bruner, J. S. 1983. *Child's Talk: Learning to Use Language*. Oxford University Press.
Bruner, J. S., C. Roy and N. Ratner 1982. The beginnings of request. In K. Nelson (ed.) *Children's Language*, vol. III. New York: Gardner Press, pp. 91–138.
Bruner, J. S. and V. Sherwood 1976. Early rule structure: the case of peekaboo. In J. S. Bruner, A. Jolly and K. Sylva (eds.) *Play – Its Role in Development and Evolution*. New York: Penguin Books, pp. 277–85.
Butterworth, G. E. and L. Grover 1988. The origins of referential communication in human infancy. In L. Weiskrantz (ed.) *Thought Without Language*. Oxford: Clarendon Press, pp. 5–24.
Carter, A. L. 1975. The transformation of sensorimotor morphemes into words: a case study of the development of 'more' and 'mine'. *Journal of Child Language*, 2:233–50.
  1978. From sensori-motor vocalizations to words. In A. Lock (ed.) *Action, Gesture and Symbol: The Emergence of Language*. London: Academic Press, pp. 309–50.
Chaiklin, S. and J. Lave (eds.) 1993 *Understanding Practice: Perspectives on Activity and Context*. Cambridge University Press.
Clark, A. 1989. *Microcognition: Philosophy, Cognitive Science and Parallel Distributed Processing*. London: MIT Press.
Clark, R. A. 1978. The transition from action to gesture. In A. Lock (ed.) *Action, Gesture and Symbol: The Emergence of Language*. London: Academic Press, pp. 231–57.
Coulter, J. 1983. *Rethinking Cognitive Theory*. London: Macmillan.
  1989. *Mind in Action*. Cambridge: Polity Press.
  1991. Logic: ethnomethodology and the logic of language. In G. Button (ed.) *Ethnomethodology and the Human Sciences*. Cambridge University Press, pp. 20–50.
Coulthard, M. 1977. *An Introduction to Discourse Analysis*. London: Longman.
Cox, M. V. 1991. *The Child's Point of View*. Second edition. London: Harvester Wheatsheaf.
Dasen, P. R. and A. Heron 1981. Cross-cultural tests of Piaget's theory. In H. C. Triandis and A. Heron (eds.) *Handbook of Cross-Cultural Psychology*. vol. IV. Boston: Allyn and Bacon, pp. 295–336.
Donaldson, M. 1978. *Children's Minds*. London: Fontana/Collins.
Dore, J., M. B. Franklin, R. T. Miller and A. L. H. Ramer 1976. Transitional phenomena in early language acquisition. *Journal of Child Language*, 3:13–28.
Drew, P. 1994. Conversation analysis. In R. E. Asher and J. M. Y. Simpson (eds.) *Encyclopedia of Language and Linguistics*. Oxford: Pergamon, pp. 749–54.
Drew, P. and J. Heritage 1992. Analysing talk at work: an introduction. In P. Drew and J. Heritage (eds.) *Talk at Work: Interaction in Institutional Settings*. Cambridge University Press, pp. 3–65.

Dunn, J. 1988. *The Beginnings of Social Understanding*. Oxford: Blackwell.

Dunn, J. and C. Kendrick 1982. The speech of two- and three-year-olds to infant siblings: 'baby talk' and the context of communication. *Journal of Child Language*, 9:579–95.

Dunn, J. and C. Slomkowski 1992. Conflict and the development of social understanding. In C. U. Shantz and W. W. Hartup (eds.) *Conflict in Child and Adolescent Development*. Cambridge University Press, pp. 70–92.

Durkheim, E. 1901/1938. *The Rules of Sociological Method*. London: Routledge.

Edwards, D. 1978. The sources of children's early meanings. In I. Markova (ed.) *The Social Context of Language*. London: Wiley, pp. 67–85.

Emde, R. N., W. F. Johnson and M. A. Easterbrooks 1990. The do's and don'ts of early moral development: psychoanalytic tradition and current research. In J. Kagan and S. Lamb (eds.) *The Emergence of Morality of Young Children*. University of Chicago Press, pp. 245–76.

Ervin-Tripp, S. and D. Gordon 1986. The development of requests. In R. L. Schiefelbusch (ed.) *Language Competence*. San Diego: College Hill Press, pp. 61–95.

Falmagne, R. J. 1990. Language and the acquisition of logical knowledge. In W. F. Overton (ed.) *Reasoning, Necessity and Logic: Developmental Perspectives*. New Jersey: Erlbaum, pp. 111–31.

Figueroa, E. 1994. *Sociolinguistic Metatheory*. Oxford: Pergamon.

Flavell, J. H. 1963. *The Developmental Psychology of Jean Piaget*. Van Nostrand: Toronto.

Forrester, M. A. 1992. *The Development of Young Children's Social-Cognitive Skills*. Hove: Erlbaum.

Francis, H. 1979. What does the child mean? A critique of the functional approach to language acquisition. *Journal of Child Language*, 6:201–10.

Frazer, J. G. 1890. *The Golden Bough*. London: Macmillan.

Frith, U. 1989. *Autism: Explaining the Enigma*. Oxford: Blackwell.

Garfinkel, H. 1967. *Studies in Ethnomethodology*. New York: Prentice Hall.

Garvey, C. 1984. *Children's Talk*. London: Fontana.

Gerhardt, J. 1990. The relation of language to context in children's speech: the role of HAFTA statements in structuring 3-year-old's discourse. *IPrA Papers in Pragmatics*, 4:1–58.

  1991. The meaning and use of the modals HAFTA, NEEDTA and WANNA in children's speech. *Journal of Pragmatics*, 16:531–90.

Giddens, A. 1976. *New Rules of the Sociological Method: A Positive Critique of Interpretative Sociologies*. London: Hutchinson.

Gleason, J. B., R. Y. Perlmann and E. B. Greif 1984. What's the magic word: learning language through politeness routines. *Discourse Processes*, 7:493–502.

Goffman, E. 1959. *The Presentation of Self in Everyday Life*. New York: Doubleday Anchor.

  1971. *Relations in Public*. London: Penguin.

  1983. The interaction order. *American Sociological Review*, 48:1–17.

Golinkoff, R. 1975. Semantic development in infants: the concepts of agent and recipient. *Merrill-Palmer Quarterly*, 21:191–3.

1986. 'I beg your pardon?': the preverbal negotiation of failed messages. *Journal of Child Language*, 13:455–76.

Goodwin, M. H. 1990. *He-Said-She-Said: Talk as Social Organization Among Black Children*. Bloomington: Indiana University Press.

Gordon, D. and S. Ervin-Tripp 1984. The structure of requests. In R. L. Schiefelbusch and J. Pickar (eds.) *The Acquisition of Communicative Competence*. Baltimore: University Park Press, pp. 295–321.

Greenfield, P., J. Reilly, C. Leaper and N. Baker 1985. The structural and functional status of single-word utterances and their relationship to early multi-word speech. In M. Barrett (ed.) *Children's Single Word Speech*. Chichester: Wiley, pp. 233–67.

Greenfield, P. and J. H. Smith 1976. *The Structure of Communication in Early Language Development*. New York: Academic Press.

Greenfield, P. and Zukow, P. G. 1978. Why do children say what they say when they say it? An experimental approach to the psychogenesis of presupposition. In K. Nelson (ed.) *Children's Language*, vol. I. New York: Gardner Press, pp. 287–336.

Griffiths, P. 1985. The communicative functions of children's single-word speech. In M. Barrett (ed.) *Children's Single Word Speech*. Chichester: Wiley, pp. 87–112.

Gumperz, J. J. 1982. *Discourse Strategies*. Cambridge University Press.

Halliday, M. A. K. 1975. *Learning How to Mean: Explorations in the Development of Language*. London: Edward Arnold.

Hamlyn, D. 1983. *Perception, Learning and the Self*. London: Routledge.

Hannan, T. E. 1987. A cross-sequential assessment of the occurrences of pointing in 3 to 12 months old human infants. *Infant Behavior and Development*, 10:11–22.

Harris, P. L. 1989. *Children and Emotion: The Development of Psychological Understanding*. Oxford: Blackwell.

Haselkorn, S. J. 1981. The development of the requests of young children: from nonverbal strategies to the power of language. D. Ed. thesis: Harvard University.

Heath, C. 1988. Embarrassment and interactional organization. In P. Drew and A. J. Wootton (eds.) *Erving Goffman: Exploring the Interaction Order*. Cambridge: Polity Press, pp. 136–60.

Heritage, J. 1984. *Garfinkel and Ethnomethodology*. Cambridge: Polity Press.
    1995. Conversation analysis: methodological aspects. In U. M. Quasthoff (ed.) *Aspects of Oral Communication*. Berlin: De Gruyter, pp. 391–418.

Holland, J., K. J. Holyoak, R. E. Nisbett and P. R. Thagard 1986. *Induction: Processes of Inference, Learning and Discovery*. Cambridge, Mass · MIT Press.

Howe, C. J. 1981. *Acquiring Language in a Conversational Context*. London: Academic Press.

Humphrey, N. K. 1976. The social function of intellect. In P. P. G. Bateson and R. A. Hinde (eds.) *Growing Points in Ethology*. Cambridge University Press, pp. 303–17.

Husserl, E. 1964 (1928). *The Phenomenology of Internal Time-Consciousness.* Bloomington: Indiana University Press.

Ingleby, D. 1986. Development in social context. In M. Richards and P. Light (eds.) *Children of Social Worlds.* Cambridge: Polity Press, pp. 297–317.

Ingram, D. 1989. *First Language Acquisition: Method, Description and Explanation.* Cambridge University Press.

Karmiloff-Smith, A. 1992. *Beyond Modularity: A Developmental Perspective on Cognitive Science.* Cambridge, Mass.: MIT Press.

Kohlberg, L. 1976. Moral stages and moralization: the cognitive-developmental approach. In T. Lickona (ed.) *Moral Development and Behavior: Theory, Research and Social Issues.* New York: Holt, Rinehart and Winston, pp. 31–53.

Leach, P. 1980. *Baby and Child.* Revised edition. London: Michael Joseph.

Leslie, A. M. 1984. Infant perception of a manual pick-up event. *British Journal of Developmental Psychology,* 2:19–32.

  1987. Pretence and representation in infancy: the origins of 'theory of mind'. *Psychological Review,* 94:84–106.

Levinson, S. C. 1983. *Pragmatics.* Cambridge University Press.

  1995. Interactional biases in human thinking. In E. N. Goody (ed.) *Social Intelligence and Interaction: Expressions and Implications of the Social Bias in Human Intelligence.* Cambridge University Press, pp. 221–60.

Light, P. 1986. Context, conservation and conversation. In M. Richards and P. Light (eds.) *Children of Social Worlds.* Cambridge: Polity Press, pp. 170–90.

Local, J. and J. Kelly 1986. Projection and 'silences': notes on phonetic and conversational structure. *Human Studies,* 9:185–204.

Local, J. and A. J. Wootton 1995. Interactional and phonetic aspects of immediate echolalia in autism: a case study. *Clinical Linguistics and Phonetics,* 9:155–84.

Lock, A. 1978. The emergence of language. In A. Lock (ed.) *Action, Gesture and Symbol.* New York: Academic Press, pp. 3–18.

  1980. *The Guided Reinvention of Language.* London: Academic Press.

Loveland, K. A., S. H. Landry, S. O. Hughes, S. K. Hall and R. E. McEvoy 1988. Speech acts and the pragmatic deficits of autism. *Journal of Speech and Hearing Research,* 31:593–604.

Lukes, S. 1973. *Emile Durkheim: His Life and Work.* London: Allen Lane.

Masur, E. F. 1983. Gestural development, dual-directional signalling and the transition to words. *Journal of Psycholinguistic Research,* 12:93–109.

Maynard, D. W. 1985. How children start arguments. *Language in Society,* 14:1–29.

McTear, M. 1985. *Children's Conversation.* Oxford: Blackwell.

Mead, G. H. 1913/1964. *Selected Writings of G. H. Mead,* ed. A. J. Reck. New York: Bobbs-Merrill.

Miller, M. 1979. *The Logic of Language Development in Early Childhood.* New York: Springer-Verlag.

Miller, P. 1986. Teasing as language socialization and verbal play in a white working-class community. In B. B. Schieffelin and E. Ochs (eds.) *Language Socialization Across Cultures.* Cambridge University Press, pp. 199–212.

Murphy, C. M. 1978. Pointing in the context of a shared activity. *Child Development,* 49:371–80.

Nelson, K. 1973. Structure and strategy in learning to talk. *Monographs of the Society of Research in Child Development* 38, no. 149.

(ed.). 1989. *Narratives from the Crib*. Cambridge, Mass.: Harvard University Press.

1993. Events, narratives, memory: what develops? In C. A. Nelson (ed.) *Minnesota Symposium on Child Psychology*, vol. XXVI. New Jersey: Erlbaum, pp. 1–37.

Nelson, K. and J. Gruendel 1981. Generalised event representations: basic building blocks of cognitive development. In M. Lamb and A. Brown (eds.) *Advances in Developmental Psychology*, vol. I. New Jersey: Erlbaum, pp. 16–42.

Newcombe, N. and M. Zaslow 1981. Do 2½-year-olds hint? A study of directive forms in the speech of 2½-year-old children to adults. *Discourse Processes*, 4:239–52.

Ochs, E. and B. Schieffelin (eds.) 1979. Developmental Pragmatics. London: Academic Press.

Olson, D. and R. Campbell 1993. Constructing representations. In C. Pratt and A. F. Garton (eds.) *Systems of Representation in Children*. New York: Wiley, pp. 11–26.

Pea, R. D. 1978. The development of negation in early child language. D. Phil. thesis: University of Oxford.

1979. Can information theory explain early word choice? *Journal of Child Language*, 6:397–410.

1980. The development of negation in early child language. In D. Olson (ed.) *The Social Foundations of Language and Thought: Essays in Honour of Jerome S. Bruner*. New York: Norton, pp. 156–186.

Peskett, R. and A. J. Wootton 1985. Turn-taking and overlap in the speech of young Down's syndrome children. *Journal of Mental Deficiency Research*, 29:263–73.

Piaget, J. 1932. *The Moral Judgement of the Child*. London: Routledge.

1969. *The Child's Conception of Time*. London: Routledge.

Pitkin, H. F. 1972. *Wittgenstein and Justice*. Berkeley: University of California Press.

Plunkett, K. and C. Sinha 1992. Connectionism and developmental theory. *British Journal of Developmental Psychology*, 10:209–54.

Prizant, B. M. and P. J. Rydell 1984. Analysis of functions of delayed echolalia in autistic children. *Journal of Speech and Hearing Research*, 27:183–92.

Ross, H. S. and C. L. Conant 1992. The social structure of early conflict: interaction, relationships and alliances. In C. U. Shantz and W. W. Hartup (eds.) *Conflict in Child and Adolescent Development*. Cambridge University Press, pp. 153–85.

Sacks, H. 1984. Notes on methodology. In J. M. Atkinson and J. Heritage (eds.) *Structures of Social Action: Studies in Conversation Analysis*. Cambridge University Press, pp. 21–27.

1992. *Lectures on Conversation,* ed. G. Jefferson, 2 vols. Oxford: Blackwell.

Schegloff, E. A. 1968. Sequencing in conversational openings. *American Anthropologist*, 70:1075–95.

1987. Recycled turn beginnings: a precise repair mechanism in conversation's turn-taking organization. In G. Button and J. R. E. Lee (eds.) *Talk and Social Organization*. Clevedon: Multilingual Matters, pp. 70–85.

1988. Goffman and the analysis of conversation. In P. Drew and A. J. Wootton (eds.) *Erving Goffman: Exploring the Interaction Order*. Cambridge: Polity Press, pp. 89–135.

1989. Reflections on language, development and the interactional character of talk-in-interaction. In M. Bornstein and J. S. Bruner (eds.) *Interaction in Human Development*. New Jersey: Erlbaum, pp. 139–56.

1991a. Reflections on talk and social structure. In D. Boden and D. H. Zimmerman (eds.) *Talk and Social Structure: Studies in Ethnomethodology and Conversation Analysis*. Cambridge: Polity Press, pp. 44–70.

1991b. Conversation analysis and socially shared cognition. In L. B. Resnick, J. M. Levine and S. D. Teasley (eds.) *Perspectives on Socially Shared Cognition*. Washington: American Psychological Association, pp. 64–103.

Schieffelin, B. B. 1990. *The Give and Take of Everyday Life: Language Socialization of Kaluli Children*. Cambridge University Press.

Schutz, A. 1962. *Collected Papers*, vols. I and II. The Hague: Nijhoff.

Shantz, C. U. 1987. Conflicts between children. *Child Development*, 58:283–305.

Shotter, J. 1990. The social construction of remembering and forgetting. In D. Middleton and D. Edwards (eds.) *Collective Remembering*. New York: Sage, pp. 120–38.

Sinha, C. 1988. *Language and Representation: A Socio-Naturalistic Approach to Human Development*. London: Harvester.

Snow, C. E., R. Y. Perlmann, J. B. Gleason and N. Hooshyer 1990. Developmental perspectives on politeness: sources of children's knowledge. *Journal of Pragmatics*, 14:289–306.

Stephany, U. 1986. Modality. In P. Fletcher and M. Garman (eds.) *Language Acquisition: Studies in First Language Development*. Cambridge University Press, pp. 375–400.

Tarplee, C. 1993. Working on talk: the collaborative shaping of linguistic skills within child–adult interaction. D. Phil. thesis: University of York.

Toren, C. 1993. Making history: the significance of childhood cognition for a comparative anthropology of mind. *Man*, 28:461–78.

Trevarthen, C. B. 1979. Instincts for human understanding and for cultural co-operation: their development in infancy. In M. von Cranach, K. Foppa, W. Lepenies and D. Ploog (eds.) *Human Ethology: Claims and Limits of a New Discipline*. Cambridge University Press, pp. 36–68.

Turiel, E. 1983. *The Development of Social Knowledge: Morality and Convention*. Cambridge University Press.

Turner, S. 1994. *The Social Theory of Practices: Tradition, Tacit Knowledge and Presuppositions*. Cambridge: Polity Press.

Varela, F. J., E. Thompson and E. Rosch 1993. *The Embodied Mind: Cognitive Science and Human Experience*. Cambridge, Mass.: MIT Press.

Vygotsky, L. S. 1962. *Thought and Language*. Cambridge, Mass.: MIT Press.

1981. The genesis of higher mental functions. In J. V. Wertsch (ed.) *The Concept of Activity in Soviet Psychology*. New York: M. E. Sharpe, pp. 23–46.

Wellman, H. M. 1990. *The Child's Theory of Mind.* Cambridge, Mass.: MIT Press.

Wellman, H. M. and J. D. Woolley 1990. From simple desires to ordinary beliefs: the early development of everyday psychology. *Cognition,* 35:245–75.

Wells, G. 1985. *Language Development in the Pre-School Years.* Cambridge University Press.

Wertsch, J. V. 1985. *Vygotsky and the Social Formation of Mind.* Cambridge, Mass.: Harvard University Press.

Whiten, A. and J. Perner 1991. Fundamental issues in the multidisciplinary study of mindreading. In A. Whiten (ed.) *Natural Theories of Mind.* Oxford: Blackwell, pp. 1–17.

Whiting, B. B. and C. P. Edwards 1988. *Children of Different Worlds.* Cambridge, Mass.: Harvard University Press.

Winch, P. 1958. *The Idea of a Social Science And its Relation to Philosophy.* London: Routledge.

Wittgenstein, L. 1953. *Philosophical Investigations.* Oxford: Blackwell.

Wootton, A. J. 1981a. The management of grantings and rejections by parents in request sequences. *Semiotica,* 37:59–89.

1981b. Two request forms of four year olds. *Journal of Pragmatics,* 5:511–23.

1984. Some aspects of children's use of 'please' in request sequences. In P. Auer and A. di Luzio (eds.) *Interpretive Sociolinguistics.* Tubingen: Verlag, pp. 147–63.

1986. Rules in action: orderly features of action that formulate rules. In J. Cook-Gumperz, W. A. Corsaro and J. Streeck (eds.) *Children's Worlds and Children's Language.* Berlin: Mouton de Gruyter, pp. 147–68.

1989. Remarks on the methodology of conversation analysis. In D. Roger and P. Bull (eds.) *Conversation: An Interdisciplinary Perspective.* Clevedon: Multilingual Matters, pp. 238–58.

1991. Obtaining an object from a young child: the social organization of a set of practices. *Sociological Studies of Child Development,* 4:155–79.

1994. Object transfer, intersubjectivity and third position repair: early developmental observations of one child. *Journal of Child Language,* 21: 543–64.

Zinober, B. and M. Martlew 1985a. Developmental changes in four types of gesture in relation to acts and vocalizations from 10 to 20 months. *British Journal of Developmental Psychology,* 3:293–306.

1985b. The development of communicative gestures. In M. Barrett (ed.) *Children's Single-Word Speech.* London: Wiley, pp. 183–215.

Zukow, P. G., J. Reilly and P. M. Greenfield 1982. Making the absent present: facilitating the transition from sensorimotor to linguistic communication. In K. Nelson (ed.) *Children's Language,* vol. III. New Jersey: Erlbaum, pp. 1–90.

Subject index

217

Author index